DUSKO DODER was born in Yugoslavia in 1937 and came to the United States after World War II. He graduated from Washington University, St. Louis, then spent a year studying philosophy at Stanford before taking two master's degrees from Columbia, in journalism and history. He worked in several domestic bureaus of the Associated Press and was a Moscow correspondent for United Press International before joining the Washington *Post*. He has worked for the *Post* in various capacities: as assistant foreign editor, State Department correspondent and foreign correspondent. From 1973 to 1976 he was chief of the *Post's* East European bureau. Mr. Doder has also reported for the *Post* from Canada, Cuba, Somalia and the Middle East. He has been awarded several fellowships, the last from the Woodrow Wilson International Center for Scholars, Smithsonian Institution, where he wrote this book. Mr. Doder is now on the *Post* staff in Washington, where he lives with his wife Karin and their son.

DODER, Dusko. The Yugoslavs. Random House, 256p bibl index 77-90287. 10.00 ISBN 0-394-42538-3. C.I.P.

The best introduction to contemporary Yugoslavia for the general reader that has appeared in years. Every public, college, and university library should have it. Doder was born in Yugoslavia, knows Serbo-Croatian and as a child came to America where he received his education and training. He was the *Washington Post* correspondent in Belgrade, 1973-76, having previously served as the U.P.I. reporter in Moscow. Anyone who has lived in Yugoslavia for an extended period and knows the country well will immediately recognize Doder's expertise. The strength of the book is in its ability to capture the feelings, spirit, and mentality of the different South Slavic peoples, although some may question the author's interpretation of certain aspects of past historical events. Nevertheless, the serious scholar will find this book just as informative as the general reader. This account should be read in conjunction with Dennison Rusinow, *The Yugoslav experiment, 1948-1974* (CHOICE, Oct. 1977), which emphasizes the complex political and economic aspects of Yugoslav developments in the postwar years.

CHOICE   *NOV. '78*

History, Geography &

Travel

Europe

DR
370
D62

THE YUGOSLAVS

Dusko Doder

Random House New York

Library of Congress Cataloging in Publication Data

Doder, Dusko.
The Yugoslavs.

Bibliography: p.
Includes index.
1.   Yugoslavia—Politics and government—1945–
2.   Yugoslavia—Social conditions.   I.   Title.
DR370.D62   309.1′497′02   77–90287
ISBN 0–394–42538–3

Manufactured in the United States of America

2 4 6 8 9 7 5 3

FIRST EDITION

To Karin, who learned all about the roots

Acknowledgments

This book is the result of a three-year assignment in the Belgrade bureau of the Washington *Post* undertaken between June 1973 and September 1976. It is based on hundreds of conversations with Yugoslavs in high and low places, and with foreign diplomats and journalists dealing with Yugoslav affairs. Only in a few instances—and these involved information or comments by high officials in the Yugoslav government or by former high officials—have I not named the sources of information because I had pledged to protect their anonymity. Otherwise, the reporting of the things that I saw and heard is as faithful as I could make it.

Since this book is intended for general readers, I have adopted some journalistic conventions, especially with respect to the spelling of names and the often complex historical details, to make it easier on them. Yugoslavia has attracted and sustained a level of scholarly interest disproportionate to her size, and there are excellent works on politics, diplomacy, the structure of economy and party among the books listed in the bibliography. I was more interested in the rhythm and texture of life as I sought to illuminate the country's emergence into the modern world.

The main source for it was my own experience. I owe debts to a number of foreign observers with whom I discussed Yugoslavia. Among them were four American ambassadors in Belgrade, James Riddleberger (1953–58), George F. Kennan (1961–63), Malcolm Toon (1972–75) and Laurance Silberman (1975–77). I owe many thanks to the Riddlebergers, who read parts of the manuscript, and to Larry and Ricky Silberman, who read the whole thing and provided useful and encouraging comments. I alone bear responsibility for the reporting and assessments in this book, however.

Many persons and institutions helped me in the course of writing this work. I wish to express my thanks to the editors of the

Washington *Post*—Benjamin C. Bradlee, Howard Simons and Philip Foisie—for sending me to Eastern Europe on assignment and for giving me several months' leave to write this book.

It was written at the Woodrow Wilson International Center for Scholars, Smithsonian Institution, in Washington, D.C. I want to express my gratitude to Dr. James H. Billington, who gave me the opportunity to devote six months to this work in the exceptionally stimulating atmosphere of the Smithsonian castle; to Frederick Starr, head of the center's Kennan Institute, who read much of the manuscript and offered helpful advice; to my colleagues at the center, Gregory Campbell of Yale, Walter C. Clemens of Boston University, and especially to Joseph S. Sebes, S.J., of Georgetown University.

I also want to mention others who took the time to read various parts of the manuscript and comment on them: John W. Anderson, Stephen S. Rosenfeld, Clyde Farnsworth, Robert Rinehart, Strobe Talbott, Peter Osnos, Jonathan Steel, Jack Seymour, Katherine Clark, Leo Pappas, Leona and Jerrold Schecter, Craig Thomas and Robert E. Bartos.

Richard Dana was my research assistant and general aide, and a great help to the book.

My editor, Robert D. Loomis, provided thoughtful comments and suggestions on the manuscript.

And I owe a special debt of gratitude to Karin, my wife, who was my best critic and indispensable adviser.

D. D.

Washington, D.C.
October 1977

Contents

Introduction

YUGOSLAVIA HAS BEEN DESCRIBED AS A COUNTRY WHERE ANYTHING CAN happen and generally does. It is unique in many respects: an independent Communist country within Moscow's keep, but beyond its grasp; the only European nation in the Third World movement, which indeed it helped organize; and a multinational federation engaged in an improbable experiment of nation building.

I went to Yugoslavia in the summer of 1973 as chief of the Washington *Post*'s East European bureau. My beat included nine other countries, from Turkey and Cyprus in the southeast to Poland in the north. For more than three years my family and I lived in Yugoslavia. We traveled quite frequently to other countries, but Yugoslavia was our home. I studied the country and its people, traveled to all its provinces and met with hundreds of Yugoslavs. Circumstances gave me some unique advantages and an angle of vision few foreign correspondents have. I was born in Yugoslavia and speak Serbo-Croatian.

Journalists inevitably tend to focus on men in power, especially when they are colorful rebels who wield absolute power. Few men in this century have held power as long as Marshal Tito. He led a successful guerrilla struggle against the Germans and Italians during World War II and emerged as leader of Communist Yugoslavia. In 1948 he refused to take orders from Moscow and took his country out of the Soviet bloc, successfully defying Stalin's determination to destroy him and exposing the myth of unchallengeable Russian strength. Ever since, he has conducted a highly visible balancing act, becoming Europe's Fiddler on the Roof. On one side was a slide toward Stalinism, on the other toward pluralism. Tito wouldn't go either way, so he claimed his path was unique.

But his long tenure—and uncertainty whether he will live another five months or five years—has become the cause of his regime's stagnation. All his potential challengers were eliminated long ago; other old-guard Communists are either retired or dead. Younger men who have shown ambition or independence have been pushed out. And some of those who are still with him fear and covertly resent him. Twice I have heard remarks to that effect, both times from government figures at the highest level. Once, just after Tito had been re-elected President in 1974, I asked one official why the term "for life" has been dropped in favor of an ambiguous phrase suggesting infinite tenure. "The old man doesn't like to be reminded of the fact that life is a finite affair," he responded acidly. On another occasion we had just seen Tito celebrate his eighty-fourth birthday. He was in a light and bantering mood and I noted to a government figure next to me that Tito looked fitter than some of his younger associates. "Yes, our youth," he replied, grinning and rolling his eyes. The morning press that day had banner headlines about Tito's birthday reading "Our youth."

The question "After Tito, what?" has been contemplated with considerable concern in Western capitals. Washington's view has been that a viable, integral and independent Yugoslavia is vital for the maintenance of geopolitical stability in Europe. Since Tito's break with Stalin in 1948, the United States has extended more than $3.5 billion in military and economic aid in an effort to make this rift irreversible and deny Moscow access to the strategically located country.

The Kremlin would like to destroy the rival Marxist church whose beliefs and practices are attractive to peoples within the Soviet empire. But strategic considerations are even more important. Yugoslavia's return to the fold would extend the empire to the shores of the Mediterranean, give Moscow control over the principal overland route from Western Europe to the Middle East, separate NATO's southern flank from the rest of the alliance, and above all, provide necessary direct air routes for export of Soviet power to Africa, Middle East and beyond.

This is not a political book, however. So often political reporting and ideological assessment obscure or ignore those slow processes which do not make the headlines, but which produce real changes in the way people live. Even a dictator's control over national life is tempered by the traditions and mental attitudes of his subjects. I have tried to look at Yugoslavia in terms of culture and civilization, not just in terms of the government. Governments, after all, come and go; cultures tend to linger for a long time.

Each year millions of foreigners, including several hundred thousand Americans, arrive in chartered jets to what is still a relatively exotic land. They spend a few days on the Adriatic coast, visit the glorious city of Dubrovnik, the picturesque town of Mostar. Their money still goes comparatively far; food and wine are inexpensive and good, entertainment reasonable, the natives friendly and outgoing. New factories and housing complexes are sprouting everywhere, and one cannot help noticing the proliferation of automobiles, girlie magazines, sex manuals, a generally Western style of life.

Journalists and officials who visit Yugoslavia see much the same picture. Moreover, senior Yugoslav officials they meet are open-minded, reasonable and ready not only to concede difficulties and problems but to provide examples of even greater difficulties a Westerner has not heard about. But such visitors rarely get to know the other side of Yugoslavia—the one beset by nationalist tensions and hatreds, frustrated by injustice, arbitrariness, inability to register serious protest, ever-rising prices, rampant unemployment.

But Yugoslavia is many things. For a country the size of Wyoming, it is burdened by mind-boggling fragmentation among its twenty-two million people. Yugoslavs often jokingly describe their country as one that has *two* alphabets, *three* religions, *four* languages, *five* nationalities and *six* constituent republics.

I was most surprised by the remarkably successful entry of Yugoslavia into the modern world. In the course of more than three decades since the end of World War II much of the old way of life has been swept away. The Communist regime has also changed in style if not in substance. Switching from a Soviet-style controlled economy to workers' self-management and a free market, the regime introduced a degree of freedom and restrained its political police. The experimentation had an exhilarating effect on the country. After the postwar years, when it was ruled through *fear* backed by force, the system evolved into one based on *hope* backed by force. During the past few years—largely due to the revival of the national question and to increased Soviet pressures—things have slowed down and hope has become mixed with anxieties. My tour coincided with the period of uncertainty and groping.

The human, delicate and, at the same time, coarse, brutal and tragic aspects of an agricultural, backward country being pulled into the modern age have been a source of continued fascination for me. I viewed them with the detachment of a foreign correspondent; but I also saw them from the point of view of the people involved, as though their hopes and motivations were my own. And I have tried to look, through their eyes, at Yugoslav socialism and also to draw a larger picture of Tito's experiment. At the heart of it, it seems to me, is an attempt to resolve the old dilemma of dictators—how to democratize life and make themselves more responsive to the people's aspirations without losing power in the process.

Although they have no intention of introducing political pluralism, the Yugoslav Communists' conception of themselves has been far and away more imaginative—and their "road to socialism" more flexible and pragmatic—than those of other Communist counies.

Having served as a Moscow correspondent for two-and-a-half years in the late sixties, and having traveled throughout Eastern Europe, I was surprised each time I arrived in Belgrade or Zagreb after a trip, say, to Prague, Bucharest or Sofia. I initially felt I was back in what used to be called the Free World. Conversely, each time I arrived in Yugoslavia from a visit to Copenhagen or Paris I felt I was entering the Communist East. It is impossible to wed these contradictory images and that's perhaps why judgments about Yugoslavia are either relative or imprecise. I admit, by way of comparison, that I'd rather live in any Western democracy I know than in Socialist Yugoslavia. On the other hand, I'd prefer Yugoslavia to any other Communist country.

THE YUGOSLAVS

1

A Native's Return

FROM THE AIR THE WHITE AND DEEP-BROWN FIELDS MAKE THE VAST
Pannonian plain north of Belgrade look like a chessboard. The sky is
pale blue and the wheat is bleached white under the long July sun.
In the distance you can see the city fanning out in all directions, its
skyscrapers cutting into the rural patterns like dazzling glass boxes
strewn about without any obvious purpose.

For one brief, dazed moment as we descended into the hot,
humid air of Belgrade airport I thought of all the times I have gone
on trips: the first long journey from home to a new home in America, a hitchhiking trip after graduation from St. Louis to California,
then later all the way back east to New York City, where I completed
my education and started my career by joining the Associated Press,
the first step in my seemingly inevitable progression—via Concord,
New Hampshire, Albany, New York, again New York City, London,
Moscow, Washington—back to my native country. A long journey,
in every respect.

When we are young we start long journeys thinking there is a
world to conquer. For me there was also a world to forget. My
sharpest memories of my youth in Yugoslavia were unpleasant and
painful. One of the scenes that etched itself upon my mind was a
cold winter morning during World War II when my mother ordered
me not to look out the window. I must have been five or six at the
time, and I disobeyed the order as soon as all the grownups had left
the room. Sneaking up to the window, I lifted the bed sheet my
mother had spread over it and looked out. The street was empty,
except for a few soldiers on patrol. But then I noticed a man hanging from the lamppost in front of our house and human figures
hanging from each tree along the boulevard. To this day I don't
know who the victims were, why they were executed and on whose
orders. But I retained that picture in every detail—a bed sheet cover-

ing the window and freezing winds swirling outside, breaking into sharp lashing whips that hit lifeless bodies and turned them into swinging pendulums; and soldiers walking around, placing their mittens over their mouths as though they were trying to push the warm breath back into their throats.

Another event that remains vivid for me took place several years after the war. I was ten or eleven at the time and I can still feel the pangs of humiliation when I recall how my mother, along with hundreds of other women from the neighborhood, was made to take part in what was in effect forced labor. They were all given shovels and wheelbarrows and ordered to go into a field and help build a road. Propagandists for the people's revolution called this a voluntary action. There was nothing voluntary about it.

There must have been numerous other events, both joyous and unpleasant, that should be preserved in my memory. But for so many years the past to me was something I wanted to forget. I was intoxicated by the spirit of America and I had an unquenchable thirst to become a genuine part of it. Nothing seemed more unlikely then—or even now—than that I would be returning to my native country as a representative of a major American newspaper. I was elated when the Washington *Post* selected me to become chief of its East European bureau in Belgrade. But on that July afternoon in 1973, as we landed in Belgrade, it was as if at one stroke all the mournful events of my youth began racing through my mind. I wondered whether I had moved not only five thousand miles to the East but also twenty years backward in time. What if I stumbled upon echoes from long-forgotten events? Would they bring pain? or would they also help illuminate the present?

By and large, my anxieties turned out to be misplaced. I had arrived in a different country from the one that I had left. Belgrade astonished me by its modernity and growth. I had not been there since 1952 and what I remembered was a rather seedy, ravaged city still in the pangs of wartime privations. There had been a general air of shabbiness, neglect and poverty, with people totally shut off from the rest of the world. I remembered red bunting and Communist slogans flying everywhere and enormous pictures of Tito, Marx and Engels covering the façades of buildings. Where are the banners? I asked the man who drove us into the city. He glanced at me quickly, then shook his head. "They don't do that stuff anymore. Economic rationale, what's the economic rationale of such stuff? Eh? Now there are a few flags and pictures when big shots come to visit."

As we rushed along the firm, straight arrow of highway we saw billboards instead. The familiar Coca-Cola sign appeared at the edge of a cornfield, with a line in Cyrillic, *osvezava najbolje* (refreshes best) under large Latin letters. Then came colorful, Western-style ads for Pan Am, Lufthansa, Volkswagen, Siemens, Avis, various hotels, washing machines, furniture, Fiat, banks, service establishments. It was as though Tito's ideology had been submerged in a flood of automobiles, washing machines, electrical gadgetry and minicomputers. The smart four-lane expressway was bisecting what was a swamp two decades ago. The six-mile stretch is now the site of New Belgrade. I was startled by the sight of the old city in the distance and a sparkling new city around us. For my wife Karin, who was visiting Yugoslavia for the first time and who cherished some romantic anticipations, Belgrade seemed like one of hundreds of new European cities that have mushroomed since the war. She noted, however, that buildings looked better designed and more cheerful than similar settlements we had seen in Russia. True enough, Belgrade has moved toward the featureless modern metropolis, but in the process it has lost its grubby provinciality and its Balkan character, which foreigners find charming but which residents are desperately trying to jettison.

Who lives in these new buildings? I asked our driver. "Peasants," he said contemptuously, letting me know that he was a native Belgrader, the type that would never consider living in suburbs. "It's a sordid place, without soul." In 1941 the population of Belgrade was about three hundred thousand, he said. Today it is about one million. "This is a city with a peasant majority."

We stayed for a few weeks at the Moskva Hotel, a stately building erected around the turn of the century and recently remodeled and modernized. The hotel is located on Terazije Square, in the heart of the city. It is comfortable and the service is good. I took a long walk late that afternoon along Prince Michael Street all the way down to Kalemegdan, an ancient fortress situated on a strategic height where the Danube and Sava rivers meet. Much blood has been spilled since Roman times for the control of that particular site.

Finding a spot at the beginning of Prince Michael Street where a number of specialty shops are located, I stood for a long time fascinated by the sight of rampant consumerism. On one corner was a shop that before World War II housed a Woolworth store; after the war it was renamed Nama (an acronym for "People's Shops"), and its principal display window contained a picture of Tito and hundreds of dead flies. Now the Beograd department store was there with escalators, color TV sets of foreign and domestic make, household appliances, Chinese tennis rackets, Greek ties, Irish linen. Other shops, too, offered just about everything you could see on display throughout Western Europe. French, Italian and West German automobiles. Givenchy perfumes. Dior scarves. Cuban and Dutch cigars. Exotic foods, ranging from caviar to snails. People were actually buying things. I watched a middle-aged couple struggling to fit a large oil painting into their small Fiat. I noticed a VW beetle hauling an oversized chest of drawers on its roof; it did not have a roof rack. The air was bad, impregnated with dampness and poisoned by the fumes from the automobiles.

And the people: well-dressed crowds in the street that might fit anywhere in Western Europe, or almost anywhere. Women wore chic clothes and makeup, even country girls whom one could recognize by their robust plumpness and pink cheeks, which had been given an extra coating of rouge. I was surprised to see blondes—almost always dyed—in the crowd. It seemed as though a Western type of consumption had brought Yugoslavia closer to Western Europe's style of social life. This made the greatest initial impression on me. Belgrade was a brisk, frivolous, noisy, crowded and dynamic city compared to the one I remember twenty years ago when its people seemed frightened, numbed by events, going sheepishly about their business, their meetings furtive, their conversations muffled.

While I was finding my bearings during those first weeks I crisscrossed the country, observing how the newly created world of the consumer society was changing life's patterns and adding new features to old forms. There was little doubt in my mind that under Tito's socialism Yugoslavia had entered the modern world. At least the physical symbols of that world were present everywhere.

A foreign correspondent is by the nature of his job placed in the position of a spectator, watching the show staged by the natives. For brief periods, despite my position, I was not in the audience but among the natives. It was then that I sensed how confused and vulnerable the people were about the changes taking place before their eyes and heard their doubts about the country's surge into the technological age and emancipation. It was then that I grasped how difficult it is, in this corner of Europe which has known so much violence, to establish that thin thread of trust on which all human relations are based—including those between a government and its people. Can Tito's paternalistic dictatorship generate such trust and make itself into a permanent way of life simply by promising an ever-rising standard of living?

There is about Yugoslavia a certain flavor of the East. It is as though the country has yet to make its choice of civilizations. Its people want to belong to the West, but they still hark back to the days of Turkish rule. On a different level, the government sees the wave of the future in the Communist East but has found it advantageous to adopt Western patterns of economic life. In the process of getting reacquainted with the country I frequently ran into these contradictions and noticed traits of Yugoslavs that I had not been conscious of before. Business relationships seemed vaguely defined, bureaucratic procedures medieval; then there existed an urge to assure everyone, but especially foreign visitors, that conditions in Yugoslavia are as good as anywhere else, if not better.

My first business contact was with a lawyer, whom I wanted to consult about the lease on a house I was going to sign. He was highly recommended by Information Ministry officials, who also supplied his phone number. I called him and outlined my problem. "Very good," he said, "let's meet at the Café Slavia and discuss the matter. What would be a convenient time for you?" Didn't he have an office? I inquired. "Yes," he said, "but we'll be more comfortable at the café." I am not sure whether that was his normal style or whether he felt embarrassed by his modest, dark office from which he conducted his business.

There was a great deal of tedious, time-consuming bureaucratic work to be done—getting registered, obtaining passes, clearing customs. I was fascinated by the *Post* bureau's rubber stamp which had to be planted on every piece of paper in order to make it official. Since various items of the *Post*'s property were brought into the country at various times, we had to keep track of the dates when annual import permits had to be renewed. Could we place all items on one customs declaration and renew it once a year, instead of having to do monthly chores for various items? Impossible, said the Belgrade customs directors.

I also discovered that as an English-speaking foreigner I stood a far better chance of getting something done than as a native speaker.

Upon arrival I wanted to rent a car. I arranged it through the hotel desk, but on the appointed hour the car was not there. I decided to phone the Avis office and order another car. I made the inquiry from the phone of the Hotel Moskva desk. The answer was a curt negative. The desk clerk smiled. "You made a mistake. Call the same man again but speak English," he said. I did what he advised. "Of course," the voice at the other end said in rudimentary English. "What kind you like? Will be right there." This became a source of continued irritation. I had to adjust to this reality: whenever I was in a hurry, I had Karin order meals brought to our room or make phone inquiries.

Yet the language was essential in order to get a full flavor of the country, especially the crucial relationship between citizens and authorities. After my predecessor, Dan Morgan, departed for Washington, we moved temporarily to the villa the Morgans had lived in. It was located in Dedinje, the posh, pleasant suburb where the political elite lives. We were a three-minute drive from Tito's residence. The first evening there we drove into the city down a deserted tree-lined boulevard. Suddenly I noted a policeman who was waving at me to turn into a narrow side street. I pulled into the narrow opening, stopped the car, leaned out of the window to ask the policeman if I was going right to get downtown. A grave-looking man, he approached the car, shouting "Move on." There was nobody around and I started telling him that I was not familiar with this neighborhood, but before I finished I saw his nightstick swinging toward my head. Fortunately, I jerked my head and the stick landed with full force on my shoulder and upper arm. "I said move on," he hissed. I had never been hit by a policeman before and I felt rage boiling up within me. Without thinking, I opened the door, intending to get out and ask for an explanation. "He'll kill you," Karin screamed. "Please drive on. Please." The policeman had pulled out his gun. I drove off, my feet trembling from rage and fear so much that I had to stop the car after a bend and recover my composure.

The next day I protested vigorously at the Ministry of Information. My bruise by then had turned dark blue and rusty-red and was painful. Officials were sympathetic, but I sensed that their embarrassment was due to a feeling that their national reputation was in jeopardy because of an unfortunate action against a Washington *Post* correspondent. However, I hadn't been in Belgrade long enough to realize that all traffic in Dedinje is halted when Tito or one of his ranking foreign guests are driven through in their limousines.

A few weeks later I had lunch with Deputy Information Minister Enver Humo. Yes, he said, that was an unfortunate incident. An investigation was conducted, he continued. "You see, he thought you were a Yugoslav."

The first weekend we drove into the country north of Belgrade, and we were pleasantly surprised to see how well the countryside looked. Rural communities lived what seemed to be a new life, rolling about in small Fiat cars, drinking in local *kafanas*. Less than 20 percent of Yugoslav farmland is under collective cultivation, the rest belonging to individual farmers whose plots are limited to ten hectares in size. These peasants' farms were prosperous, their houses freshly painted. The dominant colors were yellow and orange on older houses, blue and maroon on newer ones. The economic pull of Western Europe was evident everywhere. Since they have been permitted to travel freely and emigrate, many farmers have gone to West Germany, France or Austria. These are hard-working, decent folk who migrated for a year or two not because they wanted to broaden their knowledge, but because of their understandable desire for higher-paying jobs. They returned home with farm machinery and their savings. But they also brought back new ideas.

We ventured into the countryside for selfish reasons—Karin's passion for folk art and her interest in primitive painting. We first visited the villages of Kovacica and Uzdin, driving along the road flanked by tall poplars. I saw the trip as an opportunity to sample the quality of rural life, so we paid unannounced visits to a dozen or so homes. The pictures painted by old peasant women and younger farmers were delightful and charmingly fresh after all the op-art, pop-art stuff we had been exposed to. One old peasant grandmother, whose painting career seemed to be flourishing, had nothing to show us. "Everything is sold," she said matter-of-factly. "But you can call my agent in Rome. Do you want me to give you his number?" My agent in Rome!

Another peasant woman, whose husband is a painter as well as a prosperous farmer, conducted a thriving trade in handmade shawls, which seemed to me very machine-made. Everyone seemed to have his or her own agent in Italy or Germany. Later, while touring Slovenian countryside in the north, I met another primitive painter,

Joze Horvat-Jaki, who was not only an artist of considerable talent, but also an accomplished businessman. He owned and operated a tile factory in Italy, and each week he would spend a couple of days across the border attending to his business.

I realized, as we were returning to Belgrade, that all accounts of the Yugoslav village speak about its backwardness and that this has generally been blamed on centuries of foreign rule, which has kept the village in a state of material, cultural and political poverty. Now there were automobiles with German, Austrian, Swedish and French license plates parked in the driveways of peasant houses, and their drivers seemed to have brought back with them the flavor of Düsseldorf, Malmö and Lyons. We noticed neatly trimmed hedges, freshly painted fences, modern machinery.

I called on Oto Bihalji-Merin, a distinguished art critic and author of several books on primitive art. His *Masters of World Primitive Art* had just been published in New York, and he was excited about the high quality of reproductions in it. At age seventy, he turned out to be a likeable man, and I found his vigor and excitement infectious. Thirty or twenty years ago, he said, "I used to go around villages looking at native paintings. I don't do it anymore." There are thousands and thousands of primitive artists who are painting and selling their works and "most of it is kitsch, folklorism or souvenir art." But, as he put it, "I'd rather have them paint than drink. Out of this mass we'll have a handful of real artists such as Generalic.

"What has happened in the village?" he asked rhetorically. "It was suddenly confronted with the modern age and the changes are staggering. The village is being submerged in the spillover of impersonal European prosperity, it is being urbanized and modernized before the people have a chance to decide what is worth preserving about their old style of life. They are selling only white bread in shops nowadays, and they feed white bread to their pigs. I remember white bread as a special treat served only during holidays. Many young people have gone to the cities to seek employment, so it may be something of a long-range problem to get another generation to work the land. You have the surge for white bread and white collar."

Toward the end of my tour a chance encounter recalled echoes of a long-forgotten past that cast the present in realistic perspective. As a foreign correspondent I have been subjected to considerable police scrutiny. Since other members of the foreign community frequently received similar attention, the idea of massive police surveillance tended to be magnified in our closely knit community. What we failed to realize is how much the role of the security establishment has diminished as far as average Yugoslavs are concerned.

Just before my departure I had dinner with Dessa Trevisan, the *London Times* correspondent. In a crowded restaurant later that evening we were joined by a young Belgrade journalist, Zoran Mandzuka. I had never met him before, but I had seen his byline in the daily newspaper *Borba*. He was a pleasant, sophisticated man of about thirty, and he specialized in foreign affairs.

At one point, Mandzuka excused himself and went to the bathroom. Miss Trevisan used the opportunity to relate gossip about Mandzuka, adding that his father had been "a very important official of the Interior Ministry" but was purged in the cleanup of the security services a few years earlier.

What memories words can bring back. The name Mandzuka suddenly acquired a meaning. Mandzuka was a one-armed brute of the security police who administered savage beatings to persons under interrogation. I never saw the man, but I could vividly recall the fear on the faces of my parents when his name was mentioned. Mandzuka, the symbol of the people's revolution, had lost his hand in the war but was reputed to have double strength in his remaining limb. It broke ribs, disfigured faces. If you opposed or ridiculed the revolution, Mandzuka's arm would make you confess your errors.

"Didn't your father lose an arm during the war?" I asked Mandzuka as casually as possible after we'd ordered another bottle of wine. "Why, yes," he said, startled. "Have you met him?" I gave a confused reply, then changed the subject.

Later, as I drove into the tepid night air, I thought that each Yugoslav of my age or older must have known a Mandzuka type in those postwar years. But most of the old security police officials have been retired and replaced by younger, better educated and more moderate men. The sharp edge of the political police has been blunted to a point where it would be nigh impossible to reintroduce the type of terror that reigned for the first decade of Tito's rule.

When I started the laborious task of getting reacquainted with my native land, I naturally sought out Yugoslav diplomats and journalists I had known in Washington, Moscow or other places.

When I knew them abroad, they always appeared dynamic, open, charming and talkative. But now they were cautious, diffident, silent. Some of those who eagerly sought my company in Washington would not even return my phone calls in Belgrade, let alone invite us to their homes. We had befriended one particular couple in Washington and I thought our relationship had evolved into one of genuine friendship. Zdravko, who was forty-one, and his wife Mela had spent a total of nine years in the United States, during which they acquired fluency in English and the social mannerisms of New York and Washington. Could we have been so grossly deceived? Would social contacts with me in Belgrade damage Zdravko's career or raise doubts about his reliability? Or did the temper of things caution him against taking chances? Whatever the reason, we never heard from them.

The journalists also were cautious. I phoned a man with whom I had had a close relationship in Moscow. He had since moved to higher things. By chance I later ran into his wife on the street and received an affectionate hug. Her husband, I said, "sounded a bit frightened on the phone. And he never called me back. It's almost like Moscow," I added in jest. "*You*," she said looking into my eyes and stressing the pronoun, "you should be able to understand . . ." Was she alluding to our common experiences in Russia? "But this isn't Moscow," I said. "No, it isn't Moscow, but there are reasons—" she broke off, squeezed my arm and was gone. A week later she phoned and invited us over for dinner. It was a strained affair, our last get-together. They never accepted our invitations afterward.

I had been largely discouraged by these initial experiences when, more out of journalistic habit than anything else, I phoned another colleague who had been stationed with me in Moscow. Milan Bekic was now editor in chief of the evening newspaper in Zagreb, the second largest city and the capital of Croatia. He was a Communist party member and held a sensitive position, yet his voice over the phone was warm and genuinely cordial. He'd come over right away and pick me up, he said. Twenty minutes later he strode into the hotel lobby, a tall man with a certain languor in the droop of the shoulders, wearing a well-cut, mustard-colored summer suit and a wide, colorful tie.

We got into his office car, which was equipped with a telephone that he used all the way to the restaurant. The paper was going into a new edition; he had to approve stories that would be on page one and check any problematical material. The process, which is usually conducted in secrecy on Communist newspapers and which I had never witnessed before, was now conducted from the moving vehicle in complete openness. "Old man," Milan said to me at one point, "you catch hell no matter what you do in this job. It is infinitely better to be a correspondent, far away from chiefs, pressures and the car with a telephone." Then during another break he turned to me with a knowing smile. "But we have no Watergate here. Only in America you can have Watergates."

Ivo, the driver, joined us for dinner in the garden of a restaurant situated on a wooded knoll. It was a lovely, balmy night. We feasted on roasted lamb and sipped some mellow white *Grasevina* wine, gossiping about colleagues and recalling old memories from Moscow. Pretty girls wearing colorful Croatian aprons darted in and out of the building, carrying vast quantities of food.

"Now seriously, old man," he said later, on our way to visit his family and have coffee and brandy, "it's great you've been assigned here. Of course there will be people who will be suspicious of an American of Yugoslav stock. But what do you care? You do what you think is right. Our spooks may give you some trouble, you know what I mean. The hell with that. It cannot really affect you one way or the other." Milan's house was shrouded in darkness when we arrived. Soon his wife appeared wearing a night robe and beaming with joy. She brought out bottles of brandy, describing their properties and assessing their merits. Milan obviously was not afraid, his mind exuding the same easy European elegance as his bearing. I felt that he had refused to join the general scrimmage for aggrandizement and material success that has been taking possession of the Yugoslavs since the disappearance of the postwar revolutionary idealism.

Almost immediately after our arrival we went to visit my aunt and her family. Except for an uncle Peter, who lived in Los Angeles, she was the only surviving kin of my late father. We had lived together during the war, when her husband was imprisoned in Germany, and I had grown up with her two daughters. I imagined our visit to be one of those happy Balkan reunions. In retrospect, I am sure it would have been had I been a bank clerk or an insurance executive.

On the phone my aunt's voice was warm but somewhat distant. Instead of "hurry over, we want to see you all right away," or something to that effect, I was asked if we would like to come over at four. Of course. Perhaps she needed time to prepare a little feast, I thought. She had never met Karin or our son. There was always a clannish feeling among my relatives. We, after all, belonged to a clan that descended from the mountains above the river Piva down into the valleys of Montenegro and Hercegovina, then moved north and west into the cities before crossing the ocean.

Only about a year later, while I was covering the tenth congress of Yugoslav Communists, did I realize the most likely reason for the strange reception that we got. As the speaker read the list of the newly elected members of the party's central committee, I suddenly heard the name of my cousin. I thought back to that sultry summer day at my aunt's apartment when I had no idea that my cousin was so politically involved. Aunt and Uncle were alone. Her eyes were moist, her hug tender, and she used the nickname she'd given me three decades before that nobody ever used. She had been in her time a great beauty, fair-haired with radiant eyes and bony features. Now, plagued by thrombosis and old age, she stood before us perplexed, trying to control her emotions. Uncle, who was older, appeared far more vigorous. He soon proceeded to set the tone to our conversations, which from the beginning acquired a surrealistic flavor. While Aunt fussed around my son, went out to fetch Pepsi for him and coffee for us, Uncle pursed his lips with a gesture of mock conspiratorial air and asked me, "You must be doing something else besides writing for newspapers, eh?"

I said no, explaining that the job was going to keep me very busy, since my beat included nine other countries besides Yugoslavia.

"You know what I mean," he winked. Aunt, who brought in coffee, said, "Please stop that . . ." But he continued, and when she started to say something he interrupted her with such vehemence that I felt uneasy.

"They are all spies," Uncle began his long monologue while looking at Aunt. "Why do you think they've sent him here? And to Moscow? He speaks languages, knows the people. Two hundred million Americans and they send him." I looked at Aunt and her face seemed to signal to me that I should ignore Uncle's accusations. But did she share his views? Or was she only embarrassed by his lack of tact? Was there a pool of affection in her eyes? Or did she feel my presence might damage her daughter's career?

For once I was happy that Karin did not understand Serbo-

Croatian. But I knew she'd sensed the chill in the air, and had noticed Uncle's voice curdling with censure.

It was the time of the Senate Watergate hearings, and I attempted to explain the role of the American press. Uncle brushed my arguments aside. They seemed to infuriate him even more. Suddenly his tirade came to a halt, as abruptly as it had started. Then he started talking about Yugoslavia and Tito, whom he described as the greatest thing that ever happened to the country.

In the background I saw the familiar oil painting of Uncle in the uniform of a Yugoslav Royal Cavalry major. When did he become a Tito booster? What was the purpose of the monologue? Why were we talking about such things? I had expected a few bottles of wine and fresh goat cheese and jokes about the times when I and my two cousins played Indians during the war. Belatedly, I realized he had stopped talking and ushered in an uneasy silence. An hour had passed and my cousin, the future central committee member, appeared. From then on Uncle dropped politics and instead complained about my son's hair—"The first blond one in the family"—saying it as if he were talking about a serious deficiency. I reminded him that another cousin had blond hair. "Yes, but Bobby's was not as blond," Uncle said.

My cousin, who was a university professor, talked to Karin about Yugoslavia. Our exchanges were rambling, without direction. Our boy was hungry and Aunt began stuffing him with chocolate, which she produced from a refrigerator built into a living room bar. The other cousin never showed up. I wanted to leave. I felt humiliated because, except for those first furtive moments, not a single word passed that was from the heart.

We got up. Uncle got up, too, saying something to the effect, "It was good seeing you." My cousin asked what kind of car we were driving. Aunt's eyes were moist again, her face tender. The whole thing must have been painful for her. Yet she failed to ask us to stay for dinner, even to go through the motion of keeping up appearances. In the Balkans a centuries-old tradition requires that a guest be offered hospitality. The same tradition requires that the guest must not accept hospitality the first time it is offered, but rather wait for another, more persuasive invitation. This gives everyone an opportunity to keep an appearance of cordiality. Aunt did not do that—a break in tradition that also ran against her long-held conviction that any difficulty can be overcome by something good to eat.

We emerged into a sunny afternoon and drove to the hotel. It was during that silent interval that I resolved to avoid all contacts with my relatives for the duration of my tour. I rigorously stuck to this decision. Yes, we are linked by blood, but in the real world we have grown apart. I felt that I should not become a source of embarrassment or discomfort to anyone. I remember when another cousin, Roberta, fresh out of the University of Missouri Journalism School, visited the Old Country in 1949 and upon her return wrote an article on Yugoslavia for the *St. Louis Post-Dispatch*. I was still in Yugoslavia, and I remember my father being called in by security officials and interrogated about Roberta. Today's methods are probably not as crude or frightening. Yet I saw no reasons for testing them.

2

Searching for Identity

IT IS A BRIGHT SUNNY DAY AND YUGOSLAVS IN COLORFUL COSTUMES LINE
the streets to welcome the royal visitors. Actor Christopher Plummer,
playing Archduke Ferdinand, heir to the Austro-Hungarian throne,
and Florinda Bolkan, playing his wife Sophie, ride in an open car
along the river-front boulevard. The crackling noise of pistol shots
echoes over the low roofs of Sarajevo, and the royal couple, mortally
wounded, slump onto the back seat. The festive scene bursts into
pandemonium. It is the final scene of the movie, *Assassination at Sarajevo*, and the screen suddenly turns black to the steady beat of the
drums of war.

The movie, produced in 1975 and directed by Yugoslav film
maker Veljko Bulajic, re-creates in detail events of June 28, 1914,
when the shots fired by an eighteen-year-old Serb nationalist touched
off World War I and ushered in some of the themes that came to
characterize the contemporary world. On the screen I watched
young desperadoes as they set out to change the world, going about
their deadly conspiracy with a mixture of lightheartedness and
fanaticism. Not concerned about their possible moral guilt, they felt
themselves to be martyrs and heroes, certain that their sacrifice
would help cut the tentacles of the foreign octopus and free the
South Slavs from centuries of humiliating subservience. Never again
will the Balkans be the same, the young men were saying. The principal conspirators in this fiery inception of Yugoslavia did not live to
see her emerge as an independent state in 1918. But their hopes and
ideals have become a part of the myth each Yugoslav child has been
taught ever since.

What has happened to those hopes? Why after nearly six
decades of independent political existence are the Yugoslavs still
beset by deep ethnic and religious differences? The movie recalled
echoes of the violence that had lubricated much of Europe's dip-

lomatic tension before the South Slavs achieved their independence. Yet, only a few weeks before I went to see it there had been an attempt on President Tito's life in Zagreb. The first story I filed to the *Post* out of Yugoslavia was about a terrorist bombing attack on the main railroad station in Belgrade. There have been assassinations of Yugoslav diplomats, an endless string of bombings of Yugoslav government institutions abroad and other acts of violence. Various Yugoslav extremist groups, mostly expatriate Croatian nationalists, have been blamed for these incidents. Is this a temperamental predisposition toward violence? Does Yugoslavia, in fact, offer a harmonious future to all its ethnic groups?

Countries, like individuals, usually cut an image of some kind. Out of thousands of elements certain general characteristics or specific styles of life become associated with one country or another in a way that commands instant recognition. In the technological age advertising men have seized on visual images that convey the message. St. Basil's Church in Moscow's Red Square, for instance, has come to symbolize Russia, Eastern, authoritarian, mysterious. A poster showing a policeman halting traffic so that a mother duck and six yellow ducklings can cross the street in Denmark, a land of orderliness, tolerance and Hans Christian Andersen's fairy tales.

The image that the West and most of the world has of Yugoslavia is blurred, hazy or nebulous—except for a moment of political decisiveness in 1948. At that point, when Soviet power was spreading throughout Eastern Europe, Marshal Tito defied Stalin, and the Yugoslavs, vulnerable and alone, survived Soviet pressures. It was an act of defiance that quickly went recorded in the history books: the first crack in the mighty Soviet empire and the beginning of a major schism in the Communist movement.

But after a relatively short time I discovered that not only do the Yugoslavs have a hazy notion of their common purpose, but that there is in fact no such thing as a Yugoslav. There are Serbs, Croats, Slovenes, Macedonians and others, who in some respects seem as unlike each other as people from different countries. Although of a common South (or Yugo) Slav origin, they speak different languages, use different scripts, and had never lived within a common state prior to the creation of Yugoslavia in 1918. Their history has been one of suffering and humiliation. For centuries the northwestern half of Yugoslavia had been under the domination of Austria-Hungary, while the southeastern half was ruled by Turkey.

Imperial wars, invasions and colonial rule have left a landscape of Gothic spires, Islamic mosques and Byzantine domes stained with blood. The foreign yoke had been harsh. There is a stone in the center of Zagreb where in 1573 Austro-Hungarian authorities, as a hideous joke, executed Matija Gubec, the leader of a Croat peasant revolt, by having him seated on a red-hot iron throne and crowned with a red-hot iron crown. An equally gruesome memorial stands at Nis, about 150 miles south of Belgrade, where Turkish authorities built a tower from the heads of Serb peasants who rebelled against the Turks in 1804. Similar events have lived on in song and story for a long time, shaping the character of the peoples.

But beyond shared suffering, the Yugoslavs have been divided throughout the centuries in a more profound way. The Roman Catholic Slovenes and Croats lived in the northwestern half under Austro-Hungarian rule, which belonged to the world of European civilization. The Serbs and Macedonians, on the other hand, who are Eastern Orthodox, were plunged deep into the darkness and Oriental inertness that the Ottoman Turks imposed upon the world they conquered. Hence the Roman Catholics of Yugoslavia carry an intellectual and emotional load that differs considerably from the one borne by the Eastern Orthodox population. In the days of the Yugoslav national revival of the nineteenth century, however, the main preoccupation was the burden of centuries of foreign domination. At the beginning of the century the Serbs rebelled against the Turks and won, first, political autonomy, then independence. Their success fired up the imagination of the Yugoslav peasantry throughout the Balkans. The Yugoslav idea, which originated among the Serbs and Croats who lived under Austria-Hungary, offered a vision of the future. It was based on the questionable assumption that South Slavs were tribes of a same people that, once united, would find a common national existence.

For more than a hundred years a mad cycle of violence, insurrections, wars and conspiracies that culminated in the assassination of Archduke Ferdinand made the Balkans into what was popularly known as the "powder keg" of Europe. Out of the rubble wrought by World War I, the Yugoslav peoples finally emerged from foreign domination united. An offspring of President Wilson's doctrine of national self-determination, it was a problem child almost from the start.

All this came to me with greater clarity and impact as I tried to understand the continued animosities among the different Yugoslav ethnic groups that make the task of finding a collective image of Yugoslavia so difficult. The crux of the problem is the relationship between the two largest nations, Serbia and Croatia, where a common language but not much else is shared. In the smaller nations, Slovenia and Macedonia, they speak entirely different Slavic tongues and are not encumbered with leadership ambitions.

I found in my notes the following impressions that I'd jotted down on my visits to various parts of Yugoslavia:

The Slovenes are sober, discreet, serious-minded; they say exactly what they mean. Occupying the Alpine country at the far north of Yugoslavia, they are clearly European. Theirs is a land of spectacular mountain scenery, unpolluted Alpine lakes, and lovely Gothic and baroque churches. A nation of 1.7 million, they speak an archaic Slavic tongue not easily understood by other Yugoslavs. The Slovenes have never had their own state and have lived under the domination of Germanic people for more than a thousand years. But they hung on to their language and culture. They are pragmatic, realistic and have a clear sense of common purpose. Because they are few, they acknowledge the need for belonging to a larger state for economic and security reasons. They value the Yugoslav federation because it gives Slovenia a large market, raw materials and a sense of security against the larger, neighboring Italian and German cultures.

The Macedonians far away to the south value the Yugoslav federation for similar reasons. The 1.6 million Macedonians have always been dominated by foreign peoples. Their arid hills remain dotted with the symbols of long-perished civilizations and old conquests, but in a strange, uncanny way. Their history doesn't appear as a spectacle; you don't look back on the landscape of Byzantine prelates or Sultan Suleiman the Magnificent—you are right in it, except that the men in Turkish-style black pantaloons and heavy vests and the women in long embroidered skirts carry around transistor radios and haul their produce to the market in West German cars.

I found the Macedonians to be moody—expansive one minute, vulnerable the next. They gained home rule for the first time in their history in 1945, when they were formally recognized as a nation within the Yugoslav federation. Their language is similar to Serbo-Croatian and to Bulgarian, but it did not have a written form until after World War II when other national institutions, including a university, were also established.

The Croats, who number almost five million, are urbane, self-possessed, and given to much rhetoric and exaggeration, mostly against the oppression they have suffered at the hands of the Serbs. I found them to be dissatisfied and inclined to express that sentiment in an oblique, ambiguous manner. On further acquaintance with several Croats I found that behind the screen of ambiguity the nationalist passion burned far stronger than is generally believed. Many intellectuals complained privately about the federation, some expressing separatist views. "If Upper Volta can be independent, why not Croatia?" A proud people, they lost their political independence in the twelfth century, largely due to internal quarrels about a linguistic issue (Croat nobles and churchmen were divided over the issue of whether to have the Latin script replace the Slavic script, known as "Glagolica"). Subsequently, they were ruled by Hungarians, then Austrians, while the Dalmatian coastal areas were taken over by Venice for several hundred years. When the Croats joined Yugoslavia in 1918, they expected to be equal partners in the new state and not to have to accept a Serbian royal dictatorship in place of Austro-Hungarian oppression. But there is an animosity toward the Serbs that seems to date back to their tribal period. Centuries of subjugation have politically emasculated the Croats' elite, who dwell in a realm of intellectual opposition rather than the practical world of power. It is this negative reflex which has given an exclusivist tone to the Croatian nationalism, especially in their relationship with the more numerous Serbs, whom they covertly fear and overtly despise as Oriental barbarians.

The Serbs, who number over nine million, are self-assertive, authoritarian, talkative, sly and generous. Their medieval kingdom was destroyed by Ottoman Turks in the late fourteenth century. They are as proud as the Croats, although the swashbuckling Serbs assume that the pride in their nation is an inalienable quality of their character, because they were the only South Slav people who managed to free themselves from the foreign yoke. Moreover, the Serbs of Montenegro (and the mountainous area around it) have managed throughout centuries to live in freedom in their inaccessible mountain preserves. There is an element of latent rebellion in their makeup. Ties with the Greek Church and a Byzantine heritage have introduced a penchant for speculative thought and at the same time have left them without a clear concept of consensus-building, or what we call democratic procedures. They love freedom but appreciate an orderly society run by a benevolent despot. Much of this, of course, has changed, and many Western ideas have penetrated deeply into the Serb consciousness.

An anecdote told to me by a Serb of a more objective nature is revealing. The Yugoslavs, he said, decided to send a man to Mars and tried to select someone for the mission. The choice narrowed down to a Slovene, a Croat and a Serb. The Slovene asked for a $10,000 stipend to make sure his family would be provided for. The Croat asked for $20,000: $10,000 for his family, the other $10,000 for a fund for the defense of Croat linguistic rights. The Serb asked for $30,000: $10,000 for himself and his family, another $10,000 to bribe the selection committee to make sure he would be selected, and the last $10,000 to give to that "foolish Slovene" who wants to take the trip anyway.

Even before I began sampling opinions and feelings on the "national question," I became aware of the curious nature of nationalism in this multinational federation. A good deal of internecine Yugoslav malice was invariably reflected in various fragments of gossip and jokes that I picked up in random conversations. At a more humble level, however, I watched the behavior of crowds at sporting events. Since public outbursts of nationalism are taboo, the sporting events provide an acceptable outlet for releasing feelings that otherwise will not be allowed.

Almost invariably at national soccer championship games between top Croat and Serb teams, Croat crowds in the Adriatic port city of Split greet the visiting Serbs with shouts of "Gypsies, Gypsies." Once, at a crucial game, an entire section of the grandstand shouted insults so loudly that the television network decided to block out the sound altogether. A year or so earlier a riot broke out after a game between the same two teams. Fans who came to Split from an ethnically mixed area north of the city started a fight aboard the train on their way home. Hundreds of persons were injured and the train was demolished before the army quelled the huge brawl. Meanwhile in Split, jubilant Croats celebrated the victory of their team by throwing into the sea cars with Belgrade license plates, on the assumption that they belonged to Serb fans. "They threw a dozen or so cars into the Adriatic," the barber at Split's Hotel Marijan told me, pointing to the dock in front of his shop. "Imagine, most of those cars belonged to Croat boys who work in Serbia and who drive down here to see the game. Since that time I don't watch soccer games anymore."

At ball games one could see flashes of the animosities which lie deep in the hearts of the Serbs and Croats, but which they claim to be dead. At the same time, it's at sporting events—when a national team is playing a foreign team—that the unity of Yugoslav feeling is revealed. This is especially true when the Yugoslavs play the Russians. It seemed to me on those occasions that the entire country was gripped by such volcanic passions as if its fate, honor and independence were being tested in the sports arena.

When Yugoslavia plays the Soviet Union, people who are normally disinterested in sports become enthusiastic fans. I remember one such game: the finals of the 1975 European basketball championship. On the evening of the game I returned from a trip to Turkey. The Belgrade airport was quiet, passport control was perfunctory. Customs inspectors were inside their glass-enclosed office watching television. One of them just waved us on. About fifty taxicabs were lined up in front of the terminal, but not one driver was there. "You'll have to wait until the game is over," the lonely girl at the information counter said without turning down her transistor radio. I phoned Karin and she drove out to pick me up. We rode back into the city through deserted streets; no cabs, no buses, no people. I caught the second half of the game on TV. The spectators inside the stadium were in the grip of hysteria which, after the Yugoslavs won a narrow victory, turned into delirious jubilation. An extraordinary public outburst followed. When the defeated Soviet team came on the court again to receive their silver medals, some 5000 Yugoslav fans jeered and booed the Russians with an emotional fervor that reflected both the pugnacious character of Yugoslavs and their deep-seated fears of Russia.

Our Yugoslav maid Angelina, who was fifty-five, came home that evening dead drunk. She had watched the game somewhere in the neighborhood. Normally she neither drank nor showed any interest in basketball.

Since its creation in 1918 Yugoslavia has been plagued by a variety of problems. Most intractable of all has been the problem of ethnicity. It has consumed more of the successive Belgrade governments' attention and concern than any other single issue. That became inevitable after the Versailles Peace Conference, where the great powers mapped out post-World War I Europe and punished the vanquished Germany and Austria-Hungary—especially the latter, which was dismembered at Versailles by the giving over of the Croat and Slovene lands to the allied Kingdom of Serbia. Serbia's king, Alexander, became the ruler of the Yugoslav State. This was the source of much future trouble, for the Serbs in general and Alexander in particular looked upon the new country as an extension of the borders of their former state. Inspired by Cavour, who united Italy around Piedmont, Alexander wanted to create a single (Yugoslav) nation out of the numerous ethnic groups. But Serbia was not Piedmont, and historical and religious differences among the Yugoslavs were enormous compared to those of Cavour's Italy.

The Serbs, who set out on the great adventure of nation building, felt that Yugoslavia was the fruit of their military struggle. Roughly one third of Serbia's total population perished in the two Balkan wars (1912, 1913) and in World War I.* Besides, weren't they the strongest, most numerous?

A common vision of the romantic era, which held parts of the new state together, was a thin bond that proved too fragile to resist a revival of nationalist and religious animosities. It took only a few years before the Croats began to feel betrayed by Yugoslavia. They had a Serbian king, his army, police and administration, and the Serbian Orthodox Church as the official Church of the state. For a Roman Catholic people at the periphery of civilized Europe this still meant the rule of an inferior, Oriental culture.

Yugoslav politics soon acquired the tragicomic aspects of an operetta. Political parties were built around ethnic blocs. The Serbs, being most numerous, dominated the Parliament and ran the country in alliance with the Slovene Clerical party. Stepan Radic, leader of the Croatian Peasant party, and two other Croat deputies were assassinated in the Parliament by a Serb deputy in 1928; Croat extremists assassinated King Alexander in 1934; Radic's successor, Vlatko Macek, secretly conducted negotiations with Italy's foreign

* Serbia's total population in 1910 was about 3.5 million. In World War I alone, more than 800,000 men served in the Serbian army, of whom 369,815 were killed. Over 600,000 civilians died from causes due to the war. The other Serb state, Montenegro, lost 63,000 persons, or one fourth of its total population, in World War I.

minister, Count Ciano, about the possible break-up of Yugoslavia; Serbian politicians flirted with Hitler and eventually joined the Tripartite Pact, only to be thrown out three days later in a military coup that in turn invited Hitler's savage attack on the country.

What followed can only be described as a religious and tribal war. Hitler and Mussolini created an independent state of Croatia and placed at its head Dr. Ante Pavelic, leader of Croat fascists who had lived in exile during the 1930s. Macek and other established Croatian politicians refused to join the fascist regime. It is one of the tragedies of the Croat people that the brief reemergence of Croatia as a geographic entity from 1941–45 was made under the leadership of men who brought back the Dark Ages and who carried out genocide against the Serbs and Jews with exceptional cruelty.

The Serb nationalists, led by Colonel Draza Mihajlovic,* retaliated in kind, carrying out massacres of the Croat and Moslem population in the ethnically mixed areas. Acting in the name of preserving the nation and faith, they conducted a holy war in which both sides tried to exterminate people of the opposite faith, and they did so with lower clergy on both sides sanctioning their actions. According to official Yugoslav statistics, 1,706,000 Yugoslavs were killed, about 305,000 of whom were soldiers who died in battle. The number of dead amounted to 10.8 percent of the total population at the time. Who was responsible for this? How can one explain the fratricidal strife? The Communists, who were a third, and perhaps the most important, force and who emerged victorious from the war, placed the blame on the Croat fascists who were known as the Ustashi, and the Serb royalists, known as the Chetniks. I have spoken with a number of reliable eyewitnesses, most of whom took part in the wartime struggle of Communist partisans, who said that the number of executions carried out by the Communists in this civil war had been far greater than ever acknowledged. Moreover, these executions continued even after the war ended, since the Com-

* Mihajlovic, a Serbian nationalist and royalist, began his guerrilla uprising against the invading Axis forces in 1941, but in late 1942 he became concerned about Tito's Communists. He was made general and minister of war by the Royal Yugoslav government in exile. He was convinced that communism was a greater threat to Yugoslavia than the Axis powers, and he sought to conserve his forces for an eventual struggle with Tito. Mihajlovic was a weak but honest man who followed instructions of the exile cabinet in London. But some of his top lieutenants, who commanded Chetnik units in various parts of the country, openly collaborated first with the Italians and later with the Germans. At the end of the war he was executed by the Communists.

munists were engaged in what they regarded as a revolutionary struggle against class enemies. Whatever the numbers, nationalist forces were discredited because of their cooperation with the occupying forces and their inability to contain extremist elements on both sides from conducting a fratricidal war. The widespread use of the knife as an instrument of death revealed at what depth their tribal animosities were rooted. Although most of the impersonal instruments of death produced in our age were available to them, the extremists sought a personal involvement in the administration of death.

Out of the war-cum-civil war, Tito's Communist party emerged as the only political force committed to the Yugoslav idea based on the "fraternity and unity" of the South Slavs. The Communists had several things going for them: an able leadership with a clear sense of purpose, party members from all South Slav nations and minority groups who shared common objectives, and an infrastructure in all areas of the country that was created during the war. Moreover, they were not tainted by collaboration with the Germans or Italians. The men who took over the country in 1945 did not care about the past; they were writing upon the blank page of the future. The five top Communist leaders were of varied backgrounds: Tito, a Croat; Edvard Kardelj, a Slovene; Milovan Djilas, a Serb from Montenegro; Alexander Rankovic, a Serb; and Mosa Pijade, a Jew.*

Today Yugoslavia seems a vast laboratory in which an extraordinary social experiment is being conducted under the strict supervision of the management.

Originally, the Communists adopted the unitarist approach to King Alexander. Yugoslavia would become one nation, a socialist nation. Their rhetoric was full of bombast and vivid projections of future concord. Wasn't nationalism a bourgeois notion? This clear and uncomplicated vision flowed from the totalitarian character of Tito's regime, its reliance on raw power, and the stereotypes of Marxist propaganda that have become the Communist elite's native

---

* It is a wry twist of fate that the Communists should take over the leadership of Southern Slavs. Karl Marx and Friedrich Engels had nothing but contempt for the Yugoslavs, who, they prophesied, would never achieve a state organization. Engels felt that the German people would wipe out the "barbarian" Yugoslav ethnic groups. Marx put it this way: "This ethnic trash always becomes, and remains until its complete extermination or denationalization, the most fanatic carrier of counterrevolution."

tongue. In a deeper sense, however, it reflected the Serb outlook on politics and concept of the State. The Serbs were most numerous in Tito's wartime army and rose to key positions, especially in the army and the police.

A fictitious federation was set up with Slovenia, Macedonia, Croatia and Serbia becoming constituent republics. A region between Serbia and Croatia that contained both Serb and Croat peoples, as well as about 1.5 million Slavs who had long ago accepted Islam in order to retain their privileged positions after the Turkish conquest, was declared the republic of Bosnia and Hercegovina. And Montenegro, a small Serb state whose people were the only ones in the Balkans to defy conquest by the Turks and remain free in their wild mountains, became the sixth constituent republic.

Paradoxically, the basic thrust of this division was to weaken the expansionist Serbs. The Communists not only made Montenegro a republic but also proclaimed its people Montenegrin nationals. Djilas, a Montenegrin Serb, admitted publicly long after his fall from power that he was "particularly involved in advancing untenable theoretical explanations concering the Montenegrin nation." Moreover, within the republic of Serbia were established two autonomous regions, one in Kosovo with its sizable Albanian minority, and the other in Vojvodina, where there are a number of minorities including Hungarians, Slovaks, Czechs, Romanians, and Ruthenians.

Yet side by side with this containment of the Serbs, Serbian Communists continued to dominate the instruments of state as well as the life of the country in general. The party formally adopted the concept of a single Yugoslav nation in 1958. Among more enlightened figures in the leadership there were those who realized that the unitarist approach was bound to fail and that the progression of events required a sharp change. In the early 1960s Tito sided with the progressives. He abandoned the idea of a unitarist state and instead prepared ground for the current experiment in which all nations and nationalities were given home rule and the right to full national and cultural affirmation. The Communists finally had to recognize the fact that the idea of nation as an entity—to perpetuate its breed and to protect itself among peoples of other breeds—was exceptionally strong in the Balkans. In the end Tito set out to create not a Yugoslav nation, but a Yugoslav commonwealth composed of diverse ethnic elements which accepted a common way of life and common control over their destiny.

The idea behind the reform was promising; the material involved in the experiment was not. And after nearly a decade no one can predict the final outcome with any certainty. Can a lasting agreement of this type be reached without free debate?

I put that question to Miko Spiljak, former prime minister and one of the key figures in the party leadership. He was frank: "We are groping, we don't know the way. We have no tradition of democracy. When Americans quarrel in a bar, they use the fist to settle accounts. Our people pull a pistol or draw a knife. You cannot expect a people who have always been used to despotism to produce democratic institutions overnight."

Under the tranquilizing effect of monotonous Communist rhetoric, the reform marked both the collapse of a Serb monopoly of state power and the end of a drive toward a unified Yugoslav nationality.

The first was symbolized by the fall from power in the summer of 1966 of Alexander Rankovic, until then Tito's vice-president, who had been in charge of party personnel matters and of the secret police. His fall was followed by a wholesale purge of the security agencies and the political police, all of them organized by Rankovic, and the introduction of strict implementation of the "ethnic key" in personnel policy (or proportional representation of all ethnic groups at all levels).

The second was accomplished by defining Yugoslavia as a cooperative federation of republics with control of the federal government limited to foreign affairs, defense, creation and maintenance of instruments designed to guarantee a single market, regulation of the economic system and protection of ethnic equality.

So 1966 became the watershed year, not only because of the demise of Rankovic and his dreaded political police. The lines of a new development for Yugoslavia were becoming apparent, and the party finally was facing up to the realities of the country's ethnic problem. A great deal of effort has been made to view the 1966 conflict as a clash between liberals and conservatives—which it was, but only to an extent. Deep down, nationalism has been as strong among the Communists as among the rest of the population.

Rankovic, the man who was once feared, hated and respected, lived in a comfortable house next to our neighborhood supermarket. Authorities had built a small police station almost directly opposite his house. The ground-floor structure is obscured behind high ever-green shrubbery, hiding detectives who were supposed to keep an eye on the former security chief. Rankovic would walk around when the weather was good, greeting everybody with an exceptionally correct air of courtesy. Some of his closest associates, who have known him since his days in the party before World War II, have described him to me as a man of above-average intelligence, self-control and lucidity, possessing a tidy and exact mastery of technical detail and a talent for organization. His ideological commitment was prosaic and practical, his loyalty to Tito unquestionable. Yet his mind, for all its clarity, was conventional and in the traditional Serbian mold. His instinct was for order and regularity of procedure, and he feared that Tito's tinkering with liberalism, federalism and decentralization would undermine the entire state structure. He was a strong and forceful figure in those days, cold as ice, a man who understood power and had the capacity to command. He had the instincts of prewar Serbian bourgeois politicians who saw Belgrade as the center of a centralized Yugoslavia. This concept, in its practical aspects, had been identical with Tito's initial idea of Yugoslavia. But when in the early 1960s Tito began experimenting with economic reforms and regional Communist leaders began to push for a genuine decentralization, Rankovic felt uneasy. In an instinctive way he knew that if something like this was tried and failed, the consequences would be grave. Once begun, the course had a degree of inevitability to it; in the end his own power was being challenged. In order to buy time he conceded something on reforms; but being in charge of a huge security establishment, he could hold the line.

There was something symbolic about his power. He and his police epitomized orthodox Communism and Serbian nationalism. He was so much a prisoner of his own background that, being the principal representative of the Serbs in the country's top leadership, he increasingly saw himself as the defender of their national interests. In the autonomous province of Kosovo his police used the most brutal means of terror against ethnic Albanians who, through demographic changes, became the dominant element in an area that had been the site of a medieval Serb kingdom. Even more curious was Rankovic's successful maneuvering to deny the Macedonians their own Church.

The Macedonians, prior to the Turkish conquest, had been ruled by the Serbs and the Bulgarians. The medieval Serb kingdom at the height of its power had its capital at Skopje, now the capital of the Macedonian republic. The Macedonians were the first to come under Turkish rule. They were the last Yugoslav people to be freed from Turkish rule, in 1912, but the Serbian liberators declared the Macedonian population to be Serbian. In the kingdom of Yugoslavia the Macedonians were called South Serbs and denied their ethnic and cultural rights. After the Communist takeover the Macedonians finally received administrative autonomy and the right to cultural affirmation. But the Macedonian Orthodox Church remained under control of the Serbian Patriarch.

Almost from the very beginning the Macedonian Communists insisted that their Church be granted independence from the Serbian Church, a request Serb nationalist and church leaders adamantly opposed. This may seem a trivial matter to a Western reader, especially since all of Yugoslavia is under Communist rule, but in the Eastern Orthodox world one of the essential symbols of national existence is the unbreakable unity of Church and Nation. Although they might be Communists, men reared in the Orthodox tradition could not conceive of a national idea which did not assume that unity. "A nation is not just a body of people within a geographic entity based on a racial ground without that Church-State unity," said my informant, who has held some of the highest positions in Tito's government. "We had a lot of problems with Macedonian Communists. They constantly argued that the Macedonian Church should become autocephalous. But Rankovic would not hear of it. He argued privately that he did not want to have problems with the Serbian Church. Deep down, I am sure, he was not about to write off Macedonia."

In the fall of 1966, less than three months after the downfall of Rankovic, and at the initiative of the Central Committee of the Macedonian Communist party, the Macedonian Church became separated from the Serbian Church and Bishop Dositej became Metropolitan of Macedonia and Ohrid. The act of proclamation was made at the exquisite eleventh-century Church of St. Sophia in the picturesque town of Ohrid, at the edge of Lake Ohrid. "It was one of the most extraordinary occasions," a man who witnessed the proceedings said. "There were priests with long beards, Communist officials, and plain people and they were all crying and kissing one another. It was a scene of delirious happiness, like witnessing the rebirth of a nation." Perhaps it was.

In Belgrade I listened to the echoes of this event, which some-how seemed to belong to a nineteenth-century melodrama, yet was all too real. A Serbian Orthodox bishop spoke bitterly about the Mace-donian Church. "We will not know for a hundred years whether the Macedonians are really a nation," he said in that Byzantine oblique-ness that attaches ambiguity to every thought. Obviously he thought they were not, since he added, "What would be left of the Serbian Church if the Serbs in Bosnia and Croatia formed their own Churches?"

There is a certain enthusiasm and infectious charm about Macedonian intellectuals. They, more than anyone else in Yugo-slavia, feel threatened by jealous Bulgarian neighbors with former and present irredentist claims on Macedonian territory. Commu-nism, in Macedonia, is an incidental thing. The Macedonians are building a nation, trying to move it quickly into the modern age and doing so with considerable success. Macedonian officials seem im-bued with a positive direction and purpose. Their republic gives an impression of gentle austerity and simplicity. Their land seems more sober, paler than the rest of Yugoslavia, colored as it is in hues of terra cotta. There are a number of archeological digs that reveal active social and commercial life during the Roman age. The Byzan-tine architecture of the Orthodox churches is simple and classical in taste. But the old churches and monasteries, as those in Serbia and other parts that were ruled by the Turks, are situated at wide inter-vals and at locations far away from the principal thoroughfares, often on barely accessible mountain slopes. They are usually sur-rounded by massive stone walls which are taller and thicker than the structures themselves. You begin to understand when touring these ancient edifices what has shaped the character of the people. But the mural decorations inside the churches, especially in those around the town of Ohrid, reflect the splendor and wealth of perished ages. The portrait of St. Naum on an icon inside St. Clement's Church matches in its beauty and execution anything I have seen at Moscow's Tretyakov Gallery.

In Kosovo, an autonomous province that straddles the northern tip of Albania, political decentralization has brought marked im-provements to the Albanian national minority. Before the fall of Rankovic, many ethnic Albanians told me, their rights existed on paper only. "Those who tried to assert their rights as Albanians were in trouble," one middle-aged Albanian said. "The secret police picked up those whom they regarded as nationalist troublemakers and simply killed them. Then they would say such-and-such a man was shot while trying to flee across the border to Albania. Who could prove otherwise?"

Kosovo, roughly half the size of Maryland, is a remote area of mountain ranges and rich fields where gentle courtesy and hospitality coexist with outbursts of cruel violence and deep ethnic and religious hostilities. To all Serbs, Kosovo has a special meaning. It was the site of a medieval Serb kingdom which was destroyed in 1389 by the Turks, but legends and folk songs have kept the glories of the vanished kingdom alive. For five centuries every Serbian child has been reared on the legends and folk songs of Kosovo. In time the defeat was invested with heroic qualities, as the people felt the need to embellish the past in order to compensate for a humiliating present. It was this myth which sustained the hopes of the Serbs and gave them the strength and cohesion no other Yugoslav people had, to shake off the foreign yoke in the nineteenth century.

When I went to view the site of the 1389 battle on the outskirts of Pristina, the capital of Kosovo, I met a Serb youth who pointed to the field of lovely red peonies and said, "People believe that the vivid red of these flowers comes from the blood of Serbian soldiers massacred on that spot. Of course this is a folk tale." Then, a little later, he added somewhat sheepishly, "And yet, isn't it strange that you have red peonies mostly in that area where the battle was fought?"

Until the fall of Rankovic the position of ethnic Albanians was similar to that of blacks in the United States prior to the civil rights movement of the early sixties. They are still privately referred to as *shiptars*, a word employed by the Slav population to confer inferiority. Because Kosovo is the poorest region in Yugoslavia, the Albanians are largely migrant workers doing manual jobs in cities, such as carrying coal, doing odd jobs and collecting garbage. One of the jokes circulating in Belgrade is about the chairman of the federal parliament who declared recess but asked the delegates from Kosovo to remain in the hall. "Why's that?" the chairman is asked by a colleague. "Well, today is garbage day, someone has to take the garbage out."

Since Kosovo was granted home rule ethnic Albanians have replaced Serbs in key positions, an Albanian University was established in Pristina, and the Albanian language has become the dominant language of the province. Given the history of bloody ethnic feuds between the Albanians (who are largely Moslem) and the Orthodox Serbs, it was perhaps inevitable that the nascent Albanian nationalism would eventually take on exclusivist overtones. In Kosovo in 1968, serious rioting, which reflected general dissatisfaction, was quelled by the army. But in the 1970s unrest also included separatist tendencies, especially among younger people and intellectuals. What makes the tangled web of ethnic, religious and linguistic tensions even more complicated is the exceptionally high birth rate of Kosovo Albanians. Their annual average rate for more than a decade has stood at 29 per 1000 population, which is the highest in Europe. The ancestral Serbian province is now the home of one million ethnic Albanians, who comprise over 74 percent of Kosovo's population. The demographic picture is also being changed by a slow but steady exodus of Serbs from Kosovo. "Kosovo!" Serbs would say, after reports of Albanian nationalist and separatist demonstrations reached Belgrade, "What we need is another Rankovic." The thought of losing what they regard as the cradle of Serbdom is enough to provoke atavistic feeling against Moslem infidels.

Who are the people who have been advocating union with the country of Albania? What are the causes of nationalist agitation? The local government's public relations man, Tihomir Saljic, looked puzzled. "We have no such problems that you can describe," he said, looking me straight in the eye, then shifting toward the driver as if seeking confirmation. "Everything here is in perfect harmony." What about the "Albanian National Liberation Movement"? Scores of its members were arrested and sentenced to long prison terms in 1975 for advocating the province's union with Albania. When talking with local officials, I ran into stubborn secrecy. Saljic, who accompanied me to official interviews, was obviously uncomfortable. Thirty years old, he had just started a career with the local information office. He had not mastered the art of double-talk and his inclination was to be open. But one often comes across provincial public relations men who have been told by their superiors that the admission of weakness to foreigners is an act of treason. One of the Albanian drivers, who took us around Pristina in an official limousine, told me while we waited for Saljic to make a telephone call, "Don't believe anything he tells you."

Before Saljic and I parted company, I had a touching experience that gave me an unexpected inkling of what it must be like to be a public relations man in Pristina. We had stopped talking politics, and he had ceased attacks on Western news media for "creating" nonexistent tensions in Kosovo. A Serb whose family comes from the outlying districts of Montenegro, he looked like actor Tony Perkins, dressed in a well-cut gray suit. "Well," I said, using an old saying, "the bones of your forefathers must be turning in their graves." "Why?" He turned to me in surprise. I wanted him to know that I didn't believe much of what he had told me earlier, so I continued: "They were heroes and I wonder what they would say about your making a living by telling lies?" "My God, you're right," he said quietly. Then he caught himself, flashed a big smile and said, "You're playing tricks on me; you know damn well that I told you the truth . . ."

The paradox of Kosovo has been that constitutional changes and devolution of power to the regions which give them full rights for cultural, linguistic and political affirmation have created a unique problem. The number of ethnic Albanians living in Yugoslavia compared to the population of the country of Albania next door is the root of this problem. In addition to more than one million Kosovo Albanians, there are over 300,000 ethnic Albanians living along the border in neighboring Macedonia and Montenegro. The population of Albania itself is estimated at only 2.2 million. How long can these two large communities of the same people remain politically separated? At some point will there be demands for the national unification of all Albanians? What are the long-term prospects? My questions drew blank stares from Albanian and Serb officials, as though they had been posed in Chinese or another incomprehensible tongue.

I called on Feriz Krasnici, chancellor of the University of Pristina, an affable forty-five-year-old biologist who spoke at great length about the progress of the institution and its cooperation with the University of Tirana, in Albania. After eight years of existence the university had more than 20,000 full-time ethnic Albanian students, but not nearly enough teachers who could lecture in Albanian. One out of three teachers has to be flown in from other university centers in Yugoslavia to Pristina in order to lecture once a week, or once every other week, depending on the subject.

Krasnici, who is an ethnic Albanian, looks older than his age and speaks wistfully about his youth. His soft voice began sounding distantly repetitive as he anticipated my questions. "There's always one rotten apple in every barrel," he said, talking about his thirty-one students who were sentenced in February 1976 to prison terms of up to fifteen years for belonging to an "Albanian National Liberation Movement." The clandestine movement advocates unification of Kosovo with Albania.

"Of course we cooperate with Albania, and teachers, educators and cultural workers from Albania come here and our people go there," the chancellor continued. "But politically we go our way, they go their way."

Albania's borders are generally closed to the outside world, except for its cooperation with Kosovo which is intensive, despite generally hostile relations between Albania and Yugoslavia. Will there be, at some future date, a drive for national unification? What do the leaders of the Albanian community think about such a possibility? Krasnici's face assumed an inscrutable mask. His reply seemed to wander off in a different direction and dissolve into a collection of clichés. The questions dangled in the air, unanswered, perhaps unanswerable.

Zagreb. The capital of Croatia has the pleasant air of a provincial Austrian city. I have always found it far more attractive than Belgrade, which is somehow a modern city without much past. Old Zagreb is a mixture of Gothic and baroque, containing Roman churches with high pointed towers and elaborate façades. The thirteenth-century Church of St. Mark has been carefully restored, but small baroque palaces that once belonged to Hungarian, Croat and Austrian nobles seemed in bad repair. The Croats have kept the medieval aspect of the old town. Most of the old buildings are yellow or orange, the favorite colors of the once great Hapsburg Empire. There are female caryatids on the old buildings upholding the massive fronts. A profusion of public statues reflects a peculiar Croat predilection to honor deserving citizens in this fashion. Among the statues there are some exceptionally beautiful works of the late Ivan Metrovic, the greatest sculptor to emerge from this part of Europe. Bishop Juraj Strossmayer, the nineteenth-century Croat thinker and leader who in 1867 founded the Yugoslav Academy of Arts and Sciences in Zagreb, is fixed permanently in a pose of a careful reader. Strossmayer was one of the most articulate champions of the Yugoslav idea of unity (his academy was called Yugoslav, while the one established at about the same time in Belgrade was named the Serbian Academy of Arts and Sciences). One of the most talented Croat poets, Petar Preradovic, who was also a nineteenth-century Austrian general, is immortalized by a statue that stands in front of the Serbian Orthodox Church in downtown Zagreb. What ambiguity: the great poet in Austrian uniform! Why is he honored? For his patriotic verses? Or for his loyalty to the Hapsburg emperor? Or both?

When I spoke with some Croat nationalist leaders and intellectuals in the summer of 1975, I found them to be in a despondent mood, nursing an extensive assortment of real or imagined wrongs. There was a good deal of malice toward the Serbs. A typical sample of Croatian black humor was a joke that I heard a few days after a very serious train accident at the main station of Zagreb in which more than one hundred persons were killed, most of them Serb migrant workers. The train was a Belgrade–Düsseldorf express that—for reasons never explained satisfactorily—entered the station at seventy miles per hour and rammed into an empty train. The impact was so devastating that it sent cars of the express train literally sprawling all over the station. The joke is a one-line announcement supposedly delivered over the public address system of the Zagreb station: "The Belgrade–Düsseldorf express is due in one minute. It is coming on Tracks one, two, three and four."

A Serb who lives in Zagreb told me a one-liner with an equivalent degree of malice toward the Croats: "The Croats don't know what they want, but they want it right away."

Intensifying this malice are bitter memories of Croatia's National Euphoria period that followed the fall of Rankovic and blossomed into a Croat mass movement for liberalization and national rights. When it appeared to be moving toward secession, Tito threatened to use the army against the rebellious province. A massive purge of Croatia's Communist establishment was carried out in 1972, and new, more pliable leaders were installed.

The ouster of Rankovic prompted rejoicing among Croat Communists who saw it as a victory for their interests. Dennison Rusinow of the American Universities Field Staff tells of a friend who attended a diplomatic cocktail party on July 1, 1966, the day Rankovic fell. The entire Croat Communist leadership was in attendance. Rusinow quotes his friend: "I didn't think anyone could be more delighted with today's news than I was, but their glee was downright indecent." The ensuing power vacuum was accompanied by an atmosphere of drift and insecurity. Yet the fall of the feared police chief and the dismantling of the security apparatus were propitious omens that brought out the latent tide of Croat nationalism. A new generation of Croat intellectuals, not burdened with guilt complexes, saw the nationalist groundswell as an opportunity unique in modern Yugoslav history to achieve full partnership in the federation. The absence of a free political life had pushed the public debate into the Communist forum. But the national call was so powerful and broadly based that a group of young, dynamic and well-educated Croat Communist leaders found themselves adrift in perilous waters. At one point Miko Tripalo, Mrs. Savka Dabcevic-Kucar and their colleagues in the leadership enjoyed mass popularity as few Communist leaders ever have. They saw themselves as Croatian national leaders first, Communist officials second. "We made a tactical mistake," one Croat leader told me long after the Croat National Euphoria period was suppressed by Tito. "We tried to do it alone."

But in the complex world of multinational relations within Yugoslavia, all things are scrutinized at a claustrophobically close range by jealous regional barons. In a sense it was the Croat leaders' inability to assess political realities that led to their downfall. The National Euphoria generated self-intoxication, and the Croats just seemed unable to summon, say, the Macedonians or Kosovo Albanians—whose grievances against the Serbs and Serb centralism were more evident and perhaps even more legitimate—to a joint crusade for an all-Yugoslav cause. But the fundamental weakness lay somewhere in the Croats' inability to check the revival of tribal hatreds. The surge of nationalism turned into an amorphous mass movement that included extreme nationalists and separatists; and on the edges of that vast crowd there were voices of hate, spite and national exclusivity. Who was the enemy of Croatia? The rumble of distant drums frightened the 800,000 Serbs who are mingled with 3.7 million Croats within the republic of Croatia.

The Serbs began arming themselves. In 1974 I drove southeast to Zagreb through a region known as Kordun, which has a heavy Serb population. During World War II, the Serbs in this area had been decimated by Croat fascists. I spoke with a tall Serb from Kordun who said people in his village responded to the National

Euphoria by getting arms. "I can tell you we'll never be surprised again. Today there is at least an axe behind every door." The envenomed shrillness of voices on both sides merged into a muddy stream of chauvinist recrimination and heightened the feeling of insecurity. "Croatia should be admitted to the United Nations as a state," a Zagreb University professor told a meeting of students. About 30,000 students went on a strike in late November 1971 and ignored calls from the Croat leaders to abandon the effort. In late December Tito cracked down on the Croats, publicly announcing he would use the army to keep the country together and prevent a civil war. This was followed by the purge of the entire Croat leadership, mass arrests of nationalists and a tough policy against all manifestations of nationalism.

Whenever I visited Croatia I was led back to these events in private talks with various intellectuals. Their thoughts invariably wandered toward long-forgotten events. A middle-aged poet talked to me at length about the reasons for the collapse of the medieval Croat State, citing passages from a twelfth-century chronicle written by Father Dukljanin. We were sitting under a fragrant apple tree in his backyard, drinking a mellow red wine from Zagorje. I jotted down one line from Father Dukljanin's chronicle as it was related to me. It was about one of the last Croat rulers, Dmitar Zvonimir, who was assassinated in 1089 during a Croat public assembly. "And lying there all in blood and mortal wounds he cursed the unfaithful Croats and their descendants before God and all his Saints for his violent death saying that the Croats should never again have a ruler of their own tongue, but should be always under foreign rule."

"Well," I said, "finally you are ruled by a Croat, Tito." My companion shot back: "Tito isn't a Croat, he is a Communist."

On another occasion I called on Petar Segedin, whose book *Svi smo odgovorni (We're Responsible)*, published in 1971, is perhaps the best and most dispassionate account of Croat nationalist aspiration. He was president of the Croat Writers Union at the time, as well as a member of the Academy of Sciences and other key cultural institutions. As a young writer he joined the Communists during the war. Later he served in the administration and in the diplomatic service. Following the collapse of the Croats' National Euphoria, Segedin was pushed out of all official positions and criticized in the press.

His book does not express loathing for Yugoslavia, but rather a deep sadness at repeated disappointments that have been inflicted on the Croats. The book is in effect a call for Croat national unity, for the defense of Croat national and territorial interests which he feels are being undermined in the federation. "The biological substance of our nation is being threatened," he said, explaining his ideas, "through a low birth rate, economic exploitation, emigration of young Croats, and inequitable composition of the political authorities who are supposed to defend the people from such difficulties."

Segedin, who was in his late sixties, gave me the sense of a determinedly conservative man. Surrounded in his modern apartment by antique maps, paintings, and old furniture and books, he talked at a time when it was possible to discuss the "national question" only by implication. His language was precise, but he attached serpentine embroidery to every idea. Others expressed their dissent throught recitations of economic and linguistic grievances with the sort of partisanship that robbed the arguments of a considerable part of their force. Segedin hit the main issues. The Serbs and Croats speak the same language, but Croats generally use the Latin alphabet while the Serbs use the Cyrillic alphabet, although the Latin is becoming more and more popular. Croat intellectuals have claimed a unique linguistic heritage and show a great deal of inventiveness in introducing new words. "You must understand, the language is our last line of defense," Segedin said.

Most of the intellectuals I talked to thought that a confederation would be the only satisfactory solution for national tensions and hostilities. Among the general population, however, one could hear of dissatisfaction but little else. Sifting all information and rumors, I sensed a revival of romantic nationalism in Croatia that seemed to be a response to modern conditions: intermarriages, social mobility, unemployment and above all to the tendency in Yugoslavia to look upon the Croats in the context of wartime experiences, which places them at a psychological disadvantage. Victory ennobles all the actions taken to obtain it, and the Croats have always wound up on the losing side.

But a Croat Communist who admitted that he himself had grave doubts about some government policies offered the following advice: "I know what these nationalist intellectuals are saying. They are our problem, they like to see themselves as actors in a national epic and the struggle waged over ambiguous linguistic issues. It is simply stupid to foster an exaggerated awareness of cultural and ethnic identity. You have the Slovenes who are more advanced and ahead of us in every respect and they get along fine with the Serbs."

However parochial it might seem, the problem of Croatia has the potential of becoming a matter of international relations in a major way. A very strong, well-organized and aggressive Croat émigré community has kept the idea of a free Croatia alive through terrorist acts. Most of the old émigré leaders, however, have been compromised by their fascist affiliation and are largely responsible for the fact that the Croat case, such as it is, has achieved no sympathy from world opinion. In recent years, moreover, a few among them have publicly said that they maintained contacts with the KGB, the Soviet intelligence service. It is difficult to apply a rational yardstick to such pronouncements, coming as they do from anti-Communist émigrés. Yugoslav officials have privately voiced concern that with the United States and other Western countries supporting the integrity and independence of Yugoslavia, Croat extremists and the Russians could find a frame of reference in which to shape their parallel interests in the destabilization of Yugoslavia. A link, however tenuous, could have serious consequences in the post-Tito period. When officials privately discuss such possibilities, their genuine concern is outlined in such a way that it gives the impression that they also seek to discredit the Croat emigration before Western eyes.

But how serious is the ethnic problem? In the world of Balkan politics it is impossible to reach a categorical answer. The evidence is too contradictory. For one, the young Yugoslavs who have come to manhood during the past decade seem to comprise a race quite different from older Yugoslavs who remember the war. They have more things in common than their fathers would care to admit. Moreover, the whole country is in the throes of consumerism that sharply diverts one's focus from spiritual to material aspects of life. It is the conjunction of innumerable ordinary destinies that carries history forward, and ordinary destinies in today's Yugoslavia are wrapped up in economics, inflation, interest rates, cost of commodities, travel bargains, unemployment and a dazzling array of desirable consumer goods. The newly created world of the consumer society has created a fresh consciousness. And the men who run this experiment in nation-building believe that the country is becoming, despite itself, increasingly united. I talked once with an old Communist who had held some of the most sensitive positions in the government before he opted for the greater tranquillity of the academic world. He quoted Goethe to me: "There is a degree of culture where national hatred vanishes, and where one stands to a certain extent above nations and feels the weal and woe of a neighboring people as if it happened to one's own." He said, "We think Goethe is right. But we can achieve a higher level of culture only by raising the general standard of living. We want to satisfy the people's needs. That's why everything depends on economy. Yes, the economy."

3

Il Socialismo Borghese

FIRST IMPRESSIONS OFTEN JELL INTO LASTING IMAGES. THERE IS AN AREA
outside Belgrade that is strewn for miles with middle-class-looking
family homes. We were house hunting and stumbled onto the road
eastward along the Danube, ascending into a green belt of vine country. To the south were the hills of Sumadija, where corn, wheat and
sunflowers grow in waves; to the north of the wide lazy river, the
rich flatlands of Banat. By the time we reached the village of Grocka,
about twenty minutes away by car, it was as if a large chunk of American suburbia had been embedded in the Balkan landscape, complete
with swimming pools, wooden decks and colorful awnings. It looked
so middle-class, so unexpected, that when I look back on Yugoslav
socialism, the image of Grocka comes back to my mind.

We drove around other Belgrade suburbs where the scenery was
less luxuriant and the view less spectacular. Thousands upon thousands of one-family homes have been built in the past few years. I
noticed that those closer to the city proper were mostly duplex-type,
which in most cases meant that the owner was leasing out one apartment for high rent.

Later, I was to discover that every urban area is surrounded by
weekend retreats and holiday homes, which are known as *vikendicas*.
The proliferation of *vikendicas* brought home to me, more sharply
than anything else, the true nature of the people's aspirations and of
the course of social changes under way. For it was as if the ownership
of a home had become a symbol of one's worthiness. "What's a man
without his own house," a stocky, moustached mechanic told me
with an expressive gesture that left no doubts about the answer.
Nothing. Zero. For years one was not allowed to build private family
homes, since the Communist government was committed to the
abolition of private property, the destruction of classes and the creation of a classless society. Since the mid-sixties, though, under that

same government hundreds of thousands of private homes have been built, and the very idea of progress has become associated with Western middle-class values and materialism. What type of a society is this? I asked a prominent Yugoslav author. "We don't have a word for it," he responded. "It is best described by a phrase Italian Communists hurled at us in the past, while they were still a Stalinist party. They said this was *il socialismo borghese,* which translates into 'middle-class socialism.' " Near the end of my tour I called on an expert in the Central Statistical Bureau and, among other things, asked him whether their figures confirmed that a new middle class was emerging in Yugoslavia. "Of course," he said without wincing. "But I cannot say that in my official capacity. We do not deal in such categories . . ."

All this was to come later . . . Before I even thought of looking deeper into Yugoslav life or canvassing local values, I was confronted with the problem of finding my own living accommodations. In the microcosm of my world, real estate problems loomed large. The private housing market was confusing and brought back, in contrast, memories of our arrival in Moscow five years earlier. In Russia we were assigned an apartment by a government agency and were able to move in the first day. I had no choice because private housing did not exist. In Yugoslavia we had to find a house ourselves. The rents were exorbitant and unregulated. The laws of supply and demand seemed fully at play as in a wildest laissez-faire situation. But not quite, as I was to discover.

When the Yugoslav Communists moved away from the sterile Soviet-style economic centralism in 1965 and introduced a free market and self-management, they unleashed a force they could not fully control. It was the most normal desire of the people to improve their living standard. For two decades they had to practice the severest economy. They had weathered the rigors of endless sacrifices and privations imposed by an authoritarian government that wanted to do something about building up and modernizing the country. This meant an emphasis on industrialization, to the detriment of the consumer goods sector of the economy. It was impossible to maintain that type of economy, and the centralism necessary for it, except by violence and restrictions. With decentralization the people received some rudimentary civil rights, including the right to travel, although not freedom of speech and association. The Communist government emerged as the champion of consumerism, of a better

life now, not in the distant future. There was an enthusiastic response throughout the country; and much of the individual drive to
seek a better life was channeled into real estate, with Communists
leading the way. Those in privileged positions had already found out
how agreeable wealth could be. The largest and most luxurious
homes in the Danube valley near Grocka belong to party barons and
senior bureaucrats. Their neighbors are successful soccer coaches and
sportsmen, writers, lawyers, artists, owners of small businesses, engineers, and other professional people. Those who occupy less
exalted positions in the society have their holiday homes in less attractive areas. The growing class of small property holders has
generated a healthy respect for private property, middle-class amenities and brand-name consumerism. From time to time, however, the
Communist leadership mounts a public campaign against "illegally
acquired wealth." This seems in part a reflexive expression of guilt
some old-time Marxists feel for having nurtured into full bloom the
bourgeois sentiments which their rhetoric reviles.

Nothing much ever comes out of such campaigns except the
discovery of a handful of petty speculators whose punishment gives
dubious credence to the ideal of equality the party feels obliged to
represent. Nobody in authority raises the obvious question: Who
can build homes costing from $30,000 up to $100,000 when the
average monthly salary in Yugoslavia is about $200? But then, no-
body is truly interested in the answer. The men who run the campaigns own expensive weekend homes, fancy cars and motorboats,
and they would be hard put to explain how they acquired all that on
their salaries. After these campaigns run their course, things return
to normal. But it is common wisdom that during the campaign one
should keep a low profile and refrain from tempting fate.

In the summer of 1973, when we arrived in Belgrade, such a
campaign was in full swing. The practical consequences of this type
of market economy became immediately obvious. Classified ads for
housing had disappeared from the newspapers; we ran a want ad in
the daily Politika for four weeks without receiving a single response.
Had we come a few months earlier, we would have been swamped
with offers. Four or five months later, after the nauseating media
campaign had blown off, numerous houses and apartments again
became available.

We moved into the house occupied by my predecessor for the
remaining two months of his lease. A large living room opened out

onto a marble terrace, which was made for grandeur and which had two wrought-iron lampposts planted at each end of a twenty-foot-wide stairway leading down into a formal garden. Its evergreen hedges, flowerbeds and paths were maintained by a gardener; a small pavillion with wooden benches and tables was set in the deep shadow of fir and peach trees. There were only two bedrooms and a small dining room. The kitchen was located in a musty basement, and an ancient dumbwaiter had to be used to bring the food to the upper level. The second level of this neoclassical villa was occupied by the owner, Mrs. Ristin, and her family.

I tried to negotiate an extension of the lease and had already let Mrs. Ristin know, without much hesitancy, that I was prepared to sign two leases to her satisfaction. This, I had been forewarned, was an absolute precondition for entering into serious talks with a Yugo-from one fourth to one third of the actual rent, is signed and submit-slav landlord. One lease, which normally bears a figure amounting to ted to the tax authorities; the second, which carries the actual figure, is the binding contract between the parties. This joint violation of the law protects the owner against any litigation. But I was summoned to her salon, which was equipped with fake Louis XV chairs and genuine Oriental rugs, to be advised that she had already promised the premises to a West German military attaché. Not only was he prepared to enter into a two-lease contract with her, but he had offered $850 per month for the place.

I developed an ethnographic interest in Mrs. Ristin. She obviously came from that small segment of the population that enjoyed urban status and economic privileges before the Communist take-over. Some people from that social class—a distinct minority—never got themselves integrated into the new order of things. Although driven to insignificant jobs, they seemed sustained in impoverished gentility by memories of their former status and possessions. Their tone about the Communists was invidious and it is carried over to their offspring. I knew a film critic of moderate intelligence who during our first meeting related a long story about hardships he faced in trying to forge a career. "And that is only because my grandfather was a general in the Royal Army," the critic said, his smile on one side of his mouth enhancing his genuine charm. "And not just any old general. He was the general who, after the Nazis invaded Yugoslavia, signed the capitulation papers. That's what they can't forgive him." Months later, when I began sorting out my notes and checking them against historical facts, I discovered that the critic's grandfather had indeed held the rank of general, but that he was not the officer who signed the capitulation papers. But such an inexplicable indulgence in self-pity on the part of those deprived of social standing and financial independence is rare. The former bourgeoisie has largely come to terms with the new order, especially since consumerism and other reforms have made it possible for them to join the new possessing class. This new middle class consists of those who have exerted themselves so as to acquire some education, some property, or administrative or party positions. The price one has to pay is political: one cannot oppose or openly challenge the party.

In addition to her house in Dedinje, Mrs. Ristin and her husband owned a weekend retreat outside Belgrade, a boat, two automobiles, an orchard. In her mid-fifties, Mrs. Ristin was a formidable businesswoman. She made her own plum brandy and sold excess quantities to regular customers. She had built a chicken coop along the high concrete wall at the far end of her formal garden where she kept about thirty chickens. Her husband, who was a physician, was a man of rustic background so totally dominated by his wife as to cut a rather pathetic figure. They had just come back from Hong Kong, she told me during our first meeting as casually as if she had been in Zagreb. A business trip? I inquired. "Oh, no, we always wanted to see Hong Kong."

Colonel Gunther Holtorff, the silver-haired German attaché, told me long after he moved into the Ristin house that he was perplexed by how freely the Yugoslavs spend large sums of money. The colonel was consulted by Mrs. Ristin about the qualities of the BMW sedan, which she had promised to her son to induce him to break off relations with a girl Mrs. Ristin couldn't stand. That was too much of a temptation for the boy. Soon the colonel noticed a brand new BMW parked in front of the house. "And you know what that thing costs here," the colonel said excitedly. "More than eight thousand dollars in hard cash. No credit."

Needing to move from Mrs. Ristin's house, we found an apartment which was most unusual. A friendly Danish diplomat, who told me about the place, hinted that it was so screwy that it would be worth seeing. "A place like that in Dedinje! Less than a mile away from Tito's residence! Well, you should see it."

The address proved difficult to find. When we finally did locate the semi-finished two-story house behind a tall curtain of wild hedge, it seemed to me that I had penetrated into something very remote from Mrs. Ristin's neoclassical villa. In the yard we were face to face with the household. A number of women were sitting around a huge metal tub, peeling the skin off dried bell peppers. Children were playing around a grandmother who was pouring gooey plum jam into jars, then placing pieces of wax paper on top of them. An old man in black trousers and a black vest was sitting on a low three-legged stool, relaxing. The front yard looked like an abandoned construction site with a row of plum, peach and apple trees on one side and a pile of dirt in the midst of a dried-out mud path leading to the garage. In the back there was an outhouse, and beds of lettuce, rows of tomatoes and horseradish next to a dilapidated shack that served as a toolshed. Our invasion of this rustic scene created a considerable commotion and evident embarrassment.

I think the owners had already given up hopes of renting the apartment. They engaged in a conversation so terse and low voiced as to become almost a code. Then we were led up rough concrete slabs of steps to the second floor to inspect the premises. There was no railing on the steps nor on the four balconies of this unusual apartment, which was designed in a U-shape with the kitchen at one end of the U and the dining room at the other. The main bathroom was off the dining room; there were no provisions for heating the place except for round vents for kerosene stoves high up on the walls. But the wood floors were freshly done, doors and window trims were carefully painted and from the window, above the tops of fruit trees and wild hedges, the view of the city below basking in the clear August sun was spectacular. It must have been our repeated failures to find anything in the way of housing that made us consider the place at all. Besides, Karin dreaded the prospect of indefinite hotel life and she began to show strain, so we seized on the potential the place offered. The rear balcony looked onto a neighbor's yard with a swimming pool and a genuine English-style lawn. There remained so much to be done before the house would be finished, but—and I conjured up, with trepidation, pictures of the rustic crowd in the yard—perhaps they had it all planned. Besides, we had no other options. How soon would the place be finished?

Grandpa, for that was what they all called him, acted as though I had disturbed him in his detached serenity. He peered into my face, his eyes perplexed, his voice grave, and he said flatly: "It won't be finished unless I get a year's rent in advance." Then he reverted to his previous state, walked out of the apartment and sat on the steps outside, waiting. Karin and I went about inspecting the apartment, arguing whether to consider the place or not. What about the heating? I asked Grandpa later. He couldn't handle that at all this year, he said, but if I invested in electrical heaters he would buy them back from me during our second year of occupancy by reducing the rent.

That evening I discussed the situation by telephone with *Post* editors in Washington. They showed sympathy for my position and cabled money for rent advance; I was, however, to finance the purchase of electric heaters out of my own pocket.

The next day I went to see Grandpa. I found him again sitting on the low three-legged stool near the side entrance. Now he was wearing a dark woolen suit and he was alone. A thought crossed my mind that there may have been a tragic accident involving someone in his family. Why else wear a winter suit on a sultry August afternoon? But then Grandpa smiled at me with a touch of melancholy and his eyes looked anxious. I realized that he must have been waiting for me for hours and I immediately told him that we were prepared to advance the money. Grandpa, who was eighty-two years old, jumped from his stool, gripped my hand vigorously, then ran up the steps like a youth. Out came his daughters carrying plum brandy, candied watermelon and Turkish coffee, all of which were required to seal our verbal deal.

We sat in the shade drinking brandy as Grandpa told me the story of his house. He hailed from a village near Pirot, which is close to the Bulgarian border. He was a soldier in the first Balkan war against Turkey in 1912, then the second Balkan war against Bulgaria in 1913, then in World War I. His village and neighboring area had been laid to waste by the successive wars. He was a mason by trade, and he built himself a new home in Prizren, in Kosovo, but that was destroyed in World War II. So he moved to Belgrade, worked as a construction worker and retired in 1956. He bought this lot when land was cheap, when the Communists were talking about expropriation of private property. He had fruits and vegetables and a shack. About that time his only son fled across the border to Austria, then on to West Germany. Yugoslavs were not allowed to travel in those days, so the son, who studied to be a sculptor, never came back to visit them. Grandpa pointed to a large metal statue of a woman leaning against the outhouse, which was the only thing left of the son's. Then things changed, he said, and he started building. "With these hands," he added for emphasis. First the basement of concrete and field stones. In the basement, where the entire family used to live, the floor was still of dry, packed earth. The walls were massive, three feet thick, and offered good insulation. The room used by Grandpa and Grandma had an old-fashioned wood-burning stove, which the kitchen also had, along with a kerosene stove. He built the house slowly (with his four daughters making financial contributions for living space for themselves), while a makeshift roof hung over the shell of the second story. It must have been a gargantuan job for the old man, whose monthly pension was less than sixty dollars. "This is my memorial," the old man said. "It will stand here long after I am gone and people will say it was Vidoje Todorovic who built it."

But he saw his hopes fade and his body weaken. Inflation and high prices on material and labor upset his plans. Grandpa refused to go to the loan sharks and mortgage the house. He represented a long forgotten world where indebtedness was synonymous with moral debasement. No, he told his children. His son-in-law, the geologist, then proposed that he finish the upper level and rent it out. The rent would pay off building costs.

They had put a lot on the line that spring. Grandpa's desire to see his "monument" completed made him accept the geologist's idea. As the summer wore on he began to feel that everything would go down the drain. But, he said, staring at me with his two sharp gray eyes sunk deep in their sockets, "Providence smiled on me." He will finish his house and neighbors and relatives will know that he was somebody—somebody of substance.

Two days later I went back carrying a large sum of dollars in my shirt pocket. The contractor Grandpa negotiated with wanted to be paid in hard currency. This, of course, was of little importance to me except that I had doubts about the legality of the use of dollars as a means of payment in Yugoslavia. I engaged a lawyer to assist me in drawing up the lease and asked him how legal it was to sign two leases. Isn't it assisting a taxpayer in cheating on taxes? He brushed off my concern with the standard "*Nema problema*. Everybody does it." Two separate leases were written on the lawyer's stationery with the rent stated in dollar amounts in one, Yugoslav dinars in the other. The spirit of the irrational is very much a part of the Balkan

atmosphere. Here we were all tightly drawn in a neat little conspiracy: the lawyer, who was recommended by the Information
Ministry to assist me in doing things the right way; Grandpa, an
innocent rustic who was so preoccupied by his dream that he looked
upon the whole thing as an expression of benign Providence; and I,
trying to avoid any violations and ending up doing what "everybody" did.

After completing the paperwork, the lawyer got down to serious
matters: "Mind my words, don't give them all that money before the
work is completed in October." I said that I had to give them the
advance since Grandpa had to pay off the contractor. "You have my
best advice," the lawyer said. "Don't part with the money before the
work is finished. What assurance do you have that they will actually
live up to their promises? This paper? Have you thought about
that?"

I thought about it as I drove to the house to sign the lease and
deliver the advance rent. Again Grandpa was dressed in his finest
suit. He led me to the best room of one of his daughters on the
ground floor, where she and her geologist husband were waiting.
"Here is Dobrovoje," Grandpa said, pointing to his son-in-law, "he is
an educated man, he's helping now." *"Nema problema,"* the geologist said with an engaging, boisterous laugh. He was a tall man with
an ascetic, elongated face and stooped shoulders. I watched him and
his wife count the money. None of them had ever held so large an
amount in their hands. Grandpa's eyes were riveted on the heap of
green paper, but he seemed calm. The young couple were excited,
their eyes gleaming with greed.

We moved in three weeks later. In the intervening span of time
the stairwell was finished and the front of the house was given a nice,
well-executed finish with a West German-made plastic substance.
The light gray surface covered all the multicolored old bricks that
Grandpa had used to build the house. At least from the front the
house now looked like a modern villa. An ancient cement mixer and
the wooden scaffolding stood witness to the fact that work was in
progress. All the activity served as a tonic for the eighty-two-year-old
Grandpa. It was as if new energy had been squeezed into his shriv-
eled body. I was shocked to see him on the top of the scaffolding,
climbing onto the roof where he was going to fix something.

I felt as if we were living in the country. Ripe berries on a huge cherry tree were there for the picking; so were luscious peaches and plums. Grandma brought us a jar of peppers in oil which she had prepared a few weeks earlier and stored in the basement pantry for the winter. She had also pickled dozens of heads of cabbage in a wooden barrel and the smell of its brine wafted out of the basement into the stairwell. Everybody showed good humor. One day my son, trying the impossible task of riding his tricycle through dirt, gravel and a strip of rough concrete around the house, rode over Grandma's *filo* (large leaves of dough) which she had left out to dry in the September sun. She simply folded the leaves and put them in the basement pantry.

Grandpa, meanwhile, worked like Lucifer. The crates in which our shipment from Washington had arrived were carefully dismantled. From the wood, Grandpa, with the help of a neighbor who was a carpenter, built two sets of gates. The carpenter owned the plot next to Grandpa's, but he was not allowed to build on it because a new zoning law prohibited all new construction in the area. The neighbor had a wooden shed in the back of his plot, however, that could not be easily seen from the street. In violation of city regulations he lived there, but Grandpa's help was essential: an electric cable from Grandpa's house went through the branches of apple trees down toward the shack, thus providing the carpenter with electricity. After the gates were finished, what was left of the crates went into the making of a garage door. Every morning Grandpa went through the garbage. Since the city's garbage collection tax was determined on the basis of the number of garbage cans a household used, Grandpa kept it at a minimum. There was one can for the entire house. Grandpa's job was to sort out the garbage, burn what was burnable in a little furnace in the back of the house, and powderize glass bottles with a hammer. In short, he did what he could to make sure all the garbage would fit into one can. We occasionally made his job very difficult. When Lee Lescaze, foreign editor of the *Post* at that time, came through Belgrade, I organized a party for about eighty officials and diplomats. Cases of empty bottles were later deposited next to the garbage can on the assumption that they would be picked up by the garbage truck. I am not clear about what happened next. Perhaps the garbagemen refused to take them. At any rate, two days later we heard Grandpa smashing all the bottles into powder and packing the garbage with it.

With the advance of cold weather, the charm of our rustic life began to wear off. Even the spectacular view from our windows began to fade. The scaffolding was moved beam by beam to the north side of the house, but the contractor had not bought enough of the material to cover the rest of the house and couldn't find any more of it in the stores. The work stopped. "We'll have to wait for the material," the geologist said. "It should be here any day now."

"But then the weather will be bad," the contractor said. "The days are already getting too short." The contractor had three workers, who were employed in a state construction company from seven in the morning to two P.M. and who were moonlighting for him.

We invested about twelve hundred dollars in five huge electric heaters that blew hot air with a great deal of whirring noise. The heaters dealt a mortal blow to the electrical wiring. The solution was a ten-pound paper bag filled with fuses for the many short-outs. Karin developed, by trial and error, patterns of use. One kitchen appliance at a time if the refrigerator was plugged in, two if it was not. When the washing machine was in use, we could not turn the light on in the dining room, which was inconvenient, or in the bathroom, which was worse. By this time I couldn't reach the garage any more and had to leave my car on the street. The approach to the house became somewhat hazardous, especially on a snowy night, when one had to maneuver carefully between wooden beams, construction gear, mud, piles of stones and two automobiles that Grandpa's sons-in-law parked in the front yard. "Come spring," the geologist kept telling me with optimism, "everything will be straightened out. I know we were supposed to fix everything last October. But you must understand that it wasn't possible. Come spring, *nema problema.*"

But there were changes during the winter. Trucks brought pieces of modern furniture to Grandpa's daughters; a large and expensive electric heater was installed in the geologist's apartment; a new television set was among the gadgetry that the sons-in-law hauled to the house in their cars. Also, Joanne, a lovely Dalmatian bitch, was brought one day and tied with plain rope to a plum tree next to the outhouse. Grandpa was upset. He rarely ventured out of his basement room. The dog bothered him. "We needed a dog when we lived in the village, but we don't need it here. But you see, they want a dog because people in Dedinje have dogs. And they get a hunting dog, another mouth to feed."

Joanne introduced a jarring note into our lives. She slept inside the outhouse during cold spells, crying and howling; she wanted to run and she tugged at the rope, which left marks around her neck. We were tempted to buy a proper collar for her but thought it wiser to refrain from meddling in other people's business. The miserable creature, moreover, was fed water and bread. That was too much for Karin, and she began saving bones and tidbits for Joanne. When the weather warmed up, our five-year-old son, who loved the dog and played with her every day, somehow loosened her rope. The animal darted out of the yard, finally freed, and following her instincts went to a neighboring yard and killed a chicken. This provoked a spasm of neighborhood quarrels. Women, waving their fists, argued whether Joanne's crime had to be compensated for in cash. In the evening the geologist and the neighbor continued the discussion. (At that point nobody knew that our son had let Joanne loose.) A few weeks later the dog died, suffering terrible pains from what must have been food poisoning. Everybody assumed this was in retaliation for the dead chicken.

With the advent of spring the work on the house resumed. The material became available again. Reinvigorated, Grandpa emerged from his basement room to again climb the scaffolding onto the roof to assess where gutters should be placed. His geologist son-in-law, however, had taken over the negotiations with the contractor.

The geologist was exuberant. "We'll have a front lawn like the neighbors back there," he said, pointing to the house that had been leased by the British Embassy. "I'll cut the wild shrubbery and we'll have roses instead. Some of the trees must go, too. Eventually we'll have a pool in the back, but I can't talk to Grandpa about that at all."

"Look," I said as firmly as I was able to, "what we need up here is railing for the balconies. Roses can wait. We can't open the doors or windows for fear that our boy may climb onto the balconies."

"No problem," he said, but the vision of how the house was to look eventually haunted his mind. "When we complete the house," he said, "you know how much its value will be? More than a hundred and fifty thousand dollars! Dollars!" he added for emphasis.

A day after the house was fully covered by the smart gray plastic layer and the scaffolding came down, the geologist and three of Grandpa's daughters cut down the wild hedge. Grandpa and I tried to talk them out of this destructive effort, but they would not listen. "We'll have a proper fence and roses all along it," the geologist kept saying.

On that day I decided to find another house. The campaign against "illegal wealth" was over and the newspapers were full of housing ads. It was clear to me that the joys of buying on time had taken hold of Grandpa's household. I was fascinated by it, in a perverse sort of way. For the urge to keep up with the neighbors, to obtain symbols of the modern age, gripped everyone except Grandpa and Grandma in a way that seemed totally unexpected and ineluctable. They were decent folk, but their aspirations struck me as unmanageable, and I feared that the yearly rent I advanced in the fall had already been spent during the winter on other things.

We soon found an old house in the neighborhood that was available. I told Grandpa we had to move closer to the International School, but he knew the reason. "God knows," he said, looking heavenward in genuine contrition, "I've tried to keep our promise. But we failed. Perhaps Providence wanted to teach us humility." He never talked with me again, avoiding me systematically. I found an American engineer working for Pratt & Whitney who wanted to take over my lease. Two years later, when I was finally about to leave Yugoslavia, I drove past the house. It looked like a typical middle-class home, but roses had not been planted along the fence.

The campaign against "illegally acquired wealth" was an undertaking so vastly confused and confusing as to require weeks to unravel. The media and party propagandists talked for weeks about the evils of wealth. Some journalists went into raptures at every evidence of illicit enrichment. When everything was over, I went through press clippings and discovered that the results stood in inverse proportion to the shrill noises generated by the campaign.

In Croatia, for instance, where private real estate activity was most intensive, especially because of the beautiful Dalmatian coast, ninety-six investigative commissions, formed to look into the sources of income of perhaps more than one million small property holders, found four instances of illegally acquired wealth. In Serbia charges were brought against 218 citizens, but most appealed their cases to higher courts.

The case that got an extraordinary degree of public attention involved a tailor, Minevski, who worked for the military in the town of Cacak. His average monthly income for the period 1968–73 was equivalent to seventy-five dollars, yet he owned a house in Cacak, an expensive automobile and a nice weekend home built out of flagstone and wood at Zlatibor, a mountain resort area. It was clear to everybody that had the tailor saved all of his wages for five years he would not have been able to purchase his automobile, let alone the two homes he owned. These details weren't enough to draw much public attention because there are many tailors who work privately and make good money. Minevski, however, had a very attractive young wife, Leposava. When the investigative commission zeroed in on Minevski and brought charges against him, the commission chairman, Atanasije Maricic, who was fifty-six years old, established a "friendship" with Leposava. They met secretly at the Minevski country home. As a result, the commission chairman was arrested on charges of having received a bribe from Leposava and having succumbed to her charms. I lost track of this case, though it was clear that the question that intrigued readers was whether the tailor and his wife were working as a team, or whether Leposava acted on her own initiative when she tried to get the commission chairman to change the decision.

Most of the few hundred people who ended up in jail during the campaign resembled Minevski. They were small-time operators, artisans, entrepreneurs. Someone had to be sacrificed, many Yugoslavs told me, for a greater good. For everybody knew that those in power had accumulated their wealth by illegal means also, that they were really not interested in having a thorough investigation of tax returns, and that they were mostly in the forefront of the hectic enrichment craze.

To my amazement I found many people pooh-poohing the whole thing as a nasty farce in which a few get hurt. In comparison with what the Communists did in the past, they argued, this was child's play. Among intellectuals this perversion of justice was met with seething resentment. "What is so diabolical about this regime," one left-wing sociologist told me, "is that they have figured out how to use consumerism for their own ends. You have the entire country wrapped up in a pseudo-bourgeois culture with everybody trying to move up. You give the majority of people what they want and their attention is diverted from politics and other such things. But every now and then the regime wants to remind us that whatever we have is ours only because we have been allowed it. It is like a privilege we were granted by the regime, a privilege that can be taken away. They don't want to do that, they just want to remind us of these facts."

There, probably, lay the rub. The introduction of a market

economy in 1965 was like an injection of a dose of capitalism, a reanimating impulse after the anemic years of supergovernment. It was as though the Yugoslav Communists finally acknowledged the limitations of human nature at least in the economic field. Greed, jealousy and violence are deeply anchored in human hearts. Finally they gave up the old belief that a decree on the abolition of evil would do away with evil itself and make everyone happy, wealthy and healthy. But while the style of economic life gradually assumed Western patterns, the political life remained Eastern, Communist.

The file of press clippings on the campaign I had accumulated became an intriguing, though incomplete, source of information on the many ways Yugoslavs were acquiring wealth.

With urbanization and the growing demand for weekend retreats, peasants who owned land in scenic areas made a financial killing by parceling it out in small lots. One farmer, for instance, who owned six acres of land at a scenic spot near Barajevo divided it into twenty lots and sold each for an average price of three thousand dollars. From the profits he built one house for himself and another for his son.

Private entrepreneurs, who are allowed to employ up to five workers, are normally not bothered by the authorities except when their businesses become very profitable. I know the owner of a private restaurant just outside Belgrade who complained about his booming business. "Please don't tell your friends to come here," he told me once. I asked him why and he related how he owned a motel which did excellent business, "so much so that the authorities decided to take it over." He was reimbursed by the state, he said, "but you go over there now and you can see the place in shambles and no business."

Perhaps the best example of how the regime resents a small entrepreneur moving into big business involved the owner of a small metal-works shop in the village of Srem. The entrepreneur, Lazar Josic, realized sometime in 1973 that there were chronic shortages of a certain metal clasp for electrical systems. It was a very simple item and Josic decided to produce it for the Yugoslav market. He made a deal with the publicly owned enterprise Technoprom of Belgrade, which marketed the electrical clasp. Josic netted nearly $200,000 in less than two years, but was then denounced by local party officials and charged with bribery and speculation. The charge was based on

what prosecutors claimed was an excessively high price for the clasp
he produced. He was sentenced to eight years in prison.

Yet there are wealthy Yugoslavs whose income is regarded by
the authorities as beyond reproach. Pop singers, professional boxers
and soccer players, coaches working abroad, literary figures whose
books have been successful on West European markets, all maintain
hefty savings accounts in Yugoslav banks. Typical is the case of Josip
Katalinski, an international soccer star who plays for a club in Nice,
France, as well as for the Yugoslav national team. When he was sold
by his club, Zeljeznicar, in Sarajevo, to the French club, Katalinski
put his money into a long-term savings account in a Yugoslav bank
with a 10 percent annual interest rate. He does not have to pay taxes
on either the principal or interest. He is not alone in this privilege.
In order to encourage Yugoslavs who work abroad to put their hard
currency earnings into Yugoslav banks, the government decided that
it would not levy taxes on income deposited in Yugoslav banks.
More than one billion dollars in such remittances is deposited in
Yugoslav banks each year, but the depositors are mostly unskilled
and semiskilled workers temporarily employed in Western Europe.

Most business and professional people prefer to keep their
money in Swiss and West German banks. A joke circulating in Yugoslavia gives an inkling of the popular distrust of the Communist
banking system. A man received five thousand dollars willed to him
by an aunt who died in the United States. He went to the bank,
deposited the money and asked the teller, somewhat apprehen-
sively, whether the funds were safe. What if the bank collapses? he
inquired. The teller said that was unlikely, but all deposits are in-
sured with the National Bank. "What if the National Bank goes
under?" the man inquired. "Look," said the teller, "the bank's integrity is guaranteed by the federal government." "But what hap-
pens if the government collapses?" the man inquired. The teller
looked around, lowered his voice and said, "Wouldn't it be cheap to
get rid of the Communists for only five thousand dollars?"

The campaigns against "illegal wealth" hardly touch the men
who run the entire Yugoslav economy as if it were their own private
business. It is widely known that the most rapacious corruption and
illicit manipulation has been taking place at the managerial level.
One publicized case provided an inkling of the nature of the manipulation in these circles. It involved a former official of the secret
police, known by the acronym UDBA.

Slobodan Todorovic, the former UDBA official, was moved into an export-import firm, Progress, organized by the UDBA presumably for espionage activities. Todorovic became its deputy director and plunged into foreign trade. In a relatively short time he acquired a large downtown villa in Belgrade; an apartment house and a villa in the Adriatic city of Dubrovnik; a seaside villa in the Adriatic town of Orebic; a yacht, fully furnished, and a large vineyard near Grocka.

Todorovic must have double-crossed his employers, for having developed a liking for free enterprise, he decided to emigrate and set up his own firm in Trieste, Italy. The UDBA then sent agents to Italy to catch Todorovic and bring him back. The Yugoslav press prevaricated about the real reason for his arrest, never mentioning the fact that Todorovic was a former UDBA official and that he had been kidnapped. The authorities expropriated all his property in Yugoslavia and accused him of bribing Yugoslav officials in currency speculation deals. The bribes—and this also illustrates the home-ownership craze—were connected in one way or another with real estate matters. Todorovic, for instance, was accused of "obliging" Lazar Jancic, one of the directors general of the Yugoslav National Bank and the man in charge of its foreign currency operations. Jancic, who was in the process of building his holiday retreat at Kosmaj, the scenic mountain south of Belgrade, needed a special type of roof tiles which were not available on the market. Todorovic obligingly sent a truck and trailer with enough tiles for five houses. Jancic put his signature on a transaction which netted Todorovic, according to the prosecution, roughly $85,000 in profits.

A Yugoslav I once befriended came to me with a request to help him transfer $62,000 out of the country. He had it on him in cash. Since I had to refuse him, I did not think it proper to inquire about the origin of these funds. On another occasion, however, he told me that he earned about $160,000 annually from his business deals with West German and Swiss firms and that he keeps most of his money in a Swiss bank. "But how?" I inquired. "There are ways, if you have friends," he said, smiling mysteriously.

Friends! There evidently existed an old-boy network of wartime buddies and veteran party members who had outgrown their ideological follies yet remained bound together in the face of the tribulations and complexities brought on by the rigors of the modern age. Likewise, there are old tribal traditions of helping one's friends because one may need their help in the future. ("One hand washes another, money washes both," says an old Balkan adage.) I got the impression that a mixture of socialism and capitalism is far from perfect in an authoritarian environment, for the logical companion of a free market is a pluralistic society, and that is what Yugoslav socialists are not prepared to accept.

But most Yugoslavs prefer the confusions and dislocations of their system to the stark clarity prevailing further east. A writer in Zagreb once gave me his view of Yugoslav socialism. "Our good fortune was to have a leader who was a bon vivant," he said. "Take Lenin, Stalin, Mao or Khrushchev. They are all austere persons who lived modestly and imposed an austere way of life on their nations. Tito has always loved to live well, he adores the over-refined European styles, he relishes his dinners with kings and queens, he likes good food, elegant clothes, he enjoys wealth. "And," the writer provided the punchline, "he had to let others enjoy life, he understood them from a human point of view."

Surely this cynical appraisal was founded in an intellectual distaste for the authoritarian nature of the regime. Yet, I couldn't help feeling that there was some truth to it. Tito lives in opulence unmatched by any European king. Several other Communist aristocrats at the apex of the hierarchy also live grandly. Much of their furnishings and wealth was simply plundered during the immediate postwar years.*

The introduction of the consumer society, however, has succeeded remarkably in one thing and that has been to eliminate or at least obscure economic and social differences between the elite and the great majority of the Yugoslav population. The New Class, as Milovan Djilas described the ruling elite in his book of the same name, is still highly visible in Soviet bloc countries, with special

---

* Two former top-ranking officials in the UDBA told me in private—and separate—conversations that there existed a separate office within the UDBA that dealt almost exclusively with providing furnishings for Tito and other top men. The office was headed by a Stevo Kreacic. One informant, who was Kreacic's superior, told me that he knew of Kreacic's criminal activity but could not restrain him. "He was tied to the very top," the informant said. Among other things, Kreacic's group was responsible for the looting of jewelry stores in Zagreb for gold to be melted down and made into solid gold flatware for Tito. The group also had stolen a Rembrandt painting and presented it to Edvard Kardelj. "Kardelj kept it hidden in his home," my informant said. "He couldn't display it since all Rembrandts have been catalogued and those known to be missing are believed to have been pilfered by the Nazis."

stores, government limousines, villas and other privileges. Yet, except for a small circle around Tito—and there are fewer than five hundred persons who actually run the country—the system of economic privileges has largely disappeared in Yugoslavia. Communist party membership still carries with it legal title to key jobs in the administration, media, army, higher education and some other areas. But there are people at lower levels of the party hierarchy whose income is greater than that of their superiors. Then there are persons entirely outside the party who are making even more. From all this followed an unpalatable trend—at least from the party's point of view. The trend toward middle-class existence carries with it both a promise and a threat. The promise is that a large body of citizenry will develop a vested interest in the system, which will help weld together the Yugoslav nations into a socialist commonwealth and gradually blunt the edge of nationalist animosities. The threat lies in the long-term prospect of pluralistic evolution which is something that the party is not prepared to accept.

Poet and writer Matija Beckovic, in a wonderful sketch of his countrymen in their pursuit of material things, included the following lines:

> Yugoslavs are finally free. They've been released from their traditional complexes, taken a deep breath and now they are simply grabbing like mad. Thus on this volcanic ground of eternal rebellions and illegal activity, a new illegal movement is in full swing —for happiness, for a home with a garden full of flowers, for a bathroom full of tiles, for pep pills and deodorants.

4

Lingering Old Ways

PETAR VOJVODIC, A DEPUTY IN THE MONTENEGRIN ASSEMBLY AND ONE of the most decorated veterans of World War II, died in the spring of 1974. He was a tall man, well over six feet; bushy eyebrows and big black moustache made his face fierce-looking and memorable. He had shoulders like a bull, and his courage was legendary. He was among the first to win Yugoslavia's highest accolade, the Order of People's Hero, a rough equivalent of the Congressional Medal of Honor. He was twenty-seven years old when Nazi Germany attacked Yugoslavia in 1941, and he immediately took to the hills and joined Communist guerrillas. I have heard people who knew him at the time say that Vojvodic, armed with a pistol and hand grenade, would charge on enemy tanks by himself. There is no reason to doubt these stories about Vojvodic, since sometime in 1943 he was selected to be Marshal Tito's personal bodyguard. Only the most courageous and the most loyal were considered for that job, and Vojvodic was the one to get it. He remained Tito's bodyguard for almost fifteen years after the war, before he retired to his native province.

The death of Vojvodic was reported in the Yugoslav media, but without any references to its cause. Oddly enough, too, the reports failed to mention his long service as Tito's bodyguard. I found these omissions intriguing. In the cobweb of half truths that has grown around the Communists' wartime struggle, I had heard a story about Vojvodic that revealed the type of men who first rose to fight the Germans. It was related to me by a senior party man. Vojvodic, as Tito's bodyguard, accompanied his boss to a conference with Churchill in August 1944. It was the first meeting between Tito and Churchill, held in Caserta, Italy, in a villa overlooking the Bay of Naples. Once there, Vojvodic fixed his gaze upon Churchill and ignored everything else. Tito, noticing this behavior, said jokingly,

"Hey, you are my bodyguard and you keep staring at him. What's the matter?" To this Vojvodic replied, cuttingly, "Comrade Tito, if something should happen to you, I'll kill him on the spot."

At first I found the story amusing, but on reflection it struck me that Vojvodic was merely following a predictable chain of reasoning in his native village. They were on British-held territory, and there was nothing he could do to guarantee his chief's safety. If Tito were to meet death, retribution would be automatic. These were ancient customs that test one's manhood and that required him to act out the preordained drama, a drama of retribution and self-justification. The mountainous portion of Yugoslavia places great weight on exterior impressions. Treachery must be met by death, particularly treachery that destroys one's dignity. For Vojvodic the bodyguard, the only way out of such possible disaster was to kill the British leader, even if it meant his own life.

My inquiries about the cause of Vojvodic's death produced no results. "People die, don't they," officials in Belgrade told me. "And he was over sixty. What's unusual about that?" But I have discovered that the federal government has fully automated propaganda guaranteed to produce similar responses to nearly every question. Unlike federal officials, who had mastered the art of double-talk and knew sophisticated ways to deflect questions, Communist officials in the provinces were far more forthcoming. In public they behaved like their colleagues in the capital, but whenever I met them face to face, they found it hard to dissimulate or lie.

Nearly a year after Vojvodic's death, I went to Montenegro and found out what had happened from a senior local official. One day in March 1974, two families turned up at the city hospital in Titograd to settle a question of honor. One, led by Vojvodic, included his pregnant daughter and several of his cousins. The other included a youth of the Cetkovic clan who had been dating the Vojvodic girl for about three months, his father and their cousins. The youth insisted that he was not the child's father.

Unbeknownst to the doctors, who were supposed to pass judgment on the matter, both families were armed. The Vojvodic side felt the family would be dishonored unless a quick wedding was arranged. The Cetkovic side felt their family would be dishonored if they had to accept a girl bearing the child of another man. Whether there were any displays of ill temper while the two families waited in a hall of the hospital for test results is not known. But when a doctor emerged to advise them that the girl was in her fifth month of pregnancy, Father Cetkovic cried triumphantly, "No marriage. They have known each other for only three months. . . ."

Before he could finish, guns flashed. The old hero Vojvodic, it was generally agreed afterward, pulled his revolver first, aimed at the would-be bridegroom but hit his father instead. Both sides quickly dispersed throughout the hospital ward, firing nearly a hundred rounds between them. In the exchange Petar Vojvodic was killed.

"I am told that it was a miracle that more people were not hurt," Veljko Milatovic, the president of Montenegro, said while relating this story to me almost a year later.

Local leaders found themselves in an embarrassing position, not because it was an isolated case of vendetta—quite the contrary—but because a genuine Communist hero was involved. Publicity, they reasoned, could encourage more killings. Hence a news blackout on the incident.

I recall another murder, which took place in the village of Srpac, not far from Belgrade, that was reported in detail. It involved an old woman, Milena Martic, whose son had been killed in a car accident. She was convinced that the driver of another vehicle involved in the accident, Veljko Miljevic, would not be properly punished because of his connections with important county officials. Moreover, several judges of the county court were passengers in Miljevic's car at the time of the accident. So the old woman found a gun in her attic, ambushed Miljevic and emptied several rounds into his body.

Normally, regional leaders and the official press pour out exhortations against blood feuds, obscurantist practices, and other "remnants of the past," such as the tradition in some regions requiring young men to purchase their brides. One press campaign in 1974 disclosed that the going price for a bride in some areas of western Macedonia was the equivalent of seven thousand dollars. But, since that was the period of high inflation and erratic gold market swings, one third of the sum had to be delivered to the prospective father-in-law in gold.

For those who had expected the old ways to disappear in the advance of consumer society, progress, rapid industrial development —or whatever label one attaches to Yugoslavia's entry into the modern world—evidence to the contrary pours in daily via the press. This is especially true of the southern mountainous part of Yugoslavia, from where the Cetkovics and Vojvodics come.

Geographically, one fourth of the country north of the Danube and Sava rivers are flatlands, an area that was on the periphery of civilized Europe. Key European events spilled over these flatlands in waves of time, with all their wondrous novelties and horrors. To the south of the two rivers is mountainous, rough country. The south was for five centuries part of the inert, indolent world of the Turkish Empire. Since they had no distinct culture of their own to impose, the Turks left the natives freedom of language and religion. Some of the mountainous areas were so remote that they were left alone most of the time.

In this mountainous part of the country traditional agricultural societies survived until the twentieth century. It was almost a Homeric world of small communities living isolated lives. The center of that world was the family stove. Around it, on long winter nights, the family gathered to listen to fairy tales. I've read some of them, now written down and illustrated. Prince Marko was a medieval equivalent of Superman; his horse had wings and talked in a human voice to his master. This fearless hero killed dragons and fought evil invaders for generations, responding to the hopes, dreams, joys and sorrows of the audience. The tales never changed. Everything in them was close and familiar to the listeners. They could recognize their forests, valleys, springs and villages. Marko and other heroes knew so well the people's needs and did everything to help them. In this world of ancient epics and legends, told by grandmothers or sung by bards on a one-string instrument known as a *gusle,* the popular heroes pondered the meaning of human existence, reappraised the deeds of their ancestors and judged their own actions. The legends and folk songs shaped the way of thinking. Mountain brigands of southern Croatia, Bosnia, Hercegovina, Montenegro, Kosovo, southern Serbia and Macedonia were later incorporated into this oral literature as they died fighting the Turks. One can hear in the legends and poems not only the saber clanging, but also the precepts of a stringent moral code. The forces of evil were bound to be defeated in the end. The legends filled one with an illusion of order. The fact that evil had the upper hand at any one moment was ascribed to the moral flaws of a few Yugoslavs who had resorted to treachery.

The legends and poems have perpetuated an innocent quixotic

world of fearless warriors, an essentially masculine world in which there is no room for erotic poetry. Women were relegated to the roles of mother, brave sister or the young maiden who nursed wounded heroes back to health so they could continue the struggle.

This was the type of society, with some exceptions, that lasted until World War II. In 1938 agriculture was the principal source of income for more than 80 percent of the population. It was primitive and inefficient. Statistics published that year by the League of Nations showed Yugoslavia ranking lowest in Europe in terms of national per capita income. Nearly half of the population was illiterate; the country had less than one hundred miles of paved roads. Moreover, the entire country was on a scale of development that ran from the northwest to the southeast—from Slovenia, where there was no illiteracy and where economic life resembled that of Central Europe, to Kosovo and Macedonia, where there were few literate persons and economic development resembled that of the Middle East.*

By the mid-1970s three out of every five Yugoslavs were employed in industries or services; the rate of illiteracy was cut down to 15 percent; improved general living standards and health services had raised the average life expectancy from forty-six years in 1938 to sixty-eight in 1972; the total length of paved roads increased to 35,380 kilometers.

Government figures on purchases of durable goods such as refrigerators, electric stoves, cars, washing machines, TV sets and hot-water heaters in the period 1968–1973 show roughly a 100 percent jump over the period 1945–1968. Seven in every ten families in 1975 had electric stoves instead of the old wood-burning ones that were once the focal point of family life.

All these statistics must be viewed through the prism of mass migrations, which involved close to one half of the population. The world of consumerism has stimulated a surge toward middle-class existence and urbanization. But a majority of urban dwellers have come from the mountainous southern part of Yugoslavia. Having foresaken the relative security of agricultural society, they moved into a world replete with financial and social pressures. The strain

---

* The illiteracy rate in each of the areas of Bosnia, Kosovo and Macedonia was above 80 percent; Slovenia's rate was about 5 percent. The figures for Serbia and Croatia ranged around 60 and 40 percent, respectively.

becomes even greater with the realization that there is no return. Family unity and the sense of community made the life in a village endurable. They may have lived in crushing poverty and backwardness, but their dignity was intact. In the new world they have had to rely on the old defense mechanisms.

On several occasions I visited the remotest regions of the south, driving from Montenegro to Ivangrad, on to Pec in Kosovo, then farther southeast to Gostivar in western Macedonia. Spring is a lovely season in this corner of the Balkans. Fields along the Bistrica River were lightly greening with spring wheat sprouting among patches of snow. To the south were inaccessible mountains serving as a natural border between Yugoslavia and Albania.

A new asphalt road cutting through the mountainous terrain created a world of its own. It was an extension of modern Yugoslavia superimposed on a wild region and in dissonant contrast with it. Next to houses made of mud bricks were modern homes of glass, concrete and bricks.

Newspapers were conducting a campaign against the tradition of buying brides, which is practiced largely by the Moslem population. The village of Cergana near Gostivar has achieved notoriety in that respect. When I was there, the topic of the day was a young man from the nearby village of Forina who had bought a beautiful Cergana girl. But after the wedding she fled from her husband to another young man, whom she loved. "Now the poor man, Djemal Ejupi, son of Ismail, is working hard and saving money for another wife," the paper quoted a Gostivar resident, Nevzat Biljali, as saying.

In the Café Gostivar I overheard a long debate about a man who became engaged to a fifteen-year-old girl after paying to her father a down payment equivalent to two thousand dollars. The group debated whether he would be able to save another two thousand dollars plus an equal amount in gold before the end of the year. What if he doesn't meet the deadline? somebody asked. That he might lose both the girl and the down payment seemed to be the conventional wisdom.

Just how widespread such practices are is impossible to determine. But there was a hint in an interview that a Communist leader in western Macedonia gave to the Belgrade daily *Vecernje Novosti*. "Although this type of sale is prohibited by law," the official was quoted as saying, "the practice exists in our society and we, to tell the truth, never regarded it as a special problem."

But even in the most backward provinces the attractions of modern life seem irresistible. During one of my trips to Kosovo I was given a driver by the Information Office to make a trip to some remote villages. The driver, Cazim Josanica, turned out to be a pleasant and thoughtful man.

We spent an entire day together, driving from Pristina to Pec, then into the mountains above Pec, and later via Kosovska Mitrovica back to Pristina. Cazim, who was a Moslem, looked older than his thirty-eight years. He had a prominent forehead and gentle light brown eyes. He did not talk about himself until we were heading back toward Pristina in the evening.

"Do you have in America a small inexpensive milking machine?" he asked suddenly. One big problem in his life was to find a way to buy a milking machine. He and his two brothers could get a reasonable amount of money to pay for it.

Cazim's problem was the following: a long time ago he and his two brothers had moved away from their village, about twelve miles outside Pristina. They found jobs in the city, and all married girls from Pristina. Cazim's old mother remained on the farm, where she had several cows and about fifteen acres of land. Each week the brothers visited the farm to get milk, cheese and produce. This was essential for Cazim in order to feed his four children and to make payments on his car and on several kitchen appliances. His brothers were in a similar financial situation; they all depended on the mother. But the mother had grown old and feeble, and cow milking had become a hardship for her. "Pretty soon she won't be able to milk anymore," Cazim said. He also felt guilty. But none of the brothers could go regularly to the farm to help her. Cazim worked overtime and his income came up to $220 a month, not enough to meet his monthly payments and grocery bills.

"The problem is," he said finally, as if anticipating my questions, "that my wife doesn't want to milk cows. She doesn't even want to go out there at all. Nor do my sisters-in-law. They want the things from the farm, but they don't want to go near it. And there's nothing we can do at this stage. Nothing. Don't you see, a milking machine would solve our problem."

"City girls," he said a little later with a knowing air, as if he had known many of them intimately, "they are different."

Earlier, while driving away from the village of Radavac, he suddenly broke into laughter. "There's a happy man," he said, pointing at a peasant riding a horse on a lonely landscape, while his woman was on foot about five steps behind the animal. "You know, right after the war"—and here he slapped his hands on the steering wheel and gave me a cheerful look—"the woman walked in front of the horse—just in case they'd come across a mine field."

A classic case of the Yugoslav vendetta took place on January 27, 1975. In the evening on that day Jaksa Vuletic, retired army captain, Communist party member, prominent activist, was murdered on the doorstep of his Belgrade apartment.

Newspaper accounts of the incident and obituaries the next day dwelt on Vuletic's notable career in his country's affairs and his functions in various organizations, ranging from the Veterans Union to the Red Cross. Police had no clues as to who murdered Vuletic or why. It was clear from the beginning that robbery was not the motive. But then, this is a safe supposition in Yugoslavia, where, as I have been told by a former police official, roughly nine out of ten homicides are due to blood feuds or questions of honor. "Our people," this official added with absolute conviction, "kill to settle old scores of one type or another. Their motives are usually a search for justice, upholding of principles as they see them. They may use the same tricks as Italian Mafiosi, but the motive here is never material wealth."

Five days after the murder of Vuletic, a senior inspector in the secret police, Branko Kekovic, stepped forward in Titograd, in Montenegro, and informed his superiors that he was the killer. He had come upon information that Jaksa Vuletic had killed Branko's brother Veljko Kekovic thirty-three years earlier, on February 22, 1942. "I had to avenge my brother," Branko said.

After killing Vuletic, Branko Kekovic told an investigating judge, he hailed a cab in downtown Belgrade and for a handsome fee had the cabbie drive him all the way to Titograd, about 250 miles away. He did not want to turn himself in right away for two reasons, Kekovic said. One, he had to see his family one more time and "kiss the grave of my avenged brother." The other was to make sure that he did in fact kill Vuletic. "You should know," he said, "that I would not have turned myself in in case Jaksa Vuletic had somehow managed to survive the bullets I aimed at his forehead." Kekovic added, "I feel so much better. A great burden has been lifted off my chest."

Why would a forty-six-year-old Communist and senior secret

police inspector be so driven to murder? From the very beginning Branko Kekovic provided information in such detail that it was obvious the crime had been carefully prepared in advance.

I had already noticed that past habits of thought have lingered on in Yugoslavia. Officials I met tried to disguise that fact, acting embarrassed as if all the past was defective. At least some of those past habits seemed to me far preferable to the aping of West European customs. But one cannot find out what a country or people are like from dining with intellectuals and friendly officials who more or less share one's interests. One must deal with them in official relations to assess how they habitually behave and react. The Yugoslavs generally resent foreign criticism and are prone to attack any critical study of their system and social mores as outrageous slander. The Communists, in particular, are secretive about manifestations of tribal traditions for fear that these would be interpreted as failures of the socialist order. The Kekovic incident seemed to me a perfect case to study the changing national psyche in its full complexity.

Branko Kekovic belonged to a new breed of Communist administrators. It is hard to generalize about so varied a group except to say that they are a generation that came of age during or immediately after World War II and began their careers in a new age. Another thing that defines them is that they were given the opportunity to acquire an education. But these formative years coincided with the age of Communist innocence. To have been born a decade or two earlier, like the men who now occupy top positions, was to have been rooted in another, earlier Yugoslavia of epic legends and tales. The generation of Kekovic was the first to cope with the realities of the twentieth century, something their fathers could not fully comprehend. Their fathers went into the war under the Communist banner not because they were attracted by the ideological appeal of socialism, but because the Communist call had an emotional appeal —the struggle against foreign invaders and the hope for justice and equality. But men of the previous generation could rely on family, friends, an old morality that cherished courage in battle and justice and equality. Kekovic and his generation were in a different situation. They absorbed much of the traditional code, yet they adopted a new one—that of the party organization. And the party was wavering. Over the past decades it became, like any organization, riddled with jealousies, pettiness, careerism and corruption.

Branko Kekovic came from what used to be called a "progressive, Communist family." Two of his brothers died as Communist guerrilla fighters during the war. It was the death of one of them, Veljko, that shocked young Branko. Veljko was sixteen years his senior and a man admired for courage throughout the hills that surround their village of Zagarac. Veljko had finished high school before the war, started studying law in Belgrade, where he became a Communist, then went off to Spain to fight in the Spanish Civil War. After the war he returned to Zagarac, where he would sit his seven-year-old brother Branko on his knees and tell stories about fearless warriors who were struggling against evil in Spain. To Branko, this sounded very much like the stories their father Maso used to tell during long winters, except that Veljko's stories were more dramatic, and more real, as Veljko himself was a part of the struggle.

A year or so later, in April 1941, when Germany attacked Yugoslavia, the name of Veljko Kekovic became woven into the rich fabric of local legends. He was a soldier in the 48th Royal Infantry Regiment, and it was due to his personal bravery that the regiment managed to escape encirclement. Survivors told a story of how the commanding officer, Colonel Pavlovic, removed from his own chest his Order of the Karadjordje Star, the highest decoration the king bestowed, and pinned it on Veljko's chest. In the mountainous world where external gestures have a special meaning, the colonel's act was enough to start a legend. The old hero Pavlovic, who earned his star in World War I, passed it on to a young hero. It did not matter that the country was collapsing, that the government had fled abroad, that the entire episode, strictly speaking, was illegal since only the king was entitled to award the Karadjordje Star. What mattered was a noble gesture by a man of courage recognizing another, younger man of courage.

The royal army collapsed after three weeks. In July the Communists started an insurrection and Veljko Kekovic was among its organizers in Montenegro. He became a political commissar in a Communist-led regiment. Throughout the fall and winter of 1941 Veljko and his partisans fought against Italian and German forces and against Chetniks, as the royalist guerrillas were called. The Chetniks had started out by fighting foreign invaders but soon realized that the Communists might be a potentially greater danger. In a battle with the Chetniks on February 22, 1942, Veljko Kekovic was wounded and captured. He died on that day, under mysterious circumstances.

After the war Kekovic's father learned that a Chetnik *barjaktar*, or standard-bearer, named Jaksa Vuletic had shot his son in cold blood. The father presented whatever evidence he had to the authorities, but nothing much ever came of that. He died soon afterward.

"Until about a year ago," Branko Kekovic said at his trial, "I've lived in the belief that my brothers had died in battle." Then, he said, he heard a rumor that his brother Veljko had been tortured and slain "like a sick dog" and the murderer was living happily in Belgrade.

Being a professional policeman and holding a senior position in the security establishment, Branko Kekovic began an investigation of his own. The Kekovics exhumed Veljko's body. Branko, his three sisters, their mother Miruna and a few cousins did the work without medical examiners or specialists. Branko himself removed the heavy stone over Veljko's skull. "I was horrified by the sight," he recalled later. The skull was passed from hand to hand so each relative could take a good look at a gaping hole above the two eye sockets. The bones of his arms were broken as were several ribs, proving to the Kekovics that Veljko had been tortured and then killed at point-blank range by a pistol shot in his forehead. It was the way in which his brother seemed to have died that brought a feeling of smoldering white fury into Branko's heart. Rumors had the Commissar Kekovic, wounded and his hands tied, being tortured and murdered on the snowy slopes of the Hum mountains in February 1942. Branko was oppressed by shame more than anything else. And the closer he came to the accurate reconstruction of his brother's death, the more ashamed he felt that it had not been avenged properly.

The defense made much of this during the trial. Along the Dinaric mountain range, tales and legends do not know of a true warrior who killed a wounded, tied prisoner—even if he be a hated Turk. It was a grave violation of the traditional code. I have heard supporters of Branko Kekovic during the trial say that never in the history of Montenegrin wars has there been a case of such a monstrous slaying. Yes, until the last quarter of the nineteenth century, Slav fighters used to cut off the heads of Turkish soldiers, but always in battle, never a prisoner who was wounded, tied, tortured. God knows how true it really was, but it was true for the Montenegrins.

The rumor connecting Vuletic to Veljko Kekovic's death in 1942 started by accident. The passage of time had erased the memory of Jaksa Vuletic in Danilovgrad District. He made a career for himself in Belgrade. Using his influence in the Union of Veterans of the Second World War, Jaksa Vuletic in 1974 managed to secure a monthly veteran's retirement stipend for a woman who had not been a war veteran. The woman, Natalia Jovanovic, boasted in front of friends in the district about her powerful patron in Belgrade.

"Jaksa Vuletic," people of the district began to recall, "wasn't that the man who killed the Commissar Kekovic?" Others said, "By God, Jaksa has come a long way, distributing veterans pensions to friends."

These were the rumors that reached Branko Kekovic, senior inspector of the secret police in Titograd. For nearly one year he carefully checked every lead, obtained evidence.

In the course of assembling the fragments of eyewitness accounts, circumstancial evidence and other data, Branko Kekovic came to a firm conclusion that on the evening of February 22, 1942, while his brother was wounded and tied to a tree, Jaksa Vuletic fired a pistol shot into the late commissar's forehead. But Branko Kekovic discovered another thing that left him disappointed, hurt and bewildered. Through his connections in the intelligence establishment, he learned that an investigation of Jaksa Vuletic's crime had been conducted immediately after the war, that the assembled evidence left no doubt about Vuletic's guilt, but that the investigation's findings were suppressed for unknown reasons. That investigation had been conducted by the military counterintelligence service (KOS), because Vuletic was an officer in the Yugoslav army.

If Jaksa Vuletic had murdered the Commissar Kekovic, as all evidence indicated, then Vuletic was a war criminal. Under Articles 125–128 of the Yugoslav Criminal Code, whose phrasing is somewhat ambiguous, a war criminal does not enjoy any form of social protection. There were two other aspects of this case which were highly embarrassing for the government. One was that a former Chetnik standard-bearer and war criminal had risen to prominence in Belgrade. The other, even more damaging, was the fact that the country's top intelligence service, the KOS, had evidence of Vuletic's past all along, and did nothing about it.

From this point the Kekovic story assumes aspects of an Agatha Christie thriller. The Yugoslav government, in order to avoid embarrassing publicity and some potentially more serious consequences, decided to handle the case as a simple vendetta and to suppress information that one of its intelligence services had on the case.

In 1974, while trying to assemble evidence against Vuletic, Branko Kekovic turned to the office of the military prosecutor and to the KOS for copies of depositions made in the course of the 1947 KOS investigation. A formal notification from the office of the military prosecutor flatly asserted that no investigation of Vuletic had ever been conducted. The answer was chilling. What has happened to the system of Communist justice? Branko Kekovic, through his connection in the secret police, had already found out that an inquiry was conducted in 1947 by the military counterintelligence KOS and that the man in charge was Milisav Koljensic, a KOS colonel.

What Branko Kekovic did not know at the time was the tangled web of personal ties Jaksa Vuletic had with important establishment figures. Once during the war, before he switched from the anti-Communist Chetniks to Tito's partisans, Jaksa Vuletic saved the lives of several Communist intelligence operatives. One of them was Milisav Koljensic. So when Jaksa Vuletic was facing court-martial in 1947, these men paid back old debts by suppressing the investigation. They were in the position to do so, since at the time Milisav Koljensic was in charge of KOS affairs for an entire military district.

But for Branko Kekovic there was only one course of action. He located Jaksa Vuletic's address in Belgrade, then followed the ancient ritual of selecting the weapon for retribution. The old "Spanish" pistol, so called because his late brother had used it in the Spanish Civil War and brought it back as a gift to their father, was the appropriate instrument. He took it with him to Belgrade, waited in front of the house No. 40 on General Zhdanov Street, and then shot and killed Jaksa Vuletic in the doorway of his home without exchanging words.

Kekovic's trial was an event. In the whipping November rain people gathered daily at the Belgrade district court building, literally rooting for the defense. And the defense was demanding that the government produce documents from the 1947 inquiry.

On the last day of the trial, the military authorities supplied some of the papers from their 1947 investigation of Vuletic, which they had earlier claimed had never taken place. But this was given to the court as "top-secret material," which could not be used in a public trial. I was able to read only portions of this material, when I obtained the court records later on. But missing among the documents supplied by the military authorities were some essential papers, such as the testimony of Vuletic's power patrons, the decision to halt proceedings against Vuletic, and the testimony of an eyewitness to the murder. Even without these papers, though, the accumulated depositions and testimony assembled by the defense and Kekovic's friends in the secret police left no doubt that Jaksa Vuletic had in fact killed Commissar Kekovic. Nobody questioned it anymore.

The court's purpose in this case—as well as in any sensitive political case—was not to establish the truth. It was to dispose quickly of the case by imposing an exemplary punishment on first degree murder charges without allowing for extenuating circumstances. The party's decision to have the court proceed in this manner must have been motivated in part by institutional rivalry between the military counterintelligence service KOS and the paramilitary secret police UDBA. The KOS has over the years achieved the dominant position in the field and the military was unwilling to give itself a black eye by publicly admitting mistakes.

There may have been other considerations. For one, there were too many people around in the upper strata of Communist society with a checkered background. Some of these people, caught up in the whirl of wartime events, had belonged—in most cases involuntarily—to fascist organizations. Gustav Krklec, president of the Yugoslav Writers Union, served during the war as an editor of the fascist newspaper *Granicar*; Stane Dolanc, the executive secretary of the Communist party and a ranking figure in the country, belonged as a teen-ager in Nazi-occupied Slovenia to the Hitler Jugend before he joined the Communists in 1943. The court also had to act in a way to deter continued blood feuds and to preclude the opening of old wounds.

The defendant, father of two teen-age boys, was a large man, quiet, disarming in his simplicity and straightforwardness, with a record of excellent public service in Socialist Yugoslavia. I believe that the authorities had already decided, in secret, that he had to be sacrificed, but that after a few years down the road a quiet pardon would be arranged so that he could be released from jail. But that didn't matter to the crowd, which spilled over into the corridors. Most of them were men of Kekovic's generation. I watched their faces. They reacted as if they were strangers in a complex modern society which somehow was not truly theirs; the values they knew were on trial. When defense counsel Jovan Barovic made his final summation, his moralistic rhetoric produced a thunderous applause that lasted long and completely drowned out the judge's admonitions. Barovic later told me that when he sat down Kekovic leaned over and shouted into his ear, "I don't care what they do to me now." He was sentenced to twelve years in prison.

After the trial I talked to an elderly man with a salt and pepper beard à la Lenin. "There is a man!" he said in a deep voice. "Those who sat in judgment are only hypocrites."

There is, however, another aspect of the lingering past that has had a more pervasive impact on Yugoslav life than spectacular blood feuds. It is the general attitude of the Yugoslavs toward authority. Traditionally they have felt that public life is a fraud, regardless of who is in power, and that men seek power and influence to get rich, which they do through stealing and corruption.

This attitude, partly a historical legacy, has produced a widespread conviction that the value of public life lies in the relationship between authority and the granting of favors. This is the magic *veza*, which translates literally as connection but which means much more than that. *Veza* is influence, pulling strings, an alternative bureaucratic system comprised of networks of clan and family links, old friendships, as well as of extended graft, bribery and corruption. If a man has *veza*, then everything is possible. He can get a low-cost apartment, a job for a distant cousin, he can fix and finagle things and obtain just about any service offered by society.

The real *veza* does not involve bribes, it is merely an exchange of favors based on old clan instincts for self-sufficiency. The "average man" or *obican covjek* of the satirical literature finds comfort in the knowledge that despite the proliferation of rules one can always find a loophole, a way out.

Those who have no real *veza* have to purchase them. The practice is so widespread—since benefits of *veza* can be bestowed by anyone—that it has taken specific forms. The most common is known as "blue envelope," involving cash placed in any type of envelope and discreetly handed to officials, physicians, managers or just about anybody in the position to render services. But the sale of favors has to be obscured by an almost Oriental ritual that seems alien to the Anglo-Saxon mentality. Payments or gifts are never solicited openly, but there is always a hint about difficulties involved in the issue at hand. That is the signal. Subsequently, the supplicant is expected to discreetly hand a bribe to the office holder without explicitly saying what it is for. Both sides know perfectly well the real meaning of the exchange, yet no explicit connection can be established. A false move can easily provoke an outburst of official indignation that would make the entire effort counterproductive, or worse. I once watched a colleague, who spent more than three years in Yugoslavia, use the blue envelope system to purchase the favor of a customs official and thus expedite the shipment of his belongings back to America. My wife Karin, however, proved hopelessly inept in this respect. I frequently had to distribute bottles of Scotch and cartons of Kent cigarettes to a variety of service people, mechanics and re-pairmen. My neighbor, Mark Hopkins of the Voice of America, maintained a lengthy list of people who should be given gifts of this nature, including the phone company.

But why so many bottles and candy boxes to the state phone company? "Do you get better service?" I asked Hopkins. "No," he said. "It's always the same. But I don't want to find out what hap-pens when you break the tradition. It might suddenly get from bad to worse."

In the heady days of revolutionary intoxication, the Yugoslav Communists had hoped to stop graft and to clear the underbrush of this "alternate bureaucracy" based on the *veza* system. But the char-acter and attitudes of peoples are formed over a long period by what history does to them. The original pledge to institute a clean government—the vision of a new dawn with happiness and harmony for all—disintegrated within a few years. For a foreigner it is very difficult to penetrate the veneer of rhetoric and stylized behavior. But if in their everyday relations a conflict arises between their personal ties and their loyalty to an abstract ideology or system, the personal element is likely to prevail. What goes for the people goes as well for party members.

It is the overwhelming importance of personal chemistry that baffles foreigners. A kind gesture, a friendly joke, the mood of per-sons involved in a transaction—these are elements more likely to influence the outcome than an insistence on rules and regulations.

Nothing captured this attitude more dramatically than my appeal to a senior government figure for assistance in importing several pieces of equipment for the *Post* bureau. Under Yugoslav law our request was perfectly legal, yet the customs office was creating endless difficulties. The official, who held a subcabinet post, listened to me with a nonchalant air of amusement that was at once charming and exasperating. "Look, I'm going to help you," he said. "I have a *veza* at the customs office, I can fix it. If we go through the channels it will take weeks to argue out the case." Indeed, his *veza* came through within two days.

.

5

People on the Move

WE WERE GATHERED IN FRANJO FRIC'S LIVING ROOM DRINKING THICK black coffee and domestic cognac. His wife and mother-in-law were proudly showing off their possessions. The house itself, of course, was the prize possession. A solidly built two-story structure, made of brick and concrete, with six rooms, two baths, central heating, the latest appliances and a yard big enough for a flower garden, a pet fox and a flock of chickens. Franjo, a stocky, curly-haired lathe operator, had spent more than twenty thousand dollars to build it, excluding a good deal of his time and energy. To reproduce it in Western Europe or America would require at least three times as much.

To get the money for the house and a deluxe model Peugeot, which was parked in the garage in the back of the house, Franjo Fric left his hometown of Cakovec, in northern Croatia, in 1969 and spent two years in a Daimler Benz automobile plant near Stuttgart, in West Germany. There was no other way, he said, since in Cakovec he was making an equivalent of only ninety dollars a month. "That was too little for my family needs. I wanted a house."

He had to leave his wife and their two children behind. He was thirty-four years old and he didn't speak German. "All I wanted to do was earn money. I lived in a factory dormitory with other Yugoslavs and we were four to a room. I didn't go anywhere. I went from my room to the factory and back. I prepared my own food. I worked overtime whenever possible and I used to read in my room. I was terribly homesick for my family, especially in the autumn. But I did well there. The Germans are very good about rewarding hard work and initiative. After a month I was making the same salary as a German worker. And, because I didn't spend it I had enough after two years to come home and carry out my plan."

Franjo's house stands at the edge of a large subdivision of new two- and three-story homes that would be the envy of aspiring

middle-class home buyers anywhere in Western Europe. That afternoon, as we walked around the neighborhood, Franjo talked about
himself. He had learned a great deal in Stuttgart and upon his return was able to get a job as an instructor at a Cakovec vocational
school. He could not have endured being away from his family for
more than two years. Some of his buddies, who started out with a
plan similar to Franjo's, abandoned their original plans after a year
or eighteen months. "At first, they'd go out on a weekend to a beer
hall, then they started looking for women, you know what I mean.
And that costs money so they had to stay on, four or five years or
more. I was tempted to join them, but I stuck it out."

Many Cakovec migrants couldn't find jobs back home and were
forced to stay on abroad, wandering back and forth during the holiday season, sending money to relatives or saving it that they might
realize their dream of owning a house, a farm or a small business.
Cakovec can provide work for about 14,000 of the people who live in
the town and neighboring villages of the county. An even greater
number of Cakovec residents, about 16,000, are working in West
Germany, Switzerland and Austria, the latter being only a few hours
drive away.

At any given time about one million Yugoslavs are dispersed
over Western Europe, from Sweden to Switzerland and France,
working in every factory town in between, most of them doing the
hard, dirty jobs that the prosperous Europeans are no longer willing
to do. They man assembly lines of the Swedish, German and French
automobile plants, sweep the streets of Paris and Geneva, collect
garbage in Zurich, unload cargo in Malmö, dig subways and build
highways from Munich to Brussels, wait on tables and wash dishes in
Amsterdam and Vienna. There are also professional men: architects,
engineers and physicians (about 8,000 Yugoslav physicians and dentists are working in Germany and Switzerland alone, according to
official Yugoslav estimates), and they are trailed by whole families of
wives, children and grandmothers. All earn handsome wages, especially by Yugoslav standards.

There are no reliable figures as to the exact number of Yugoslavs who became a part of the human wave from Southern Europe
that since the early 1960s has surged toward the industrial centers of
Northern Europe. Along with Italians, Spaniards, Greeks and
Turks, the Yugoslavs comprise an army of several million migrant

workers that the highly industrialized countries of the North have come to depend on for the operation of their factories and public services. A majority of Yugoslav expatriates stay abroad for about five years. Some, by living frugally—frequently in degrading self-deprivation—save enough for a home or a farm in two years or less. And there are some who seem destined to remain wanderers for the remainder of their working lives.

Western Europe, with its chronic labor shortages and low birth rates, owes much of its spectacular economic expansion to the steady supply of cheap foreign labor. But Yugoslavia, as one of the main "suppliers of flesh," has benefited enormously from the migrant system. The expatriate Yugoslav workers send home about two billion dollars each year—the single largest source of hard currency as well as one of the most important balance-of-payment factors for the Tito government.* The migrants bring with them even more money when they return home for good and most of it is pumped into the economy. Moreover, Yugoslavia has well over 500,000 unemployed, and the migrant system is the only thing preventing this perilously high rate of unemployment from becoming intolerable. It is inconceivable to assume that Yugoslavia's economy could survive the double burden of reabsorbing one million expatriate workers and losing their remittances over a short time span without catastrophic consequences.

The sheer size of Yugoslav participation in Western Europe's economic and social integration is staggering. The one million workers account for roughly 5 percent of Yugoslavia's total population, and 20 percent of its labor force. If there is one single factor that has helped Yugoslavia emerge from the gloom of its backward past into the light of the technological age, it is this involvement in Western Europe. Psychologically, the West has become Yugoslavia's new frontier: men driven by ambition or by desperation trek northward into a life of personal sacrifices and uncertainty. Most of them have the best and finest times of their lives, a clear sense of purpose, and they make the most money they had ever made. I have seen Yugoslav migrants, carrying cardboard suitcases and the stamp of Balkan life, arrive in northern industrial cities. My *Post* colleague in

---

* According to Zagreb University's Research Center for Migrations, Yugoslav workers had, at the end of 1977, seven billion dollars in savings deposits in West German banks alone.

Bonn, John Goshko, once suggested that they look very much like figures out of old turn-of-the-century photographs of new arrivals at Ellis Island. But then I saw these men returning home in different clothes, their bearing exuding confidence, their faces reflecting the indelible stamp of West European life. While still working abroad they spend their holidays in Yugoslavia, spending a great deal of money. I recall reading in the press that two Yugoslav dentists and their families spent their vacation in the exclusive Adriatic resort of Sveti Stefan, each renting $300-a-day luxurious bungalows normally used by Italian movie stars and Western industrialists. Both Yugoslavs were employed in Switzerland. I also recall sitting next to a semiliterate man from Bugojno, on a flight from Munich to Zagreb. He had been out of work when he decided, reluctantly, to go to Germany. But, he said, "It takes less than two hours from Munich to Zagreb by plane"—less than it would take him, had he remained in Bugojno, to go to the industrial town of Zenica and hold a job there. "And I make seven times more money in Munich than I would have made in Zenica."

The migrant system has transformed the Yugoslav countryside. It has given the opportunity to semiskilled and skilled workers to earn money abroad and acquire the symbols of middle-class existence—a home, a car, a piece of land. Which in turn has helped obscure many of the economic failures of Yugoslav socialism and has provided the government with a safety valve with which to relieve the pressure of unemployment. The mixing and the confluence of all these elements has had a profound effect on the entire country, and consequently an equally significant effect on government policies. Through the expatriate workers—"our seventh republic," as the weekly *NIN* headlined one of its accounts about the million-strong workers' army abroad—Yugoslavia has been sucked into a relationship with Western Europe that goes beyond economics. For all the revolutionary rhetoric and social experiments of Tito's regime, and all the great promises of a socialist future, Yugoslavia in the mid-seventies seemed in a basic way far closer to the bourgeois West than the Communist East.

Government officials dealing with labor affairs have reached the conclusion that nothing can be done about the migrant system—at least in this decade—and that the whole issue will be manageable by the end of the 1980s. Privately, their immediate problem is the brain-drain. Milan Manojlovic, deputy labor minister, told me, "The people we want to come back, the highly qualified, are not coming back." Most of the returning migrants are unskilled or semiskilled laborers and, with about 11 percent of domestic workers unemployed, they only aggravate the problems.

A special Institute for Migration has been established at the University of Zagreb. Its chief, Professor Ivo Baucic, a serious and cautious man, confined his conversations with me to the statistical and sociological analysis of the problem and refused to be drawn into its political aspects. But he suggested I visit Imotski County for a dramatic view of the migration system and its consequences.

At first sight I found it difficult to believe that Imotski is one of the poorest of Yugoslavia's 513 counties. By April the vineyards and tobacco fields in the Imotski valley are green under the hot Mediterranean sun. The gray limestone hills that surround the valley stand out sharply against the dark blue sky.

Imotski is located in the hinterlands of the Dinaric range, which stretches along the Dalmatian coast. The road that rises from the Adriatic Sea, like a ribbon cut into the rocky Biokovo Mountain, dips in a long sweep toward Imotski through what could well be the lifeless, stony surface of the moon. Then, from the height of about three thousand feet, the town of Imotski (population 4500) appears at the northern edge of a valley with eighteen lakes and forty hamlets and villages. A fertile oasis in a stone desert.

Before I took off for Imotski I read the only history of the area, which was published in 1953. Its author described people living in one-room houses with dirt floors. Families ate, slept and lived in that room, and during the winter they brought their cattle inside at night to keep warm. They used large pans to cook food in the fireplace, then ate from the same pan. What I saw when I drove into the valley was a far cry from that description. It seemed to me as if Imotski had been submerged in an avalanche of Western prosperity which had erased poverty and changed its character.

But things are not what they seem in Imotski, as I learned after a couple of days in the valley. For one, the county is without water, since it lies on the porous *karst* plateau. Winter and spring rains do fill the lakes and underground caverns, frequently flooding the entire valley. But springs dry up each summer in the heat and Imotski families have to collect rainwater for drinking. Moreover, Imotski's prosperity and building boom are not what they seem to be.

The county's total population is about 48,000, but it can provide jobs for fewer than 3,500. About 10,000 Imotski men are working in Western Europe, 90 percent of them in West Germany. Since 1968 they have built more than 7,000 villas with money earned abroad. Big money, by local standards, has been pouring in for a decade. Banks in Zagreb and Sarajevo have opened their branches in Imotski. And as the county began absorbing West German marks, Swedish crowns and French francs, visions of wealth and comfort replaced the traditional austerity. Until the 1973 recession in Western Europe the Imotski migrants were spending money as if there were no tomorrow. Since then they have become a bit more cautious.

For generations Imotski men have been forced to look for work outside the valley. They are proud, restless, emotional and easygoing —poets and soldiers at heart. In the eighteenth and nineteenth centuries many of them were *hajduks,* or mountain brigands, fighting Turkish or Venetian authorities. The county has produced one of the great *hajduk* leaders, Andrija Simic, and one of the greatest Croat poets, Tin Ujevic. The women of Imotski have been known as serious and self-disciplined, accustomed to waiting for their men. The men, when home from their wanderings, have wrested patches of land from the inhospitable nature, but it's the women who have worked these patches of soil trying to coax enough food to sustain life.

In the late nineteenth century, while Imotski was under Austro-Hungarian rule (as was the rest of Dalmatia), many of its men crossed the Biokovo Mountain, took boats going to North America, and later sent for their families. In the first decades of the twentieth century this type of permanent emigration increased. Statistics reveal that between 1905 and 1907, more than 1,500 men migrated to North America; in 1928, when the valley experienced one of its worst drought periods, more than 6,000 persons emigrated to Western Europe and South America. This pattern of emigration was interrupted by the outbreak of World War II.

In the first decade of Tito's rule, while Yugoslavia was a Communist prison, the regime claimed that the need for migrations had disappeared. Yet hundreds of young men of Imotski would frequently cross the Biokovo Mountain and try to escape by boat across the Adriatic Sea to Italy. Then, later, the prison doors were flung wide open, and the people were issued passports to travel wherever they wanted. Since 1963, when Tito's government made

the decision to permit workers unable to find employment in Yugoslavia to go abroad and seek jobs, the fiction of full employment was
quietly shelved. From 1964 on, Western countries, trying to recruit
workers for their industries, maintained labor offices in Belgrade,
Zagreb and other Yugoslav cities. They offered good wages, incen-
tives and prospects for adventure, at least by Imotski standards.

So young men of Imotski, who always had had dreams that took
them beyond the valley, joined Europe's migrating throngs—but this
was different from earlier exoduses. Unlike their forefathers who
had clawed their way to America and Australia and stayed for years
(sometimes forever), young Imocani in the 1960s went to neighboring Western Europe, mainly to West Germany. They were not
emigrating; they were merely moving temporarily to Germany to
earn enough money for a new home, a new car or a piece of land. In
the old days men had to think hard and prepare for a long time
before taking off for America. It was a significant turning point in
their lives. In the sixties, however, young men simply drove with
friends to Munich or Augsburg, or Stuttgart. It was no longer a
matter of making a crucial decision. Munich, after all, was only a day
or so away by car, less than two hours away by jet.

Just who built the first modern house in Samici, the tiny hamlet
set on the rocky hillside in the least fertile part of the county, is a
matter of dispute. But once one villager built a modern home, it
became a matter of pride for others to match it.

Samici is not on the map, but is located half-way between the
villages of Cista and Lovrec, off the old Roman road. It has about
eighty homes and its name comes from the Samija clan that lives
there. The family name of most villagers is Samija, but their clan
structure has weakened during past decades and only old women
remember the precise nature of family ties that existed at the turn of
the century.

Samici had endured centuries of impoverishment since the
Croats first settled the inhospitable valley. The hamlet had been so
poor that it couldn't afford a church, or even a small Roman Catholic chapel. Now it seemed prosperous and empty, left to old women
and young children. A few old men remaining had gone off into the
field, or down to the *kafana* in the nearby village of Velika Cista,
about thirty minutes away on foot, where they sat in the warm sun
and exchanged stories.

I found Marija Samija sitting on the front steps of her home.

She was dressed in peasant garb with a black scarf hiding much of her head. Her husband Ivan, who spent years as a migrant worker in Europe before and after World War II, finally settled down nine years ago after losing two fingers of his right hand in an accident in Germany. He was sixty-six at the time and without a pension. Her only son, Ljubo, forty-five, has been working in Germany for the past fourteen years. She showed me the house built with Ljubo's wages— its shiny modern kitchen, modern appliances, running water, tiles, flush toilet and septic tank. A house like that had been the object of wild dreams in Marija Samija's life. But now, at age seventy-three, she was preoccupied with a sense of foreboding, a feeling that her world has been shattered in a modern age whose attractions her children found irresistible but whose demands she viewed as excessive and incomprehensible.

Marija Samija brought out a jug of homemade wine from a cool place under the cistern for rain water. The previous year, while Ljubo was vacationing in Samici, he installed an electric pump. "It goes on like that year after year, one summer a new floor, the next a pump, then something else again, curtains for the second-floor rooms," she said with a toothless smile. "I often sit out there in the sun and ask myself, was it worth it; and then I think how the best years of our lives are gone and all we have is this house."

Ljubo's wife, Slava, is a strong woman with a dark, angular face. She thinks of Germany as a dark, soulless country where her Ljubo earns a living by operating heavy construction equipment. Before their house was completed, the distance between them was bewildering but bearable. She counted the years, but she also saw their dream becoming a reality. But now the distance has become unbearable. Slava has taken a job in a newly opened textile factory about thirty minutes from her home. She makes an equivalent of ninety dollars a month, but all of it goes to support and clothe their two sons, one attending a trade school in Split, about fifty miles west of Imotski, the other attending high school in Imotski. After fourteen years she wants Ljubo to come home, but each time he returns for a visit, she said, "I tell him he's got to go back for another year. A few more years, until the children get out of school."

I heard other, younger women in Samici speak about "a year or two longer." Stipe Samija's wife, who was in her early thirties, was among them. She had joined Stipe in Germany for a year, then had decided to return home to supervise the building of their ten-room house and to be with her children. For unmarried women, a man working in Germany is a person of substance, someone they'd like to marry. Only old women are genuinely apprehensive. Old Marija Samija has long abandoned the illusion that soon the men would come back for good. The young have become more greedy than their forefathers ever were, more involved in their shiny new possessions than other values in life. "How can a Mercedes or a color television set be the highest good?" Marija Samija asked incredulously.

Twice a year, during the summer and at Christmas time, the Imotski men come home, bringing their savings, their cars filled with gifts, toys and trinkets. The hamlet comes to life—it is the time entire families live for. The men spend money—in the valley are their roots, their community; it is there that they have to demonstrate their importance after months of anonymous existence in cold northern cities. The Samici men are German enough by now to start on their own summer project of improving a dirt road that leads from the old Roman road in a long curve toward their village, just as they are Yugoslav enough to drink and be boisterously merry and compensate for all the privations and frustrations of their wandering existence.

Each Christmas, in particular, families get together like in the old days. Except that they have more food on the table now, with a pig roast in the middle, and numerous gifts under the Christmas tree. And they are better dressed for the long walk to the midnight services at Lovrec or Cista, the two neighboring villages along the old Roman road.

Imotski has changed a great deal since the days of subsistence economy. The cost of construction, land and just about everything else has gone up sharply. And it is not cheap to maintain the fancy new homes. About a thousand migrants, who had made their fortune in Germany, have come back for good. One man from Velika Cista, a village of about 2000, decided to put his savings into a restaurant business. He built a structure in the shape of an ocean liner, with the decks serving as summer terraces and the bar located underneath. The idea of running their own restaurants had occurred to sixteen men from the village of Arzana (population 1300) with the disastrous result that when I visited the village there were sixteen separate cafés or eating establishments, this despite the fact that Imotski is beyond all normal tourist routes.

I went to Zdilar's, a tavern in the valley that is the hub of local social life and the center of county gossip, at the urging of Andrija

Mikulic. Mikulic, a forceful man in his late forties, is director of the Pionirka textile factory, Imotski's largest employer and its only industrial enterprise. He established the state-owned Pionirka as a workshop with seventy employees in 1962 and had built it into a factory with 1,300 workers by 1976. Its annual production in 1976 was valued at eleven million dollars.

The migration system, Mikulic said, has had an anesthetizing effect on Imotski's economic and social problems. It offered temporary solutions to unemployment while creating an illusion of domestic wealth. Salaries of expatriate workers are being invested, unproductively, in houses, cars, garages, cafés, in land, and gadgetry of all sorts. He knew of several cases, he said, where migrants paid as much as $1500 each to build elaborate stone tombs. At the same time, the system has subverted what used to be a subsistence agriculture. Young men dream of great fortunes and have no intention to be farmers.

"And the worst thing is that this is a vicious circle," Mikulic continued. "The only way out is to create productive capacities here in Imotski. How else could we reintegrate these people?" I had earlier heard the same kind of talk from Srecko Puljiz, a soft-spoken agronomist who has been a county executive for four years. "How do you go about creating new jobs without money?" Puljiz said. "Right now we need about 15,000 more jobs."

The men like Mikulic and Puljiz—and indeed most other natives of Imotski—show an attachment to their impoverished valley that an outsider finds baffling and perhaps irrational. As far as money is concerned, the three bank branches in Imotski itself had a good deal of hard currency in savings accounts that the migrants and their families had opened. Mikulic in the early seventies began to think of how to get his hands on that money and expand the Pionirka's capacity. The answer he came up with had a distinctly heretical ring to Communist ears. Why not have the migrants invest their savings in building factories in the county? Why not bring a West German manufacturer to Imotski?

Mikulic's idea found backing among county political leaders. It had to be dressed up in "socialist" clothing, however, since the workings of Tito's system are different from, yet akin to, the Russian system. The Yugoslavs have allowed private business on a very small scale (with a private entrepreneur permitted to employ the maximum of five employees) but have remained adamantly opposed to private ownership of businesses in general. Mikulic's plan amounted to issuing special bonds: the migrants to invest their savings, against 8 percent interest and a guarantee of jobs when they returned home and the plant was completed. No equity ownership was involved.

In 1972 and 1973, Pionirka began its drive toward attracting migrants' savings, building factories in Arzana (employing 100 persons), Velica Cista and Cista Provo (employing 140 persons in each village). Many of the workers in these new plants are wives of migrants still in Germany. In 1974 the county polled 4,000 men when they came home for Christmas, asking whether they would invest more for a major expansion; more than 3,500 of them endorsed the idea and expressed readiness to invest $1,000 to $5,000 in the enterprise.

The "Imotski model" of generating capital was soon copied by other communities with a large number of migrants in Western Europe.

It is not really surprising that the ruling group—despite its general pragmatism—was alarmed by these experiments. Such private initiatives posed a political challenge in the long run. The obvious was disguised in a series of ideological arguments. Some attacked the idea of "buying a job," as the newspaper *Politika* put it. Others saw it as a manifestation of inequality in a supposedly egalitarian society. Does it mean that only a man with a hard-currency savings account can get ahead? What about unemployed Yugoslavs without hard-currency accounts? Can a man who has contributed his life savings to build a factory be fired by that factory? Does he have greater rights than the next man?

Only once has Marshal Tito spoken favorably about workers' being allowed to own shares in Yugoslav firms—and he did that during an official visit to West Germany in 1975. The idea was quietly dropped, and the communities testing the "Imotski model" continued to operate without clearly defined legal guidelines. Mikulic, meanwhile, was given a gentle slap on the wrist and his deal with a German firm to establish a joint venture in Imotski—with Imotski migrants working in Germany to be transferred home to work in the joint plant—has been blocked by Yugoslav authorities through the refusal to waive high duty on imported capital equipment.

Over lunch one rainy day at Zdilar's, where I shared a table with the manager of a local bookshop and a few of his friends, I got a dose of local enthusiasm for the migrant system. These were simple men, factual and straightforward, and they all had managed to organize their lives through earnings they had made in West Germany. "We've never lived so well," Antun Zdilar, fifty-eight, a farmer, told me.

When I talked with Mikulic, Puljiz and some other educated men who held positions of responsibility in the county, I discovered a different view. The migration system, they said, had done nothing to help their county counter its underdevelopment. In fact, it may have kept it underdeveloped by fostering illusions of well-being.

This, in effect, is the dichotomy of views reflected throughout the country. Most people saw the system of *Gastarbeiter*, or guest workers (a euphemism for the migrants), as a "good thing," a way out of poverty toward middle-class status. Intellectuals, however, especially those critical of the regime, consider the *Gastarbeiter* as victims of Tito's economic system, which combines a market economy with a confusing system of workers' self-management in an authoritarian political environment. That both of these contradictory views seem valid reveals the desperately intertwined character of Yugoslavia's shaky economy.

The struggle for economic development has encountered more than the well-known obstacles of ignorance, inertia, corruption and disease. Despite the regime's will to reshape attitudes and institutions, there was the constant threat that population would increase faster than output, thus producing a decline in per capita income and reductions in capital formations. It could be argued that Tito's economic reform of 1965—the replacement of his rigid, Soviet-style state socialism with a more relaxed, Western-oriented market socialism—would never have gotten off the ground had it not coincided with the greatest labor recruitment drive by industrial countries. The Yugoslavs had to shut down state firms which, because of their inability to compete profitably, had been subsidized by the government. White- and blue-collar workers had to be laid off to increase efficiency and reduce underemployment. What were the tens of thousands of workers going to do?

As far as capital formation goes, the figures on savings accounts in Yugoslav banks are illuminating. In 1974, for example, there were more than 2.2 million hard-currency savings accounts representing assets of more than $1.5 billion.

Migration patterns within Yugoslavia reveal a symbiotic relationship between underdevelopment and population shifts. Slovenia, as the most advanced region, was forced to recruit more than 120,000 workers from poor Yugoslav areas to keep Slovenian industry running.*

At the opposite end of Yugoslavia, in Macedonia, unemployment is high, between 10 and 15 percent, depending on who is providing the figures and why. Moreover, the wages in Macedonia are about one third of what they are in Slovenia. I recall staying in the lovely new hotel, Deserat, on the banks of Lake Ohrid. Since the beauty of its setting and architecture stood in sharp contrast to the poor quality of services, I decided to have a talk with the manager. Not wanting to offend his feelings, I complimented the hotel, but then added that if an American businessman were running it, he would have selected a few able persons and sent them for training to a first-class establishment, then have them train the rest of the staff.

"But we did just that," the manager said in the most amiable manner. "We've sent eight men to Germany for training. After they finished training, seven of them took jobs in Germany for high wages, the eighth returned home to become the manager of a hotel at Sar Mountain."

For the residents of the developed areas of Yugoslavia, especially the Slovenes, Western Europe has lost much of its former attraction. But for the people in economically depressed areas, the West retains its magnetism and promise. In addition to migrants who work in Western Europe and who are officially described as "Yugoslav workers temporarily employed abroad," the traditional pattern of overseas migration of families has continued. More than 200,000 Yugoslavs have migrated to North America and Australia in the past two decades, most of them to Australia. I have been told by both Yugoslav and Western officials that the largest group of permanent emigrants comes from Macedonia.

Perhaps the most devastating statistical fact I obtained from the Center for Migration Studies in Zagreb was the one stating that only about 40 percent of the total number of expatriate Yugoslav workers

---

* Most of these workers are from Moslem areas of Bosnia and Kosovo. In 1976 the Slovenian government decided to build a mosque in the baroque city of Ljubljana for its new Moslem residents. A senior Slovene Communist official explained the decision by saying, "Many of our new residents are devout Moslems. We want to make them feel at home."

have held jobs in Yugoslavia before taking employment abroad. This means that three out of five migrants are young men whose first job was in Western Europe.

Despite two decades of a steady and impressive economic growth —averaging more than 6 percent annually—Yugoslavia is finding it increasingly difficult to provide work for its people. My initial reaction was to attribute this failure to Marxist economists and their dogmatic tinkering with the economy. This is true, but only to an extent (as will be shown in the next chapter). A good deal of the problem is due to the "pangs of development" that accompanied Yugoslavia's postwar industrialization. In 1940 less than 6 percent of the country's population—a shade over 920,000 persons—were employed in administrative, service or industrial jobs.* Due to the destruction and dislocations of war, the number of employed people in 1945 was under 500,000. The total number of employed persons in 1975 stood at 4.3 million, or about 20 percent of the total population.

Whatever the reasons, however, it is difficult to exaggerate the social and economic impact of this mass movement of people. One expert said: "What you have here is the younger men coming to venerate the life styles of the North, the purposeful, quick, calculating manners in human relations that had made them feel uncomfortable when they originally migrated but that they have gradually absorbed as behavioral norms. They come back and they look upon our easygoing, imprecise Balkan ways as backward and irrational." There are also tens of thousands of children who have spent their formative years in Western Europe but who have to accommodate themselves to new values in their native land. Finally there is the political aspect. The expatriates have seen democratic societies at work, and they become acquainted with the notion of social consensus. In Sweden, for example, they have been permitted to vote in local elections even though they are foreigners. They are not likely to accept authoritarian decision-making processes without a challenge.

This complex set of influences has had a restraining effect on authoritarian impulses of Tito's government. The migration system has precipitated a number of changes such as liberalization of federal

---

* The Yugoslav term for employment includes persons holding jobs and drawing salaries for their work. It excludes self-employed persons such as craftsmen, farmers, free-lance artists, performers, etc.

banking laws, the passage of legislation to facilitate the return of migrants through customs and tax benefits, and the modest measure of promotion of the private sector of the economy.

Regional authorities, especially those in Slovenia and Croatia, have adopted practical measures to keep their skilled or professional workers at home. The Slovenes, for example, have instructed state banks to grant loans for home construction—a step necessary to keep at home those workers who might have otherwise gone abroad to earn money for a new homestead. (But the concept of home mortgage remains alien in other parts of Yugoslavia.) Slovenia and Croatia also adopted regulations permitting private practice to physicians and dentists. Most of the expatriate Yugoslav medical specialists come from Serbia, Bosnia and other parts of Yugoslavia where they are not permitted to engage in private practice.

The 1973 oil crisis and the alarm it produced throughout Europe induced the Yugoslav leadership to consider changes in the law that would allow private entrepreneurs to employ ten, twelve or more workers instead of five as currently permitted. (Mika Spiljak, a member of the party's top leadership, told me without specifying any dates that this change was inevitable.) But gradually the initial fears gave way to a realization that there could be no wholesale packing of migrant workers onto trains bound for the South, that they have entrenched themselves so firmly in Western Europe that the economies of the advanced countries could scarcely function without them. In short, the Yugoslavs realized that the migrant system is here to stay for some time.

As the logical extention of this realization, the Yugoslavs have moved to institutionalize the continued presence of their workers abroad through bilateral agreements with industrial countries on matters ranging from social security and pension systems to education and information. It is an essentially damage-control effort. For there is nothing the Yugoslav economy could do—as it is constituted today—to open up new opportunities. I knew a young architect, an energetic, independent man of twenty-six whose hobby was music and who couldn't find a job upon graduation. After a few months he left for Munich, where he is making a living as a saxophone player.

Another young man, who held a good job as manager of a travel bureau that I patronized, called on me in early 1976 to talk about North America. He and his wife, he told me, had decided to emigrate to Canada. A few months later, when his papers had been processed and the whole family was about to depart for Montreal, we invited them to dinner. Why, I asked him, did he decide to migrate overseas? He looked a bit sheepish. First he talked about his brother, who was an electrical engineer and who had migrated to Belgium and married a Flemish girl. Then he added: "I'm twenty-nine, I have two children and a good job. It's not that simple to become manager at such an age. But I could see my life for the next twenty years if I remain here. I could move on to a state tourist agency, or to the JAT airline. But it would all amount to the same thing. I want to have my own business, I want to do things. I want to start all over again. That's why we are going to Canada. When you are beginning anew, you have to do it in a place you like."

6

Most Wonderful Ideological Conspiracy in the World

> We are taking part in the most wonderful
> ideological conspiracy in the world that
> is called in socialist parlance the
> experiment in self-management.
>
> —*Komunist*, Belgrade
> April 1970

IT WAS SOME TIME BEFORE I WAS ABLE TO TAKE ACCOUNT OF ALL THE things that made Yugoslavia so different from the rest of Communist Europe. On a long swing through Eastern Europe I felt as though its various people had been partly lamed by an irrational great power and an ideology which had long lost its moral and intellectual force. Czechoslovakia, after 1968, was a very sad place, its people obviously crippled by an alien hand. There were no Soviet troops in Romania and yet that country appeared to me like a vast camp, with widespread corruption. I called on an acquaintance, who was serving as ambassador of a Nordic country in Bucharest, and he showed me with a touch of revulsion a bundle of American dollars he was about to hand to a Romanian official to obtain an exit visa for a Romanian Jew who had married a Nordic girl. In 1973 the going rate for this sort of bribe was seven thousand dollars. In Poland, an old country with a proud tradition, I saw the regime fearing its people and both the government and the people being apprehensive about Russia. During a two-hour interview with Communist leader Edward Gierek, my *Post* colleague John Goshko and I discovered that Gierek's confidence and authority, so evident in his discussion of Poland's domestic politics, would give way to extreme caution and uneasiness whenever we raised matters related to his political and economic relations with the Soviet Union. Even in Hungary, which by comparison seemed the most relaxed country in the Soviet bloc, one faced stern police controls and a variety of restrictions.

What makes Yugoslavia unique in the Communist world is her unconventional internal system—a mixture of socialism, capitalism, utopianism and Balkan anarchism.

Yugoslavs call it *samoupravljanje*, or self-management. To listen to officials tell it, everything about Yugoslavia is self-managed: the country is a "self-managed commonwealth of nations"; each citizen is a "self-manager" (or *samoupravljac*); together they make decisions in a "self-managed manner," which suggests the image of a New England town meeting going wild. Except for their homes, cars, land and personal possessions, everything else is owned by society in name—banks, factories, theaters, newspapers, railroads, mines, public utilities, retail shops, etc. The authority on the functioning of each enterprise, distribution of its profits, its capital investments and long-term plans, is supposed to rest in the hands of its employees, unlike elsewhere in the Communist world where state and party bureaucrats make the decisions.

Before Tito's economic reforms and decentralization of 1965, Yugoslavia in practice had had a system of economic planning almost identical to the Kremlin's. The Plan was the key to lever for management of manpower and resources. It was drawn by experts at the party and government headquarters who sought maximum growth. Along with growth, the Plan has produced inefficiency, waste, rigidity, asymmetrical development and chaotic distribution.

The replacement of Soviet-style economic centralism with self-management provided a release of new energies and introduced the dynamism of a marketplace. Self-management seemed to be well suited for the rapid economic as well as social development of the country, although it has injected a different type of chaos.

Purely by accident, I got a dramatic insight into Yugoslavia's economic system. I was driving from the Adriatic coast toward Titograd one warm spring morning in 1974. About half way up a steep incline I came upon a column of heavy-duty trucks blocking the road. Their drivers had halted there to cool off their engines. I stopped my car and struck up a conversation with a couple of drivers. They were carrying bauxite from India for the Titograd aluminum plant.

One of the drivers, who had a curling moustache and a sharp sense of dramatic values, kept grumbling about self-management. I learned from him that there are large bauxite deposits at Niksic, forty miles north of Titograd. "There is enough bauxite there for a century," he said, his eyes flashing. Then his voice changed, acquired a mocking tinge, "Bauxite from India! Titograd buys Indian bauxite and Niksic sells its bauxite to Russia. How could that make sense? It's got to be crazy! But that's self-management."

I was not able to ascertain the profitability of the aluminum works, nor was I able to get any explanation of why the Titograd plant would import bauxite from India, which is about eight thousand miles away, instead of getting it from the neighboring town of Niksic only forty miles away.

Not that one could ignore the happy state of anarchy and lack of organization in other industrial enterprises. In dealing with Yugoslavs generally I could never figure out where Balkan habits left off and self-management took over. But at the same time I was led through some spruced-up industrial firms where intelligent representatives of workers' councils discussed successes and shortcomings of the self-management system. In some developed regions—notably in Slovenia—the system seemed to function smoothly and efficiently. A Western diplomat, who had served three tours of duty in Yugoslavia before becoming his country's envoy in the 1970s, told me once, "The economy is chaotic but life is getting better. All I can say is that self-management is one hell of a lot better than what they had before."

As I was trying to focus on something resembling a theoretical position which could be studied and interpreted, I came upon a flippant definition of self-management in the normally stodgy, dull, official weekly, *Komunist*. Self-management, it said, is an "experiment" and "the most wonderful ideological conspiracy in the world." That was it. Self-management, in the history of Communist Europe, was a revision of Stalinism that took the Communist party and state bureaucracy out of the business of running the economy. It provided an ideological justification for Tito's regime.

Another aspect of self-management has a larger scope. Many intellectuals outside Yugoslavia, still dreaming about a radical transformation of human relations and social institutions, have taken

Tito's experiment as a serious attempt to deal with the management of industrial society and as an alternative to the two tested systems— capitalism and communism. The rhetoric of self-management certainly offers hopes in both directions. But its practice in Yugoslavia in the 1970s could hardly be called a serious option for either, save that of offering partial democratization of life for a Communist society, and of stonewalling on the central issue of political and economic liberties.

Today, Yugoslavs are prone to describe self-management as a system which grew out of their wartime revolutionary struggle. But in fact *Komunist*'s definition is accurate: self-management was hatched as an ideological conspiracy by Edvard Kardelj and Milovan Djilas in 1949, when in the aftermath of Tito's feud with Stalin it was obvious that the rift had become irreparable and that the principal players had passed the point of no return. After all those years of instilling Stalinist discipline and control, making Moscow's policies the touchstones of Yugoslav communism, Tito, Djilas, Kardelj and Rankovic were confronted by the venality, the deviousness and the falsity of the Russians. The worst thing of course was their excommunication from the Communist movement. Control was getting away from all of them. What they had held on to—the Marxist-Leninist ideology—was slipping away amid unprecedented Soviet propaganda charges. Prominent Communist leaders in Eastern Europe were forced to "admit" to being Gestapo agents or American spies and to testify that top Yugoslav leaders had been in the pay of the Nazis and of the Americans as well. There was no doubt that had they fallen from power at that time, Tito and his colleagues would have lost their lives in the manner of medieval heretics who denied the dogma. It was, in retrospect, a desperate situation. Reflecting upon it much later, Djilas told me how he began rereading Marx, Engels and Lenin in those days, searching for an ideological rationale different from the Kremlin's. They had to sneak the country out of the Soviet-dominated Communist world while slowly reshaping the thinking of the Yugoslav party. Djilas seized on Marx's idea of free association of producers as a possible alternative. Marx had wanted the workers to run their own lives. The entire society could be organized in that manner with the federal government retaining responsibility for defense, foreign policy and other "essential" functions. Kardelj and Djilas had to sell the idea to Tito. Sitting in a limousine parked in a narrow street on Dedinje, Tito's two lieutenants discussed the merits of their proposal on a spring night in 1950. What they were arguing for was a departure from Stalinism, a new Socialist path which could win supporters in the international Communist movement. When they confronted Tito with the idea of self-management, his first reaction was negative. In the long debate, however, Tito suddenly recalled Lenin's civil war slogan: "Factories to the workers." And that was it; Lenin's slogan legitimized the proposal in Tito's mind and he announced a new law on self-management in June of 1950.

For Western readers these ideological subtleties may seem trivial, but in the Communist world they cut deep. Tito had to show himself as being closer to Lenin's teaching than Stalin. The liturgy of self-management, which was trundled out daily and urged in a torrent of words, seemed enough of a demonstration to rank-and-file party members that Stalin's charges against the Yugoslav leaders were false. Gradually, the party was reindoctrinated. As Djilas put it, "I was responsible for twisting the brains and Rankovic for twisting the arms" of wavering party members. Yet, for more than a decade self-management was little more than an "ideological conspiracy" and a convenient propaganda device. Like in Russia, the state owned all enterprises in Yugoslavia. These were managed from the center by the party bureaucracy with workers' councils having no decision-making powers of any importance.

It has been argued, with a great deal of accuracy, that only a determined totalitarian government could have industrialized in two decades such a backward agricultural country as Yugoslavia. But by the 1960s the old ideological debates were becoming increasingly irrelevant to the complex managerial decisions of modern society. The Yugoslavs had survived Stalin's blockade, then were publicly vindicated for their anti-Stalinist stand by Stalin's successors. Tito had consolidated his political position. His regime had created a solid industrial base. The only problem was that the economy was not functioning well. Low productivity, absenteeism, shoddy quality, corruption, inefficiency, waste, growing pressures for better living standards, all tended to complicate government plans. In essence, the country was going broke maintaining padded employment in factories and firms that could not begin to meet their costs. It was clear that the real issue was a conflict between ideology and administration.

In discussing how a new system was created it is almost impossible to exaggerate the importance of the narcissistic tendencies of Yugoslav leaders, especially of Tito. Tito's vision of the uniqueness of *his* socialism had led almost imperceptibly toward the evolution of self-management. But there were compelling practical reasons favoring a more rational approach toward the economy. The regime was faced with growing popular dissatisfaction. Despite tough repressive measures and total control of the information media, strikes spread throughout Yugoslavia. From January 1958, when more than four thousand coal miners staged a three-day strike at Trbovlje, in Slovenia, demanding higher wages—this was the first known strike in Tito's Yugoslavia—the number of significant work stoppages grew rapidly each year. According to incomplete figures compiled by Dr. Neca Jovanov, there were 225 strikes during 1962 and 271 in 1964.* The Economic Reform of 1965 ended federal participation in economic affairs and introduced a market system. By shifting decision-making powers to regions and to individual enterprises, the government in one stroke transferred the responsibility for the operations of enterprises onto the shoulders of the employees. Left to the mercies of a market ruled by the laws of supply and demand, they had to sink or swim on their own.

At first factories stopped hiring, then began laying off workers. Tens of thousands of Yugoslavs who lost their jobs, or had no prospects for jobs to begin with, soon began migrating to the industrial centers of Northern Europe. Those who retained their jobs in Yugoslavia were suddenly forced to compete profitably. The shock brought self-management to life—factories were operating directly under workers' councils and were responsible for their survival in a free market. The number of strikes over the next few years declined sharply.

The real architect of self-management was Kardelj, a decent, efficient, pragmatic, intellectual Slovene who embodied more than any other leader the basic contradiction of the Yugoslav system—the chasm between good intentions and the determination to wield power. The fact that he has survived in power throughout the period testifies to his loyalty to the cause and to Tito. He has been an ideal number two man and his mark on Yugoslav socialism was his

* See *Savremenost*, No. 4, August 1973.

ability to give political forms to an idea. He did not dissent from Tito's totalitarian years, but he had thought there was a better way. He had agreed with Djilas in 1953 about the need for democratization of the country's political life, then withdrew his support when it became obvious that Djilas would lose power.* Quietly and patiently Kardelj continued to press for liberalization, eventually outmaneuvering his archrival Rankovic and other Jacobins in the party hierarchy.

Kardelj is a small, bespectacled white-haired man, absolutely without magnetism, looking as insignificant as a man can look. In public there is something a bit wooden about him. He looks like the school teacher he was before turning to politics. But in private conversations the impression he makes is a very good one. His mind is sharp, logical, Western; there is nothing of the Balkan braggart in him. This is not only a stylistic difference with other top leaders, it is something deeper. Once the idea of self-management was advanced, he saw in it the way to resolve the tension between the means and the ends through a system in which the economy and all other aspects of life would be regulated by agreements between various groups in the society. With painstaking pedantry he wrote laws and constitutions—four of them since 1945, the last being a book of about three hundred pages—elevating the "Ideological conspiracy" to the level of a major social experiment. He had never been a Stalinist, but it never entered into his calculations that self-management would spell the end of Tito's communism. The system was to function under the party's guidance, with the party serving as the ultimate arbiter. He simply ignored the paradox that direct grass roots democracy based on self-management is irreconcilably at odds with the Communist one-party rule. Moreover, despite his pragmatism he failed to take into account the frailty of man and the intransigence of institutions.

It was Tito's practical mind that saw different possibilities in the system of self-management. He finally seized upon it not so much as a way of dealing with the problems of alienation and productivity, but as a way of resolving Yugoslavia's ethnic problems. Ethnicity has

---

* Some years later while on an official visit to Sweden, Kardelj told Agda Rössel, distinguished Swedish diplomat, "You know, Djilas said a lot of things that are right. But he said them at a wrong time."

been the plague of Eastern Europe in this century. The Hapsburg Empire collapsed on this issue; its successor states have inherited the disease. Yugoslavia is a multinational state par excellence. Tito and his colleagues discovered that Communist centralism was no remedy. By decentralizing the economy and granting home rule to all ethnic components the Yugoslavs adopted and modified an idea that was kicked around just before the collapse of the Hapsburgs. Self-management and decentralization, they felt, was not only a convenient way of disarming nationalist elements, it was the most promising way to create a more stable commonwealth—a garden of nationalities, to use Herder's phrase—each being a distinct flower, bound together by commitments to a common way of life.

Perhaps, just perhaps, Kardelj's self-management may have worked in a highly advanced, ethnically homogeneous country; or, at least, in a Yugoslavia in which all nationalities, having buried internecine hatreds and animosities, had developed an exceptionally strong tradition of civic responsibility and were in a compatible phase of economic and social development.

That was not the case. In theory—and for nearly a decade in practice—the Yugoslavs had utilized a system which was the very antithesis of their former Soviet-type centralism. In the 1960s workers' councils became mini-legislatures. The acquisition of home rule, which developed parallel with self-management, produced a state of laissez-faire economy and cutthroat competition. This resulted in the release of unsuspected energies and business talents. Industrial managers and regional bankers quickly abandoned obscurantist practices of the previous era for traditional business methods. Graft, corruption, wheeling-dealing followed. The country was rushing headlong into the bourgeois world.

There was a good deal of chaos to it all. Some saw even a touch of madness. The system quickly created regional interests, practically destroyed the unity of Tito's party, and revived his ingrained fear of nationalism and the centrifugal forces it could spin off. In 1972 Kardelj was charged with making amendments to create controlling devices that would prevent the system from acting up again. He gave to Tito's self-managing socialism an ironclad sense that Yugoslav unity could be preserved only by achieving an equilibrium among its many regions, nationalities and faiths.

It is on the lowest level that difficulties arise. How could all employees, from the cleaning woman to the director, participate equally in the management of an enterprise? I recall asking that question during an interview with the leaders of a large agricultural equipment plant in Zemun. The acting director, Alexander Calic, the chairman of the workers' council, a representative of the trade unions and several other experts all assured me that that was possible. One of them produced a hefty mimeographed document of about eighty pages of single-spaced type. "This," Calic said, handing the document to me, "is read by all workers before they take a vote." As I was leafing through the document, which was full of technical jargon and figures, a woman employee walked into the room. "Have you read this?" I asked the lady, handing her the document before she was introduced. For a moment she looked at me in surprise, then began to giggle. "Are you kidding? Who can understand that stuff?"

Pretensions aside, self-management has injected some real changes. It has legitimized self-expression and criticism. It also has sought to involve workers in a broadly based consultative process. I once spent a day at an electronics firm—one of the officially advertised self-management successes—where I found that most workers knew a good deal about the structure of their firm, the economy, and society as a whole. It was clear that the workers were kept informed about changes that are likely to affect them and about important decisions involving long-term planning. But it was also clear that the hierarchical power structure in the firm was a descending line from the director down to the cleaning woman. I interviewed one of the firm's top managers. He was a bright middle-aged man, self-assured, fast and analytical. He had spent a year or so in the United States, and he let on quite frankly that he regarded any interference of workers and nonspecialists in corporate decision-making as a calamity to be avoided at all costs. Self-management, he said, is helpful for smoothing industrial relations. But what is really important is that his firm was making solid profits and that the workers were making good wages.

Before I left his plush office, the manager told me a story that illuminated management attitude toward self-management. He had at his disposal a Lear executive jet, he said, winking roguishly. When traveling abroad and requesting permission to land, the pilots are routinely asked to identify the owner of the craft. "I have trained my pilots to reply to these queries, "The jet belongs to the working people of—' " and he gave the name of his enterprise, breaking into convulsive laughter.

The problems abound when a firm is operating in the red. The workers of a large refrigerator company at Cacak were happily voting themselves higher wages and bonuses until the summer of 1975, when it was discovered that the enterprise was heavily indebted and had lost more than eleven million dollars that year. Everyone quickly blamed the company's former director, who had left the firm at the end of the previous fiscal year.

A prominent Yugoslav economist commented privately: "When an enterpirse is doing well and making money, we call it a triumph of self-management. But, once it goes into the red and starts making mistakes, we ascribe these faults to management."

If such stories could be idly dismissed at the time, they appeared again in different forms. The workers' council of a Kotor firm, Trgovina, in a fit of generosity extended home-construction loans to sixteen employees with an annual interest rate of under 2 percent. The self-managers of Titograd's customs office voted to give their deputy chief an $18,000 loan at 2 percent annually. Three years later, in 1975, when the party reasserted its controls, criminal charges were brought against the men involved in the two cases. Both were tried in the same court: the Kotor group of sixteen was acquitted, while six employees of the Titograd customs who voted the loan to their deputy chief were given prison terms from six to twelve months.

All this sounded too absurd, yet the trend of the events was evident. What was the point of having "inalienable" self-managing rights when, for example, the director of the catering enterprise *Surcin*, Branislav Ivkovic, can be hauled into court and sentenced to two years in prison for having accepted a $2500 grant voted to him by his workers' council? The party committee of Zemun brought charges against Ivkovic under Article 255 of the Crimnal Code, which deals with stealing and robbery. Who was challenged? The workers' council which exercised its constitutional rights? Or was it a case of a vendetta against Ivkovic? The director appealed to the Supreme Court, which in turn instructed the lower court to review the case and specify the laws broken by Ivkovic. The lower court reviewed the case and found that the "spirit of socialist relations" was violated, and reduced the sentence to eighteen months. The Supreme Court found this unacceptable and overturned the decision. But Ivkovic had spent two years of his life battling the case.

Even against such examples, which convinced me that self-management did not live up to what it was cracked up to be, the Yugoslav system of mixing communism and an open, Western-style economy has been a relatively successful hybrid in the economic field.* It has created an atmosphere for a greater degree of personal freedom, opened the country's borders in all directions, restored a measure of private initiative and markedly raised living standards.

The main accomplishment of self-management lies in the fact that Yugoslavia has managed a smoother transition to industrialization than any other East European country. There have been no food-price riots and bloody clashes between workers and the police, as in Poland, and no famines and widespread misery as in the Soviet Union, Romania and other countries. Yugoslavia's entry into the modern world has been achieved in a comparatively relaxed environment, without police coercion of the Soviet bloc type. From a few contacts with blue-collar workers I realized that while they may be disinterested or bored by Kardelj's theories, they *are* interested in profits and productivity, on which their personal income depends. Improved productivity is evident wherever production performance can be measured. One of the amazing statistics about Yugoslavia's labor force—apart from the massive migration of workers to the West —is that three out of four persons employed in Yugoslavia hold at least two jobs.†

Self-management has also provided the framework for imaginative regional leaders to discard some rigid Communist attitudes toward private enterprise. An entrepreneur can, for instance, set up a business by entering into a "self-management" agreement with workers. Typical is a factory producing agricultural equipment in the village of Planina na Kozjanskom, in Slovenia. It was established by two brothers, Joze and Stanko Span, who invested a total of

* The system has failed in agriculture, however. Although 85 percent of agricultural production is in private hands, the law limits private holdings to ten hectares, or 24 acres, per family. The result is that from a country which exported agricultural products before World War II, Yugoslavia has become one of the major importers of food. In 1974, when according to official figures the country registered a record harvest, food imports amounted to $944.4 million, including one million tons of wheat, and considerable amounts of sugar and meat. Total exports of Yugoslav agricultural products in 1974 were $396.9 million.

† The newspaper *Politika* said in its January 7, 1977, issue that about 3 million Yugoslavs held a second job. The total number of employed was 4.2 million.

$120,000 in the plant and equipment. The plant, established in 1974, realized a pre-tax profit of $1.3 million in 1975. It employs sixty-seven workers, who have signed a ten-year agreement with the Span brothers. The average worker's pay is about $2900 per year. The two brothers—one is director and the other his deputy—earn $26,000 per year each. As private entrepreneurs, the Span brothers could not own a firm employing more than five persons. By creating a self-managing factory they have entered into a contractual arrangement under which they will recover their original investment with handsome profits over the ten-year period, after which they will lose all property claims on the factory.

I have heard many Yugoslavs ridicule and criticize the system; yet, paradoxically, most of them seem to support it. A Yugoslav journalist I knew explained why, despite all their misgivings about the chaotic and constantly changing experiment, most people were grudgingly for self-management. "It is not important whether it works or not," the journalist said. "What is important is that whatever personal freedoms we enjoy rest on self-management. What is the alternative? A return to the Eastern-type centralism."

The belief that they should be happy with limited freedoms and, above all, the fear of reverting to a Soviet-style centralism are what keeps the system going. This is also its great weakness as a model for West European leftists. For self-management is not just a system for the control of industrial enterprises by workers. It is supposed to be all pervasive, going right down to the shop floor, the hospital ward, the theater, the prison and the university.

For nearly a decade the system was moving toward a greater autonomy of local organization, until Tito and his colleagues realized that the reins of power were slipping from their hands. The Communist party and the state—which Marx had said should wither away under communism—very nearly did in Yugoslavia. Tito first purged the party; then he halted the evolution of self-management, which could not be done openly. Instead, the fragmentation of self-managing bodies promising even greater democracy was adopted by the 1974 constitution. It provides for a complex electoral process involving nearly two million delegates at various levels. Moreover, a Law on Associated Labor was passed in 1976 extending the self-management rights of workers from their enterprises into such areas as social security, medical care and education. Within a single factory, for example, there may be several workers' councils, each representing what is formally called the Basic Organization of Associated Labor (BOAL), each under obligation to draft its own written regulations. The BOALs are required to negotiate agreements with other BOALs, as well as with local authorities, on matters ranging from wages and prices to schooling and pension-fund problems. This free exchange of labor between self-managing units in different areas of social activity requires an enormous amount of negotiating, and all sorts of committees and boards. From the BOAL level, matters are taken up at commune and regional levels, with negotiations supposedly taking place at each step of the way until, finally, regions or republics negotiate the federal plan and budget on areas of common interest.

Except for several specialists who in 1976 were involved in drawing up this complex legislation, I have not met a Yugoslav who understood the system. And those engaged in drafting the law were primarily concerned with political matters. I interviewed Roman Albrecht, a member of the party's presidency and one of Kardelj's key associates, on the subject of a new banking law. I left with the impression that he did not have a deep understanding of capital formation problems, an impression which was confirmed by a governor of the National Bank who privately described Albrecht and his associates as a "group of idiots experimenting with things they don't understand."

"They are no idiots," a sociologist told me. "Quite the contrary. They are trying to salvage the rhetoric and hope of self-management while partially restoring the old order. Self-management logically leads to political pluralism. The ruling group was not about to let power slip from their hands. Now they have expanded the system by thousands of ambiguous rules and by greater fragmentation. But the invisible factor in all this is the Communist party. The party can control the fragmented and complex system far better than a few years ago."

"Our problems," Jogan Savin, a Slovene Communist official told me, "is that self-management has been imposed from above. We are trying to go to the floor level and explain to the workers what their rights are. But that will take time."

Much of the official rhetoric in the mid-1970s focused on the experimental character of self-management, its perpetual renewal, and its evolution into a system somewhere between bureaucratic centralism founded on nationalization of the economy and capitalist societies of the West. In short, a new type of socialism. Whether Yugoslav self-management can eventually evolve into a cogent system which would reconcile socialism with a democratic society is an open question.

7

Party as Schoolmaster Who Rarely Uses Stick

THERE IS A POPULAR JOKE ABOUT A MAN FROM BOSNIA ATTENDING A self-management meeting. He is urged by colleagues to speak and criticize management policies in his enterprise, but the Bosnian keeps mum. On the way home he is ridiculed by a colleague for not speaking out. "I have a friend, Mujo," the Bosnian replied, "and Mujo attended a meeting at his enterprise and they urged him to speak and criticize. So Mujo started talking and criticizing, and he talked until they called the police. And Mujo is still in jail."

This is a quintessential Yugoslav joke. The hold that Tito's government has on the average Yugoslav seems like that of a choke collar on a dog. The leash is very long indeed, so long in fact that you don't feel it unless you forget it exists. But then, when you step too far out of line, you realize that the leash is held carefully.

The Yugoslavs would seem to have been poorly suited for Tito's regimentation but, ironically, the Communists have done more to encourage participation in politics than any earlier bourgeois regime. Having long been under foreign rule, the Yugoslavs never felt a part of the body politic, and survival instincts dictated that they fence themselves off from their rulers. They are not detached from politics —quite the contrary. But there is a gap between the citizenry and the government, a gap which an average Yugoslav feels cannot be bridged except by outwitting the government through personal resourcefulness and cunning. Generally they are far less concerned with national politics than with local issues, and the latter are most often narrowed down to ethnic issues rather than class questions.

The very sense of class is extremely weak, since hereditary authority and autocratic privileges had belonged to foreign elites for long periods. Only in cities such as Belgrade and Zagreb does one find groups described as "better families" or "old houses" that have maintained urban status for several generations. But by and large Yugoslavs have a strong sense of equality which reflects inbred attitudes drawn from the past. On the individual level—they are fiercely independent—they don't like to be ordered about. They are individualists, or, as one Soviet diplomat once told me, "anarchists, anarchists, there's no other word for them!"

So self-management, when it was applied in earnest in the sixties, appeared ideally suited to the regime's objectives. Quite clearly, the ruling oligarchy has never contemplated the introduction of democracy which would spell the end of their monopoly on power. The system, however, liberalized life, introduced elements of civic and economic responsiblity at the local level, and above all, eased ethnic tensions. As one Yugoslav sociologist put it, "We realized that ethnic groups are irreducible units which like molecules in chemistry cannot cohere to produce a new structure but which you can use to make an emulsion by associating them in a federation or confederation."

This was one half of the coin of Tito's alchemy and it showed well. It almost seemed that he could reconcile Communist authoritarian rule with a major liberalization of the country's political life. Except that when self-management and decentralization took hold, the other half of the coin showed in an upsurge of nationalism among regional Communist party organizations. The crisis in Croatia was a major jolt. There, the young and pragmatic Communist leaders saw themselves increasingly as Croatia's national leaders, not as members of Yugoslavia's Communist leadership. On the fringes of a coalition of Croat nationalists and Communists that came into being in early 1971 one could hear public calls for secession.

And all this was taking place with the apparent blessing of Tito.

It is important to recognize that traditional patterns of clique politics gradually give way to genuine pluralism within the Communist party. At one point in the early 1970s there existed, in fact, eight Communist parties within Yugoslavia—one in each of the six republics and the two autonomous regions—each with its own regional interests and power elites. It was at that point that the common ideology appeared surprisingly brittle and that the traditional source of Communist authority—the party machine, the military chiefs, the veterans—found themselves outside the political process.

As events progressed and as the inevitability of political pluralism became obvious, Tito and the old Communists around him saw that restraints were disappearing. The entire system was moving closer and closer to a pluralistic confederation, and yet to some it seemed nearer and nearer to collapse. It was then that Tito drew the line. It was one thing to make industrial jobs more interesting and give the workers more responsibility for what they do than Charlie Chaplin had in *Modern Times*. It was quite another thing to see centrifugal forces threatening to shatter the party and the power of the ruling oligarchy. The party, Tito declared in December 1971, must resume its role as the central authority of the land. And he set into motion a wholesale purge of young and liberal regional officials.

"We had to do it," one senior party official told me, explaining the massive purge of Communists at all levels of the party and government bureaucracies during the 1972–74 period. "We were close to complete anarchy."

Ironically, one of the ranking Communist affairs specialists in the American government told me at roughly the same time: "Dammit, they're right, they've got to have a strong party. What else could keep this place together?"

The effect of the tightening gradually introduced a somewhat more repressive atmosphere in the mid-seventies. Yet the Yugoslav system, taken on its own terms, measured up well against other authoritarian systems. Yugoslavs continued to enjoy a good deal of latitude in criticizing various aspects of public life, with the exception of direct criticism of Tito and his basic policies.

Despite the impression of political drabness and the absence of serious public debate on key issues, there is within the Yugoslav party a good deal more informal and private consultation than occurs in some political parties in the West. Economy, of course, is the main area of politicking. Even in matters of foreign policy various ethnic groups are able to exert considerable influence.

The Slovenes, for instance, are vitally interested in the fate of Slovene ethnic minorities in neighboring Italy and Austria—an issue of little consequence for the Bosnians, Montenegrins, or for that matter most other Yugoslavs. But the Slovene Communists have been exceptionally successful in influencing the federal government in Belgrade to argue vigorously for the interests of Slovene ethnic minorities, and the problem of the Slovenes in Carinthia has been a source of chronic trouble in Yugoslav-Austrian relations. Mitja Gorjup, the executive director of *Delo*, the largest Slovene daily newspaper, told me, "Frankly, we have to push Belgrade on this issue. We do it on this paper by featuring front-page articles about the plight of Slovenes in Austria."

The Macedonians also generate articles about the plight of the Macedonian minority in Bulgaria, but they are not permitted to raise the question of Macedonian minorities in Greece and Albania because Yugoslavia diplomatic ties with these two countries are more important and complex. I had an off-the-record conversation on the subject with a leading Macedonian Communist who flatly denounced the Foreign Ministry and spoke about the continued difficulties the Macedonians face in trying to push the federal government to change its stand.

But the sharpest and most significant conflicts of interest are in the economic field. Slovenia, with 8.3 percent of Yugoslavia's population, accounts for 16.5 percent of the country's GNP and for more than 20 percent of its foreign trade. Large Slovene enterprises, which already dominate Yugoslav markets, have been turning increasingly toward Western markets in an effort to expand their production and profits. Why don't they invest in the poor regions of Yugoslavia? Communist chiefs from these regions are asking.

In Kranj I visited a large Slovene telecommunication firm, Iskra, which operates subsidiaries in West Germany, Italy, Switzerland, Britain and Venezuela. In 1975, Iskra realized an after-tax profit of $23 million on a total turnover of $450 million and the firm's management has decided to expand its overseas operations by entering additional joint ventures in Equador and Venezuela. For Iskra planners, foreign investments are likely to produce greater profits than investments in Kosovo or Bosnia. "It is quite simple," one Iskra manager told me. "We already have most of the Yugoslav market anyway; we have to go international."

Iskra's influence on the local Slovene government is equivalent to, if not greater than, the influence of AT&T or ITT on the American government. There are also large companies in Kosovo, Macedonia and Bosnia which—although they have difficulties in meeting their payrolls—exercize great influence on their local governments.

Since December 1971, Tito has been moving toward recentralization without really coming to terms with it. The forces pressing against him came from different directions. Those upset by the chaos and political permissiveness urged the rule of a firm hand. Others, among them Kardelj, sought to salvage the self-management experiment, arguing that a sharp halt would be a poor long-term solution and that it would not be possible anyway. Tito took the middle course. He had never contemplated the possibility of his party giving up power; hence he moved to reinvigorate it and impose discipline on the membership. Yet self-management, *his* path to socialism—the ideological rationale for his power and prestige for nearly three decades—had to be retained.

The Yugoslav party is one of those curious organizations that defies commonplace notions of a Communist party as a tightly knit secular order imbued with a high degree of ideological fervor. Quite the contrary. I have spoken with hundreds of party members but have never found one who, when speaking privately, was a true believer. The hum of propaganda has created the façade of party conformity but Marxist political lingo has been so overused that it has been drained of all meaning. Party members openly have their children baptized and hold church weddings. The mother of Djemal Bjedic, who served as Prime Minister in 1975, was given a religious funeral that year with top state and party leaders marching in the traditional Moslem funeral procession. (The pictures of the funeral were shown on national television.)

Undoubtedly, among 1.4 million party members there must be some true believers, but it is difficult for any outsider to discover who they are or whether in fact they exist. I have inquired into this aspect of Yugoslav life with greater persistence than it probably deserved, asking numerous Yugoslav acquaintances whether in their circles they knew of any true believers. The question invariably produced a period of reflection and the answer "no." Once, a Slovene engineer whom I befriended responded by saying that he had long thought the arm-waving circus posturing of a young colleague reflected sincere idealism until he had an intimate talk with him and discovered a cynical young opportunist.

An even more stunning admission came from an old Communist, who is a federal judge and the author of a series of books on "socialist legality." He had spent some time in Sweden on an exchange program and came to the conclusion, as he told me, that "Sweden is the only place I know of where you have socialism. We and the Russians only talk about socialism without knowing much about it."

And yet, all these men in public are making daily bows to Tito, self-management and nonalignment. These are the basic elements of Yugoslav socialism, the stable frame of reference in constantly shifting Marxist rhetoric and experimentation. There are still a number of writers who compose obscure articles about the ideology. Published mainly in the party's weekly and monthly journals, they seem one of the last political rites and rituals of an earlier era. Even in terms of political symbolism, the cult of Tito is maintained without any reference to Marx, Engels or Lenin. Tito's home in his ancestral village is a secular shrine, and his birthday on May 25—not the International Workers Day on May 1—is the principal ceremonial event of the regime.

The weakness of ideological fervor among Yugoslav Communists, in fact the total lack of it, is hardly surprising. The 1948 feud between Stalin and Tito was a landmark event in Communist history not only because it created the first important schism among ruling parties, but because one of them—the Yugoslav—was forced into a systematic reexamination of the dogma. The Yugoslav interpretation of Marxism was to assign the party the role of a "socialist critic" within a self-managed society and to commit itself to a gradual withering away of party and state bureaucracy. That is why in 1952 the party changed its official name to the League of Communists of Yugoslavia, an act symbolizing their difference from the Russians. But the ideological conflict with the Russians left the Yugoslavs disoriented. The ruling quadrumvirate gradually split on the issue. First Djilas was ousted in 1954 for advocating political pluralism. Then, in 1966, Rankovic was expelled from the party for opposing pluralism within the party. Finally, the positions of Tito and Kardelj were challenged in the 1970s by younger, more liberal Communists in Croatia and Serbia. These major shifts, along with a series of minor zig-zags, have left ideology devoid of vigor and the rank and file confused and cynical.

It was largely a matter of Tito's prestige combined with his skillful handling of the party and the army that enabled the old marshal to impose discipline on regional barons. Several hundred thousand new members were admitted to the party in 1973–74 to replace the ousted cadres. A panoply of institutions was set up to create the illusion of diffusion of power—self-managing councils, trade unions, self-defense units and others, all involved in endless consultations. Party membership was again made a prerequisite for all top jobs in the administration, universities and communications.

I called on another ranking party man, former Prime Minister Miko Spiljak, who is a member of the party presidency and chief of the Yugoslav Trade Unions. If the workers are managers of their enterprises, why trade unions? How do they protect workers' interests? And against whom? Spiljak, an exceptionally intelligent and forthright Croat who was a trade union organizer before World War II, seemed perplexed by such questions. At first he veered off into generalities, but then he made his point. "We are not about to permit a multi-party system in this country. But we want to have democracy. At the factory level every criticism is possible. We want to have the greatest number of people influencing policies. We have not reached that as yet."

Another senior figure, Finance Minister Momcilo Cemovic, was, perhaps unwittingly, even more candid. The party, he told me, is "like a schoolmaster who doesn't use his stick often, but instead patiently tries to persuade his pupils to do what they should do. And," he added with emphasis, "our patience is great indeed." In an instant I recalled the famous Richard Nixon interview in the Washington *Star News* the day after his 1972 reelection in which he talked about Americans as "children" to be guided by the President.

The extraordinary thing about the Yugoslav party is its complete submission to one man. The apparatus of power is the office of the president—in short, Tito himself. The party and the country have accepted his style of leadership, a charismatic leadership which is also sought by the leaders of some Western democracies. Tito's rein over his party is almost absolute; he uses it to act as a broker between corporate and regional interest, and in an important way he has turned Yugoslavia into a corporate state. He has let local leaders deal with local situations, but he has never instituted at the federal level a clearly defined decision-making process. This is a vital clue to the Yugoslav political system. The average Yugoslav is far from being impotent at the local level where personal contacts, the *veza* system, and an easygoing inefficiency of self-management all combine to blunt the rigidities of a one-party rule. But his influence on federal policies is nonexistent. At the federal level, regional Communist elites haggle over the budget or peddle their favorite development schemes. There are endless discussions; in 1976, for example, the

Federal Assembly was nearly six months behind the deadline for adopting the federal budget. In the end, an agreement was imposed from above, just like in all cases where crucial decisions are required. As one senior Yugoslav official put it, "If there is an important matter to be resolved, everybody knows that Tito will have the final word."

8

Rebel Who Became Uncrowned King

SHORTLY AFTER THE END OF THE 1973 YOM KIPPUR WAR, MARSHAL TITO traveled to Kiev to discuss the Middle East with Soviet leader Leonid Brezhnev. Although it was not a formal visit, protocol required that Tito lay a wreath at the monument to victims of World War II. The steps leading up to the massive monument are unusually high, and the Russian hosts assigned two Soviet army officers to assist the octogenarian Yugoslav leader in ascending. The two discreetly flanked Tito when he approached the steps and tried to support him by his elbows. But the old man swung his arms, shoved the two officers aside and marched up the steps without assistance.

A member of the Yugoslav delegation, who told me the story, explained: "The Old Man knew he mustn't show any signs of weakness, because it would be exploited. We saw the Russians watching the entire episode carefully. His physical vigor was duly noted."

In politics—especially in the authoritarian world of Eastern Europe—the appearance of strength must be maintained at all costs. Tito's instincts in this respect have been exceptional. A Communist since 1917, he became Yugoslavia's uncrowned king and autocrat in the fashion established by Prince Milos in the early nineteenth century—as leader of a guerrilla uprising. He has forged a modern state and brazenly led it down a unique path, improvising a new brand of socialism at home and his own type of neutralism abroad. Although he had only four years of primary education, he sensed intuitively the epic nature of history and the importance of myths in politics. In the twilight of his life, he is regarded at home and abroad as the pillar of the system he created.

Among diplomats the state of Tito's health is almost equated with his country's political health. I recall a conversation with three Western ambassadors in December 1974. They had just come back from an annual hunting party hosted by Tito for the chiefs of diplomatic missions in Belgrade. Following a daylong hunt, the ambassadors dined with Tito at his hunting lodge. The sumptuous dinner lasted more than five hours. "We watched him all the time," one envoy said. "Tito was drinking a great deal, but he never left the table. Frankly, it is impossible even for a younger man to consume that much liquor and sit through a five-hour dinner."

All countries have their great men who tend to see themselves as indispensable; dictators have the advantage of using the instruments of state to make others believe it. Tito has done just that to create his myth, but then again, his life has been the stuff of which myths are made: a courageous guerrilla leader wresting control of Yugoslavia during the war; later, a tough local hero defying Stalin in 1948 and successfully resisting the malevolent giant; finally vindicated on the world stage when Stalin's successors took a step unprecedented for the rulers of Russia by traveling to Belgrade to seek reconciliation with a man they had called a "fascist murderer" and an "American spy."

Tito also was a contrast to his contemporaries—the crafty, bloodthirsty Stalin, the fatuous Mussolini, the manic Hitler, the erratic Khrushchev, the unimaginative Franco. He was more humane, less murderous, willing to experiment. Although he considered himself a Marxist, he was bored by abstractions, never taking ideology very seriously, at least not as a means of interpreting the actions of others or his own reactions to problems. He was a practical politician with a Byzantine mind. He enjoyed the pleasures of power, openly and unabashedly living in the style of his royal predecessors. He proclaimed the country's destiny: independence, socialism and nonalignment. Above all, he abandoned the suffocating Soviet-style policies and repression that he introduced upon taking power and ushered Yugoslavia into the modern age.

Yet his long tenure—and uncertainty when it will end—has placed his regime in a peculiar state of limbo. He had simply outlived most of his colleagues. Ambitious, younger men were pushed out the moment they were perceived as potential challengers. With age Tito turned more secretive, relying on a few trusted aides. His power has been absolute.

In his mid-eighties Tito was still darting around the world. I heard him speak extemporaneously in the spring of 1976 and found his vitality, clarity and speed of mind amazing. His immense self-confidence reflected his conviction of his own greatness. Close up, he gave an impression of strength; his mien that of a medieval despot, his sky-blue marshal's uniform or his business suit elegantly tailored, a large solitaire diamond ring on his left hand. I noticed his hair was dyed, but the shades of color were not consistent from one occasion to the next. I felt his face obscured such a depth of conceit that there seemed to be no possibility of two-way communication between him and lesser mortals.* He was a living deity, a myth, a benevolent grandfather and wise ruler rolled into one. This, I have been told by some astute Yugoslav observers, has widened the gap between Tito and the men who run the country under—very much under—him, generating a feeling among the elite that nothing can be done until after Tito.

But out in the country Tito has a real hold on the people. It was my impression that if by some miracle free elections were suddenly held in Yugoslavia, Tito would get a majority of the votes, even if his Communist party would not.

I talked with a young textile worker in Pirot, near the Bulgarian border. "I am for Tito. As long as he is alive I know the Russians will not come here," he said. But why would the Russians come here? He motioned eastward toward Bulgaria, "Ask them, over here."

A fifty-eight-year-old clerk in Slovenia, who was a devoted Roman Catholic, put it this way, "God bless his soul. Had it not been for him we would have been another Bulgaria or Czechoslovakia today."

An elderly lady of bourgeois background told me in Sarajevo, "Honestly, the people have never had it so good. He lets them live and enjoy life." And a librarian in a small town near Zagreb said, "I don't like him. But I guess we all respect him for having stood up for the Russians and kept us out of their clutches."

Later, as I started assembling information and opinions on Tito, I encountered among intellectuals stern critics of the leader,

* During Tito's official visit to Sweden, Prime Minister Olof Palme asked his guest about the fate of a group of Marxist philosophers who earlier were fired from their jobs for criticizing Tito's policies. "Imagine," Tito replied, according to a Swedish official present at the discussion, "they thought they knew better than I what the country needs!"

especially among left-wing Marxists. They cited his great vanity and the monotheistic cult he has permitted to be built around himself. He has, they charged, identified his interest in playing a role on the world stage as being in the interest of Yugoslavia. His thirst for power has been so strong that he has not been able to step down and pass the torch to a younger generation. He actually relishes the "After Tito, what?" editorials that sprout throughout the world press after periodic reports of his illnesses.

All these harsh judgments were highly personal and, of course, private. For in a country whose leader enjoys the status of a deity, thoughts on such matters must not be publicized. But these conversations reinforced my belief that one could not understand present-day Yugoslavia without understanding the remarkable career of Tito.

You don't have to be in Yugoslavia for long to realize Tito's unique place in the society. All the major TV news shows I saw over the three years inevitably began with the president's daily activity. Sometimes, while he was vacationing or doing nothing that would merit general attention, a presidential message of congratulation to another head of state celebrating a national holiday or a birthday would be the lead item.

Nor could one joke about Tito. I recall a unique incident during my tour of duty in Yugoslavia. In the fall of 1974, Mica Popovic, a well-known and accomplished painter, was to have an exhibition at the Kulturni Centar gallery in downtown Belgrade. A crowd of people invited to the opening had gathered in front of the gallery, when at the last minute the exhibition was banned. The reason for this unusual action was one painting whose ironic content offended the office of the presidency. It was a large canvas with life-size portraits of Tito and Queen Juliana of Holland, both wearing full regalia, sashes, decorations and all. Popovic had painted it from a magazine color-photo display of Tito's state visit to Holland. It was the realistic nature of the painting, its attention to details, its colors and especially its size that offended the authorities. "You made Tito look like a king," an official told Popovic, rejecting the painter's argument that he had merely painted from a photograph published in an official weekly magazine.

Among the intellectuals, as well as among some party members, Tito's proclivity for pomp and other trappings of power provokes snide remarks and sneers. Upon taking power he had not only assumed all royal prerogatives, but he had enlarged them considerably. Seventeen castles, villas or hunting lodges around the country are maintained for Tito, although in some of them, such as the one on Mount Romanija, he has spent only one night. A special "blue train," a specially equipped Boeing 727 airliner, the royal yacht *Galeb* and a fleet of the most expensive limousines are other visible prerogatives.

A colleague once asked an old mechanic near Tito's lakeside mansion on Lake Bled in the Slovenian Alps what the difference was between Tito and Prince Paul, the regent, who had owned the mansion before World War II. Both rulers, he said, have used his services. "But Prince Paul used to come here with two cars, and one of them was old. Tito comes with thirteen cars and all of them are new."

I once drew a hostile stare when I asked an official to provide me with figures of the annual budgetary allocations for the president. He viewed my inquiry as proposterous. I got a similar reaction when inquiring about the president's traveling schedule, although this was understandable. During the summer, however, I discovered a sure method for determining when Tito was in Belgrade. Tito, who lives in the Dedinje area, on Uzicka Street No. 15, was bothered by mosquitoes that abound in the summer season. Hence, authorities used small planes to spray the area with pesticides. Since we lived in the neighborhood I knew with a good deal of precision when the president was in or about to come to the capital.

The Uzicka Street presidential compound comprises four large villas, which belonged to four different owners before the war, but were combined into one estate with a large garden for Tito. Inside the compound there is a bunker, in case of a sudden air attack. The compound is surrounded by a ten-foot-high stone and concrete wall and a high hedge which makes it impossible to get a glimpse of the houses inside. It is a veritable fortress guarded around the clock by a special squad of presidential guards dressed in blue jackets, dark trousers with red stripes and white gloves. One is not permitted to walk on the sidewalk past it. I was told by people who have been inside the compound that the houses are furnished with heavy, ornate furniture that could have been selected by Samuel Goldwyn. The compound is surrounded with buildings occupied by security and intelligence units, which operate a communications center. The

White Palace, as the former royal residence is known, is used by Tito as his office.

But Tito spends most of his time outside Belgrade. He has hunting preserves and lodges at Karadjordjevo, near the Hungarian border, and at Bugojno, in Bosnia, where he goes bear hunting; an elaborate seaside villa near Dubrovnik; a castle, which formerly belonged to King Alexander, at Brdo, in Slovenia; and residences in other major cities, including two villas in Zagreb. His favorite resience, however, is on the Adriatic island of Brioni, off the Istrian coast.

Even some of the wealthiest Americans who have enjoyed Tito's regal hospitality on his private island came away impressed. In addition to his mansion and a building to house a supporting staff, the Yugoslavs have built guest houses for important visitors. On the island Tito has his own zoo and botanical garden filled with exotic plants and birds. A small nearby island, Vanga, is his personal retreat, where he has orchards and fruit groves, and a wine cellar where, to his delight, special visitors taste his own wines. He also has a tool shop where he likes to exercise his old trade. (He was a metal worker before he went into politics.)

No other Yugoslav official is accorded tokens of rank and privilege that come remotely close to those enjoyed by the president. The cream of the ruling elite, about twenty persons, are assigned middle-class homes and chauffeur-driven limousines and only the home of the defense minister, Col. Gen. Nikola Ljubicic, is guarded by soldiers. Ljubicic lived in our neighborhood and my son, to avoid a long circuitous route to school during the winter, made a daily shortcut through Ljubicic's backyard, inevitably chatting with the guard and sometimes with the general himself. The executive secretary of the party, Stane Dolanc, lived in a downtown efficiency apartment and commuted to his home in Slovenia on weekends.

Foreigners often miss the crucial importance of the regal life style, which symbolizes the absolute power of the ruler. Tito in fact has his court to which only a few persons are admitted on a regular basis. This inner circle runs the country by controlling the party and government in Tito's name. Tito grants audiences to regional barons, but this is a special privilege. The presidential protocol is strict in that respect. Even the dress requirements are entirely out of character for a Marxist ruler. Edgar Clark, an American journalist based in Belgrade in the early 1950s, told me about the first white-tie occasion—Tito's reception in honor of Emperor Haile Selassie of Ethiopia in 1953. The request came on such short notice that it caught off guard many brave peasants who rose to high positions during the war, but who were suddenly faced with insurmountable sartorial predicaments.

Two years later Tito's protocol was so formal that, according to Egyptian editor Mohamed Heikal, it annoyed President Nasser, who otherwise liked Tito. Tito, Heikal wrote, was "the first Communist king."

With the exception of some leftist intellectuals, most Yugoslavs don't seem to mind Tito's life style. They know, of course, that this is not the way a Communist leader should live, but they have gotten accustomed to it. Only the most severe critics of the regime are outraged by his governing style. As one Marxist historian told me, "It's far better to have a bon vivant type of dictator like Tito than an ascetic type like Stalin. Our man enjoys the good life and understands that we want to live better as well."

Those who have known Josip Broz Tito during earlier stages of his career say that he has a shrewd mind, an instinctive genius for manipulating people and events, and a powerful drive to succeed.

One of fifteen children of a Croatian peasant farmer and Slovene mother, he was born in the village of Kumrovec, northwest of Zabreb, in 1892. At age fifteen he left his village for the town of Sisak, where he worked as a waiter, then a locksmith's apprentice. His natural curiosity and lifelong passion for travel took him to Ljubljana, Trieste, Mannheim, Pilsen and Munich before he settled down as a mechanic at the Daimler Benz auto works near Vienna. In 1913 he was drafted into the Austro-Hungarian army and became a sergeant major. After the outbreak of World War I, he fought on the Serbian front; then his unit was transferred to the Russian front where Tito was captured in 1915 and taken to the Volga region to work.* When the Russian Revolution first broke out in Petrograd, he was in the Urals. (He escaped to Petrograd and took part in the

---

* The fact that he had fought as a sergeant major of the Austro-Hungarian army against the Serbs in 1914 is one of the best kept secrets in Tito's life. Had that been known at the time Tito assumed power in Belgrade, or earlier, Tito most likely would not have been able to consolidate his personal authority as smoothly and successfully as he had.

July demonstrations, the Bolsheviks' first attempt to overthrow the provisional government.) Tito was arrested and sent back to Omsk. When the Bolsheviks did seize power in October, he joined the Red Guards, later also Lenin's party. In 1920 he returned to Yugoslavia with other former prisoners of war, joined the Yugoslav Communist party and worked as a mechanic at a village flour mill for nearly five years. When the Comintern, as the Third International established in Moscow was known, began advancing the cause of world revolution in the mid-twenties, Tito gave up his job. He became a trade union official, party organizer and conspirator. He was eventually arrested in 1928 and sentenced to five years in jail. He drew the high sentence because of his stand in court where, in line with Comintern instructions, he defiantly propagated party ideas. Once out of jail in late 1934 he went underground, sneaked out to Vienna, and then went on to Moscow.

For a while he was the Yugoslav desk officer for the Comintern, then a Comintern agent in Western Europe, organizing among other things the transport of Communist volunteers for the International Brigade in the Spanish civil war. He was back in Moscow in 1938, when the entire Yugoslav Communist leadership along with thousands of other Communists perished in Stalin's great purge. Why did the Russians select Tito for the post of secretary general of the Yugoslav party? Nobody knows. Tito was a quiet, hard-working Comintern employee and he played the part of a new and junior member of the Comintern crowd that lived in Moscow's Lux Hotel.

His ambition and self-confidence were both enormous. In the spring of 1976, while conducting a ninety-minute televised monologue on his youth, Tito selected episodes from his mystical relationship with the October Revolution. He was serving with Lenin's Red Guards near Omsk, guarding a railway line. As he recalled the adventures, he suddenly remarked, "At the time I entertained the idea of emigrating to the United States. And you know, had I done it, I would have become a millionaire." Probably. But he opted for the world of power. The Bolshevik revolution had fascinated him. He had witnessed a huge empire crumble before the onslaught of a group of determined men. He was confident that he would succeed one day.

Veljko Vlahovic, one of the few Yugoslav Communists who survived Stalin's purges, recalled dining alone with Tito in the restaurant of the Lux Hotel. It was in late 1938 and Tito had not yet been confirmed by the Russians as secretary general of the Yugoslav party. Internationally known Communist figures were in the restaurant, among them Bela Kun of Hungary, Walter Ulbricht of Germany, Maurice Thorez of France, and Palmiro Togliatti of Italy. Vlahovic recalled how he pointed out to Tito that nobody wanted to sit at their table. "It is of no importance," Vlahovic quoted Tito as replying prophetically. "One day they will be falling over each other's chairs to sit with us."

Once his appointment was made, he returned to Yugoslavia in January 1939 and plunged into organizational work. The party had fewer than 2,500 members. By the time he initiated an organized armed struggle against Nazi Germany in 1941, the membership figure stood at nearly 12,000 persons. He had a gift for attracting and using bright young men. He selected three lieutenants, all roughly twenty years younger: Edvard Kardelj, a Slovene school teacher; Milovan Djilas, a Montenegrin writer and student leader; and Alexander Rankovic, a worker from Serbia.*

Milovan Djilas once told me that Tito all along made the final decisions. "He rarely had original ideas," Djilas said. "But once ideas were advanced he was, frankly, the only one who knew what to do with them. It was as a practical politician that he eventually became a major figure in world communism."

Familiar by now is the well-known story of Tito's wartime success and his commitment to the Yugoslav idea, in contrast to the divisive fanaticism of Serb and Croat nationalists that led them either reluctantly or enthusiastically—depending on the factions involved—into the arms of Nazi Germany. Tito's guerrilla force, by far the largest and best organized, emerged as the only one waging

---

* "The four of us," Kardelj said in an interview with the newspaper *Delo* in 1974, "were the real political secretariat of the party before the war, during the war, and after the war's end." Several other men were included in the politburo: Mose Pijade, a journalist, painter and man of wide culture who translated Marx's *Das Kapital* into Serbo-Croatian and whom Tito had met in prison; Vladimir Bakaric, a Croat whose father had been a royalist judge in whose court Tito had once been tried; Ivo Lola Ribar, son of a prominent Croat democratic politician; Svetozar Vukmanovic Tempo, a Montenegrin lawyer; Andrija Hebrang, a Croat activist; Boris Kdric, a Slovene intellectual; and Sreten Zujovic, a Belgrade bank clerk. There was never any doubt as to who was in charge, however.

an uncompromising struggle.* As such, the Communists won recognition from the United States and Britain in 1943.

What strikes me as crucial elements both in wartime and in subsequent decades are Tito's broad concept of Yugoslavia and her place in the world, and his uncanny talent for maintaining personal power.

Once he took over the entire country in 1945, Tito rigorously pursued Stalinist policies at home. But his foreign policy was too independent for Stalin's taste. The Yugoslavs worked for the creation of a Communist Balkan federation under Tito's leadership that was to include Yugoslavia, Bulgaria, Albania and possibly Greece. Some of the key leaders of Bulgaria and Albania endorsed Tito's plan. "At the time we did not perceive the fatal contradiction between Moscow's rhetoric and Soviet foreign policy," one of Tito's top aides told me. "The Yugoslavs, who were convinced their policy was in the best interest of world communism, discovered that the Russians were quietly trying to infiltrate key Yugoslav organizations and planning to replace Tito and his colleagues with more pliable men."

When Stalin turned against Tito in early 1948, he used every method short of war to bring about his downfall. "The Old Man said," one former official recalled, "when the car is skidding on an icy road, turn the wheels in the direction of the skid." Tito fought back by adopting an even harsher Stalinist line: his anti-imperialist rhetoric reached new heights and he launched a massive effort to communize the countryside. At the same time, thousands of real or suspected Soviet sympathizers were jailed. With nearly two thirds of their trade being conducted with Soviet bloc countries, the sudden economic blockade by Moscow inflicted enormous suffering and dislocations. The regime maintained itself with police terror.

Tito moved toward the West in 1950; his country was facing famine, its economy was in shambles and the peasantry was growing

* Walter Roberts, in his *Tito, Mihajlovic and the Allies 1941–45* (Rutgers University Press, 1973), reveals that at one point Tito unsuccessfully attempted to reach a cease-fire with the Germans. Roberts, who used German archives, said Tito responded to German feelers for an "accommodation" but that the entire idea was scotched by Nazi Foreign Minister Joachim von Ribbentrop. The only result of the talks between the two sides was an exchange of prisoners. I have asked Djilas, who was the Yugoslav negotiator at the talks, whether an "accommodation" with the Germans was ever planned. He vigorously denied this. But he was in general very reluctant to discuss the matter with me.

rebellious. He signaled his intentions a year earlier by sealing the Greek border, which brought the Greek civil war to a speedy end. Gradually he relaxed the terror tactics, abandoned collectivization of the countryside and began improvising a system of his own. The Yugoslav Communists were still Marxists, but as C. L. Sulzberger once put it, their dogma "may have been written by Groucho, not Karl."

Whenever he was thrust into a crisis situation, Tito always surprised his colleagues by showing unsuspected reserves of political ingenuity and diplomatic skill. He turned his attention toward the newly emerging countries of Asia and Africa. He had normalized relations with the West and became indirectly linked to NATO by virtue of the 1954 Balkan Pact with Greece and Turkey, both of which were NATO members.* But after Stalin's death this was clearly a temporary convenience for Tito. He was anticipating a change of policy in Moscow. Indeed, Khrushchev soon began making private overtures for a rapprochement with Tito.

If Tito had never wavered in his views and considered a return to the Soviet bloc, it must have been during the period that followed Khrushchev's visit to Belgrade in 1955. He was publicly vindicated and given a triumphal tour of Russia the next year, and began to have a direct influence on Soviet policy. His dream of becoming lord lieutenant of the Communist world seemed to be coming true. But the Kremlin's acceptance of Titoist heresy and Khrushchev's de-Stalinization produced unrest throughout the Soviet empire that culminated in the Hungarian revolt. Khrushchev, under the pressure of Kremlin hawks, soon had to put a distance between himself and Tito. Hoping to retain direct influence, Tito had approved the Soviet military intervention in Hungary, but concealed his stand behind a smoke screen of cryptic public utterances.†

Since 1957, however, Tito's basic policy line toward the Soviet Union has remained basically unchanged. He expressed Yugoslavia's

* C. L. Sulzberger, in *A Long Row of Candles*, recalls a conversation with Djilas in April of 1951 when Djilas asked Sulzberger to relay a message to King Paul of Greece that the Yugoslav government would be willing to enter talks on a mutual defense pact.

† Svetozar Vukmanovic Tempo, in his *Memoari*, revealed for the first time that following the Tito-Khrushchev meeting at Brioni, "our side gave its consent for an intervention of Soviet armed forces to prevent a counter-revolution" in Hungary.

fundamental needs as national independence, economic development and socialism. The Cold War sustained his balancing act between East and West. With Nasser of Egypt and Nehru of India he
began organizing a third force, the so-called nonaligned movement.
The first conference of nonaligned heads of state was held in Belgrade in 1961. Earlier he had renounced further U.S. military aid
but had carefully sought to maintain equally good relations with
both Moscow and Washington. "He feared Cold War confronta-
tions, yet he feared Soviet-American detente even more," one former
associate told me.

It is difficult to speak with assurance about the motives and
intentions of politicians, especially complex and secretive ones such
as Tito. Although he is constantly in the glare of public light, Yugoslavs know very little about his personal background. What they do
know has been served to them for the purpose of buttressing the
image of Tito that he himself had chosen.

Tito's biographies, for instance, never mention that he worked
as a waiter, or that he was a loyal sergeant major in the Austro-Hungarian army and commander of a scouting platoon on the Serbian
front in 1914. (His biography says Tito organized "an antimilitarist
demonstration" in 1914, thus implying he was sent to the Russian
front as a punishment.) Malcolm Browne of the *New York Times*
told me that he was subjected to harassment and ostracism by Yugoslav officials after he mentioned in an article that Tito had been a
Comintern agent. (Tito's biography only mentions that he had
attended a Comintern congress.)

He has been married three times, always preferring women
much younger than himself. At the end of World War I he met a
beautiful Russian girl in the Urals. Pelagia Belousova was sixteen
when she married Tito in January 1920. The wedding took place at
the Russian Orthodox Church of Bogolyubsoke, near Omsk. It was
typical of Tito's pragmatic attitude: he was raised a Roman Catholic
and had become a card-carrying Communist in 1918, but he would
let no religious or other formalities stand between him and Pelagia.

After Tito was sentenced to five years in prison in 1928, Pelagia
and their son were sent by the party to Moscow. When Tito came
out of prison in 1933, he was looking forward to his return to Moscow and a joyous family reunion. Instead, his release inaugurated a
period of unremitting personal anguish. Pelagia would not see him.

While Tito was in prison, she had established a series of intimate associations with members of the Soviet bureaucracy and had let their boy be brought up by another woman. For such a proud, vain and ambitious man as Tito, this must have been a bitter emotional experience.

His second wife, Herta Has, was a party activist in Yugoslavia. This relatively short marriage was interrupted by World War II, when Herta was seized by Croat fascist police as a suspected Communist and put in the Jasenovac concentration camp. While she was in the camp, Tito fell in love with his secretary, Zdenka, a former university student who was frail, attractive and younger.*

When the Communists in the winter of 1942–43 captured several high-ranking German officers, representatives of Tito and the German command met in Zagreb to discuss an exchange of prisoners and other matters. Djilas, who was the leader of the Yugoslav group, told me that prior to his departure Tito ordered him, "Don't come back without Herta." The Germans of course were not aware that Herta was Tito's wife and they released her along with several senior Communist officials in exchange for several high-ranking German officers. "We all returned to the headquarters and Herta went to Tito's tent," Djilas recalled. "After about one hour she came out, put her head on my shoulder and crying quietly said, 'It's all over.' " She remarried after the war.

Tito continued to live with Zdenka until she died of tuberculosis just after the Communists captured Belgrade in late 1944. Tito was heartbroken. But unbeknownst to him, Kardelj, Rankovic and Djilas, the three top men, met privately that winter to discuss the problem. "We didn't know what to do," Djilas once told me. "Tito was now head of state and we couldn't let him go to town to look for women. Rankovic proposed that we get several attractive and reliable Communist girls and place them to work in Tito's household, then let nature take its course."

Jovanka Budisavljevic, a beautiful blackhaired girl with a winning smile, was one of the girls. She was twenty-one years old at the time and had served in Tito's partisan army for the last three years of the war. Tito announced their marriage in 1953, shortly before his first official visit to Britain. "We were afraid at the time," Djilas added, explaining the leadership's secret involvement in Tito's per-

* Her real name was Davorjanka Paunovic.

sonal life, "that Tito might fall for one of the bourgeois girls—you know, groomed, proper manners, education, perfume, et cetera. We didn't want that to happen."

The very fact that she was at Tito's side for more than three decades made Jovanka a power behind the throne. Officials, trying to interest the old president in one idea or another, frequently sought her help. It was her role as a power broker that apparently led to an end of the relationship. Toward the end of 1977 Jovanka vanished from public view and was said to be under detention in the presidential palace. Rumors suggested that she was being investigated for misusing her influence on Tito, apparently in matters concerning senior military appointments, but there has been no reliable explanation for her mysterious disappearance.

That many aspects of Tito's private life and pre-1941 career have been systematically suppressed during his regime reflects Tito's shrewd assessment of the country's mood. Partly, only partly, it was his vanity that led him to conceal some actions and obscure his inadequacies, these being in general the inadequacies of most normal men. The main reasons were political. He was never a romantic revolutionary or a dreamer. More than anyone in his entourage he understood the importance of myths in politics—especially in Balkan politics. Had the Serbs known in 1941 about Tito's loyal service in the Austro-Hungarian army against the Serbs in World War I, the prejudice against him would have never disappeared. And the Serbs, in the final analysis, were the key to power in Belgrade.

And when the rebellious Yugoslav peasantry took to the mountains following the Nazi attack in 1941, Tito, suddenly, shockingly found himself leader of a liberation movement. His main objective was to gain political power for himself and his party by following Lenin's recipe. But he realized he needed military victory to achieve that goal. More importantly, he understood a whole syndrome of attitudes and sentiments that had a strong pull on large numbers of peasants.

In reaching out to his people he came closer—at the expense of Marxist doctrine—to the point of view of the peasants. The doctrine had to be adjusted to the primitive mentality of the Yugoslavs, who saw the world in terms of old heroic epics and legends, sins and retributions, a yearning for justice. He realized he could reach them not through appeals to their class-consciousness—they had none—but through his movement's sympathy for all South Slav nationalities, the idea of brotherhood and fraternity, and physical courage, which they respected and to which they responded.

There is, for instance, a story about Tito's dog Lux saving his master's life during a German bombing attack in 1943. The story, which has been repeated in virtually all biographies of Tito, relates how Tito threw himself to the ground during the raid, and the dog, crouching near his master's head, received a bomb fragment which otherwise would have killed Tito. A Yugoslav leader, who was with Tito at the time, told me that the dog was nowhere near Tito when it got hit. "But you see this is a kind of story that can inspire our people. A faithful dog risking his life to save his master!"

That same year, 1943, Tito accorded himself the title of marshal, for he realized that the trappings of power have a hold on the mentality of an army of rustics. The title of marshal inspired a respect that the title of secretary general of the Communist Party could never muster. By one stroke he put himself on the level with the king and indicated that he wanted to play in the big league.

Political work during the war posed a difficult problem since Marxist terms meant nothing to illiterate peasants. Hence the idea of Slav Russia, whose image as protector of the South Slavs lived in the collective memory, was emphasized heavily. Stalin was projected as a benevolent, powerful father—"our sun from the East"—even long after the war's end. This was homemade Marxism whose ideas were propagated in the ancient rhythm of folk tales and in simple five-tone songs.

But the glorification of Stalin and Russia soon came to haunt Tito in what became the greatest crisis of his life. The origin of Tito's national communism lies in that fierce struggle against the Russians, when Tito, to save his life, had to destroy the idol he had urged others to worship. Later he improvised his own brand of socialism and his nonaligned foreign policy. But in the bitter struggle during the 1948–49 period Tito reverted to the old patterns. Life in the Balkans had been too basic for too long for him to do anything else. Long years of foreign rule had produced an atavistic tradition of distrust toward politics. What people understood was a benevolent, yet firm ruler. In short, he became a national leader and an autocrat. In time, the struggle against Stalin became the crucial component of Tito's mythology.

Today, the very idea of being a Soviet satellite produces a feeling of apprehension and fear in the hearts of Yugoslavs. The fact that they managed to stand up to the Kremlin is perhaps the major unifying force in this multinational country. War was a traumatic, but divisive experience, including a fratricidal struggle between the two principal nations, the Serbs and the Croats. The memory of the shared ordeal in resisting the Russians dulled the memory of nationalist animosities as well as of Tito's terror in the immediate postwar years. Time had made all that seem like a part of a terrible nightmare from which the country escaped thanks to the wise leadership of the supreme arbiter. All this was given greater force when Khrushchev came to Belgrade in 1955 to apologize and to formally, yet reluctantly, acknowledge Tito's right to his own brand of socialism, thus beginning a process of reconciliation that has lasted until the present.

The easing of pressure from the East has enabled Tito to carve a unique place for Yugoslavia in the world. It is close to the Soviet bloc yet not part of it. It is strongly committed to the Third World movement and yet on good terms with Western countries. At home he had introduced "consumer socialism" and workers self-management, and opened the country's borders. This special standing in the world has created a sense of pride in their country among younger Yugoslavs. Even among Yugoslavs in the United States, those who have migrated before or immediately after World War I, there is a measure of sympathy for the regime. I can recall my uncle Peter, who fought in the Montenegrin army in World War I and who migrated to the United States in 1916 from Corfu, where the defeated army had been taken by the Allies, saying occasionally, "Honest to God, Tito has put Yugoslavia on the map. Before Tito, Yugoslavia was a pipsqueak Balkan country nobody ever heard about." My uncle was by no means a Communist sympathizer.

And yet, during my tour of duty I heard many thoughtful Yugoslavs—many of them in the party—privately question this unique balancing act. Tito's diplomatic skill is responsible for its success. This is his policy. But many suspect that the on-again, off-again process of reconciliation with Russia was designed by him to ensure his personal authority at home by playing often and subtly upon the deep fears of the Soviet threat, and also to provide him with a forum for personal involvement in world affairs.

Moreover, these critics believe that Tito, riding on his power, legend and diplomatic skill, had involved the country in a game with excessively high stakes. The Kremlin's intervention in Hungary and Czechoslovakia are still vivid memories of the people. "Quite simply," one former Yugoslav diplomat told me, "his talents and ambitions exceed by far the economic and military muscle of Yugoslavia."

A university professor in Zagreb diagnosed the problem this way: "Tito's struggle with Stalin had made him a historic figure. He devoured the world-wide publicity and respectability that it brought him. Even Henry Luce, yes Henry Luce, the archconservative, called him one of the authentic heroes of the twentieth century. All that was too much for the boy from Kumrovec; it was like a powerful aphrodisiac which left him permanently addicted. He has gained a place in history, but he wants his place to be that of a major reformer within the Communist movement, not that of a renegade outside the movement. His vanity is monumental."

However, the measure of the man as a national leader is not his vanity and other human failings but rather the sort of conception he has about his country and its place in the world. He has set forth nonalignment abroad and national independence and self-managing socialism at home as his image of Yugoslavia. As a practical politician he developed these goals empirically, then projected them into the future.

Already in 1945—in a speech which infuriated Stalin and prompted him to lodge a sharp protest—Tito had declared he had no intention of letting big powers use Yugoslavia "as small change in their bargaining." After his expulsion from the Soviet bloc he began desperately to look for new friends outside the two blocs. With Nasser and Nehru he formulated the idea of nonalignment.

Later, he began to view the contemporary world in terms of the post-Napoleonic period, when great powers established a balance to keep the peace. Beneath the ensuing international tranquillity, he argued, there were such issues as emerging nationalism and the drive for social and economic equality that worked to destroy not only the order imposed by the great empires of the period, but also those empires themselves. He is now convinced that the military importance of superpowers will inevitably decline over the coming decades and that issues such as underdevelopment, the gap between the rich and the poor, and the drive for a "new world economic order" will eventually influence international climate far more profoundly than

Soviet-American relations. Therefore he opted for the Third World and has made nonalignment of Yugoslavia a provision of the constitution.

Although he had moved away from the totalitarian practices of the postwar years, Tito in the crunch always reverted to force. In three major crises of his regime—the ouster of Djilas in 1954, the dismissal of Rankovic and purge of his security establishment in 1966, and finally in the ouster of the reformist Croat Communist leaders in 1971–72—Tito was ruthless. Having first encouraged these associates, he drew back the moment he detected that they might undermine his personal authority. For Tito, the wisdom of their views mattered less than his regime's stability. But subsequently he appropriated some of the ideas for which his opponents were dismissed and cautiously worked them into the system. His experience told him that ideals and institutions were obstinate, that effective changes took place more smoothly by quiet accommodation than by sudden shifts.

Yugoslavia's socialism has been a experiment on a national scale. The introduction of a market economy has provided an element of rationality in the system; consumerism has diverted attention away from political grievances and toward materialism, which is lustily pursued by almost everybody. Repression is used sparingly, and only toward serious political challengers. My telex mechanic would say, "We've never had it so good. If you don't mix up in politics, you can live well, you make a good living, you travel anywhere you want." The remark was typical.

Moreover, decentralization has created a plurality of interests among the six constituent republics and two autonomous regions, and workers' self-management has legitimized the right of self-expression, albeit within the prescribed context. The two factors combined cultivate the illusion that all problems can be resolved at the local level.

In his vision of Yugoslavia—which he added to his mythology— he sought to give the country an image that would balance the weight of ethnic differences and hatreds. That is the image of a country of diversity united by allegiance to basic common goals.

But in the process of creating a unique socialist system he had created a continued challenge for the guardians of Marxist ideology in the Kremlin. Tito's heresy still rankles the Russians. This is why, in addition to his temperamental liking for "high politics," he has focused his energies almost entirely on foreign affairs. And foreign affairs became his personal property. I found it illuminating that such a senior figure as Politburo member Svetozar Vukmanovic Tempo conceded that he had absolutely no idea about the Tito-Stalin feud in 1948 before it surfaced in the press. Tempo was a member of the ruling politburo and happened to be in Moscow when Djilas and Kardelj went there for the final show-down with Stalin and Molotov.

During the Cold War period Tito turned his balancing act between East and West into a form of art, obtaining economic benefits from both sides. His view of the United States, as one distinguished former American ambassador to Belgrade put it privately, was that of "a milk cow not a bull—all teats and no horns." He cultivated good relations with Washington and received more than $3.5 billion in U.S. aid without giving much in return. Yet the very existence of an independent Communist state in Europe was of enormous political, military and especially ideological value.

The Soviet invasion of Czechoslovakia in 1968 disabused Tito of any lingering hopes that the Russians would accept Yugoslav-type reforms in Eastern Europe. Moreover, the so-called Brezhnev doctrine of limited sovereignty for socialist states, which the Kremlin advanced to justify the invasion, continued to carry the implicit threat of Soviet involvement in Yugoslav affairs at some future date. To make things worse, Tito was deeply disappointed to discover the basic weakness of the nonaligned world. Nasser, an old friend whom Tito had supported without reservation, told him frankly that he could not severely condemn the Soviet invasion for fear that the Kremlin would take punitive measures against him and halt the flow of Soviet arms supplies for Egypt. "I cannot be completely nonaligned," Heikal quotes Nasser as saying to Tito at that time.

The advent of Soviet-American detente revived Tito's ancient suspicions. In a variety of ways, he played for the long term. Three years before Jimmy Carter stated during his presidential campaign in the fall of 1976 that he would not commit U.S. troops to defend Yugoslavia against a Soviet attack, Tito cautiously introduced a more conciliatory note in his dealings with Moscow and a more militantly nonaligned stand in the United Nations.

When Secretary of State Henry Kissinger visited Belgrade in 1974 he raised the question of lack of even-handedness in Belgrade's dealings with the two superpowers. Tito replied, "You know, they are near and you are far, far away." The remark provides an important clue to Tito's thinking. He still wanted to cultivate good relations with America, but he sensed changes in Washington in the wake of Vietnam and Watergate. The substance of his relations with Moscow has not changed. He exerted all his energies to have the Russians renounce the Brezhnev doctrine and for the first time attended the conference of European Communist parties in the summer of 1976. But Soviet-Yugoslav relations, as one ranking Soviet diplomat in Belgrade put it, privately, are "cordial and insincere."

There is a good deal of admiration among Yugoslavs for Tito's diplomatic skill. Most of them are convinced that he knows how to "handle" the Kremlin and that as long as he is around, the country can rest at ease. But the personalized conduct of foreign relations has become a source of anxiety among the elite. One foreign ministry official told me that, for instance, Tito ordered a break in relations with Israel in 1967 without consulting anyone. Tito's commitment to the Arab cause also led him to urge Sadat in 1973 to bomb Tel Aviv when Egypt's Third Army came close to being destroyed by Israeli forces during the Yom Kippur War. Tito's message, which was monitored by U.S. espionage agencies, caused profound annoyance in Washington.

Nobody in the leadership dares oppose him openly. His power has been absolute whenever he has chosen to exercise it. In 1973 he dismissed Colonel General Ivan Miskovic, head of intelligence and security, by instructing an aide to "tell that general not to come to work anymore." Miskovic told friends the cause for the dismissal was a remark about Tito's health that the general made in front of Tito's wife.

I recall a surprise visit by a prominent Yugoslav politician, who turned up at the Washington *Post* Belgrade bureau in September 1974. My secretary had already left for the day, and I opened the door and invited him in. No, he said, I should join him for a walk. I presumed he thought that we could not have a private conversation in the office.

"I know I should not do this," he said as we walked toward an open peasant market. "I want you to know that I would not have come to talk about state matters with you, I would not discuss such matters with a foreigner unless they involved a matter of foreign threat." He proceeded to tell me a complex story which stripped to its essentials concerned the following: Yugoslav police had accidentally discovered that an underground Communist party of Yugo-slavia had been established on Yugoslav soil; that it was supported by the Russians via anti-Tito émigrés living in the Soviet Union and other Soviet bloc countries; and that the party had managed to hold a clandestine party congress at Bar, in Montenegro, earlier that year, where it had elected a central committee and adopted a program which denied the legitimacy of the Tito regime. Nearly forty persons had been arrested, he said, and "the Old Man is furious and has sent Kardelj to Moscow to see Brezhnev.

"Don't you see what this means," he continued. "It is an old Russian trick. If there is trouble in the future, they can always say that there has been a legitimate anti-Tito Communist party in exis-tence for a long time and that the true flame of Yugoslav com-munism was burning in Titoist prisons and stuff like that."

The reason for leaking the information to me was illuminating. My informer felt strongly that the matter should be brought into the open. Tito, he said, was "furious but had decided to avoid all public-ity" and await the outcome of Kardelj's discussions with Brezhnev and other Soviet leaders. A few days after the story had appeared in the Washington *Post*, Tito himself confirmed its content. His speech was followed by a series of arrests of suspected pro-Moscow plotters and a media campaign which revived the grim days of 1948. Tito displayed toughness toward Moscow, yet stopped short of the un-pardonable insult. This was again Tito the master tactician.

None of the men he had selected to succeed him possess his political instinct or broad experience. Only two of his old comrades —Kardelj and Bakaric—are still with him, but they are old, sick and while perfect as lieutenants, they are not leaders. But many thought-ful Yugoslavs told me that the country will inevitably move toward a new type of leadership once Tito leaves the scene. For Tito—despite his vanity, hypocrisies and imperial style—has opened up a new era of political consciousness in the South Slavs. Although he saw the country's political future within the socialist world, his people have become more and more linked—spiritually and economically—to Western Europe, where millions of Yugoslavs during the past de-cades have traveled or worked. The importance of countries such as Italy, Greece and Austria, and especially West Germany, Britain and the Scandinavian nations, has increased dramatically.

Yet, Russia remains the key variable in Belgrade's political equation. The Yugoslavs do not expect any overt Soviet attempts to regain a controlling influence in Yugoslav affairs. What they fear is a revival of destructive nationalism which could provoke one power group or another to invite Soviet assistance. "Nationalism," a Yugoslav historian told me, "is irrational. And the spirit of irrationality is very much a part of our scenery." For a long time Yugoslavia, like Belgium, will be a country with a national problem. And it will take more time to determine whether Tito's image of Yugoslavia can gain a firm and countrywide acceptance.

I have heard many persons both curse and celebrate Tito. One of his Western friends, Sir Fitzroy Maclean, who led the British Military Mission to Tito's partisans during the war, portrayed Tito as gradually becoming less of a dictator and more of a human being. "There is a saying in the Balkans that behind every hero stands a traitor. The difficulty, as often as not, is to determine which is which. Take Tito himself. Seen from one point of view, he can be represented as a traitor to his king and country, as the agent of a foreign power, who ultimately betrayed even that foreign power. Seen from another, he appears as a national hero twice over."

9

Nation in Arms

WHILE MILITARY STRATEGISTS IN MANY COUNTRIES OFTEN ENTERTAIN scenarios of barely credible enemy attacks, the Yugoslavs have experienced a series of threats of foreign invasions, actual attacks and other types of pressure that make the possibility of their recurrence all too real. Their history has been a saga of chronic tensions.

The brilliant English writer Rebecca West, in her *Black Lamb and Grey Falcon*, has given a moving and detailed account of the political and cultural climate in Yugoslavia from its inception in 1918 until the outbreak of World War II. This was a period of great irredentist hopes. Italy actively sought parts of Slovenia and the Dalmatian coast. Hungary openly claimed northern sections of Croatia and Serbia. Bulgaria coveted Macedonia. Hitler finally dismembered the country in April 1941, giving chunks of it to his allies and incorporating the rest into the Reich either directly or through the establishment of Quisling governments.

It was not long before the postwar Yugoslav state was besieged by new and far more substantial foreign pressures. In the North the Yugoslavs were involved in a sharp dispute with Italy, this time trying to take a part around the city of Trieste that had a considerable South Slav ethnic population. Then, in 1948, Stalin unleashed his furious attack on Yugoslavia using all means short of war to bring down Tito. The term "Titoism" became a symbol for treason, a deadly sin which led to cataclysmic events throughout Eastern Europe. A series of leading Communists in Soviet bloc countries was tried and executed for allegedly harboring Titoist tendencies.

To several neighboring Communist countries, Stalin's attacks on Yugoslavia provided an atmosphere in which to solve their nationality problems regarding South Slav minorities. Hungary carried out a rapid Magyarization of its minorities; the Romanians were exceptionally ferocious in forcing ethnic South Slavs to become Romanians and shifting them to the Black Sea area. But the Bulgarians were to come with a most serious blow. Not only did they attempt to force ethnic Macedonians to declare themselves Bulgarians, but staked a long-term claim on Macedonia, which is one of the Yugoslav republics, by denying the existence of a Macedonian nation.*

Even after Tito's rapprochement with Khrushchev, the Soviet Union continued to apply more subtle means of pressure on Yugoslavia in an effort to ultimately regain foothold in the one country which seceded from the Soviet empire.

So, Yugoslavia's neutrality was shaped under exceptionally trying circumstances and in a part of the world which has been traditionally dominated by great powers that used Balkan states as chips in the big international game. The Yugoslav Communists felt they could not seek security in the West, although they flirted briefly with a NATO security umbrella by virtue of their military alliances in the Balkan Pact with Greece and Turkey.† The westward orientation would have inevitably entailed an internal drift toward pluralism and undermined the Communists' monopoly on power. For Tito, this was an unacceptable risk in the long run. Yet, the main threat to Yugoslavia's security then, and today, has been the Soviet bloc. As a result, the policy of neutrality was initially thrust upon Yugoslav Communist leaders as the only viable alternative.

The virtues of neutrality soon became apparent to the Yugoslavs, and they exploited it skillfully during the Cold War. Tito, moreover, opened Yugoslavia toward the newly emerging countries of Asia and Africa. In a spirit of devotion to his Communist ideology, he saw nonaligned allies as members of a "progressive" and "anti-imperialist" third force outside the two power blocs. In that period Yugoslavia's neutrality seemed assured in the context of East-West competition.

The advent of detente, however, slowly changed the strategic needs of the superpowers and reduced ideological competition. Moreover, the terrors of general war became so massive and fully understood by both sides that only a most brazen act of aggression

* The 1956 Bulgarian census shows 178,862 Macedonians living in the Pirin region of Bulgaria; the 1960 census puts the number at 8,750; all subsequent censuses show no Macedonians living in Bulgaria. In a variety of ways the Bulgarians have been suggesting that Macedonians were ethnic Bulgarians.

† The pact, signed in 1954, became a dead letter within a year due to political changes in the Kremlin and the Greek-Turkish dispute over Cyprus. Under its terms, any party could have cancelled it in 1974—but none did so.

affecting vital interests of one bloc could lead the other into a deliberate confrontation. This change carried disturbing implications for
small neutral countries in general, and for Yugoslavia in particular.
As a socialist and nonaligned country, Yugoslavia could not count
realistically on American protection.

Yugoslav strategists in the late sixties began drawing their balance sheet with special reference to two questions: Can a small
country, without recognized protection, maintain its independence
in a Europe divided into two military blocs? And what are the problems if the country in question is ruled by a Communist government
which achieved independence by bolting the Soviet bloc?

The brutality of Russia's invasion of Czechoslovakia in 1968
provided a powerful impetus for the establishment of a new defense
concept. The Brezhnev doctrine, advanced as a justification for the
invasion, was even more disturbing for Yugoslavs because of its long-
term implications. In February of 1969, the Yugoslav Parliament
passed a law on General People's Defense, making the nation-in-
arms concept the basis of Yugoslav defense strategy.

The new policy displayed both imagination and consistency.
On the military side it envisaged a universal citizens' militia, or
territorial army, which would merge with the regular armed forces
in case of an invasion and defend each factory, village, city, school or
housing complex. According to General Stane Potocar, "as much as
seventy percent" of Yugoslavia's 22 million population would be
involved "in various forms of resistance." On the political side this
would serve as a potent deterrent against aggression.

By shifting to the preparation of the entire country to conduct
defense in depth, Yugoslav strategists returned to the virtues of old-
time religion, incorporating into the national defense policy a means
of struggle that had brought Tito to power. It recognized the country's topography, its historical traditions and it anticipated the character of potential threats.

Psychologically, it was an important change. By laying stress on
self-reliance and defense of the mountainous heartland, the government fed the army, the veterans and the people a new dose of their
favorite myth—that the gallantry and heroism the South Slavs have
displayed in fighting guerrilla wars against foreign enemies make
them invincible. The myth itself is a part of psychological warfare.

I recall covering the visit to Yugoslavia of Soviet Premier Alexei
Kosygin in the fall of 1973. He and his party were flown all over the
country except for a stretch between Sarajevo and Mostar, which

they traveled by car. The two-lane road winds up and around some
of the forbidding and inaccessible-looking mountain ranges of
Bosnia and Hercegovina. Sarajevo, which is one of the largest Yugoslav cities, lies in a valley about 1600 feet above sea level.

Driving up the perilous road, I was taken with the beauty of the
innumerable precipices and awesome peaks that looked unassailable
and wild, and in whose shadow our motorcade appeared absurdly
small. When we descended into the gorge of the Neretva River, we
passed near the spot where the retreating partisan army surprised
attacking German forces by building a bridge and evacuating
wounded partisans. Beyond, I knew, were the even more inhospitable mountains of Sandjak, Montenegro and eastern Bosnia. My
driver pointed out to me a steep limestone mountainside rising from
the river. Halfway up the mountain, in what I thought was an inaccessible spot, somebody had written "Tito" in huge red letters.
"Here," the driver said confidently, "we've fought the Germans
during the war. Here we can fight anyone." Earlier I had expressed
my admiration for the rugged beauty of the region, which reminded
me of Switzerland without chalets, roads and other amenities of the
modern age. But my driver saw in these surroundings a natural
fortress, a difficult terrain where tanks and airpower could hardly be
used to advantage.

A Yugoslav official told me later that the Sarajevo-Mostar road
journey for Kosygin and his associates was deliberately planned.
"Our people wanted the Russians to take a real close look at those
mountains," he said, smiling knowingly.

The Yugoslavs adopted the concept of territorial defense to give
added credibility to their nonaligned foreign policy.

Nonalignment signifies the determination both to remain outside the two large power blocs in peacetime and to stay neutral in
any armed conflict between them. But unlike the traditional neutralism practiced by Switzerland and Sweden, nonalignment does not
mean disengagement from international politics. Quite the opposite.
It implies constant involvement in foreign affairs, something that in
the Yugoslav case, at least, provides the country with a great deal of
visibility and with numerous ties with other countries. A resulting
diplomatic web is supposed to serve as a deterrent against any potential aggressor and—in case of aggression—to cause a groundswell of
international concern and pressures to stop the fighting.

In maintaining its international posture, Yugoslavia faces

unique difficulties. Other European neutral's have pursued military neutrality while they remained a part of the West in terms of their spiritual, economic and political development. Yugoslavia is a Slav country whose leaders profess to be Communists and whose political and economic development evolved along the patterns practiced in the "socialist commonwealth." And yet, the principal threat to Yugoslav security comes from the "socialist commonwealth."

The country's location—"our cursed geography," as some Yugoslavs describe it—is of great strategic importance to Moscow. A reassociation of Yugoslavia would provide the Soviet empire with reliable Mediterranean ports and with air routes to the Middle East, Africa and Latin America. The air routes have become increasingly important with the expansion of Soviet global interests.* Moreover, Tito's heresy still rankles in Moscow and the Soviets would like to stamp out a rival model of socialism which European Communists find more attractive than the Kremlin type.

But underlying tactical goals of Moscow, which both the Tsarist and Communist regimes have pursued, impel the Russians to concentrate on the security of their empire as well as of their internal political system. The very idea of neutrality of a socialist country is alien to the men in the Kremlin. They could accept a lack of direct control over Finland's affairs because that country's system is bourgeois parliamentarism, and poses no ideological threat to them. Yugoslavia, on the other hand, has been a source of ideological trouble for Eastern Europe.

Against this background, the Yugoslavs are trying to preserve their independence through a combination of complex and seemingly contradictory policies. In the formation of their defense posture, however, they have been heavily influenced by the experiences of two other small countries—Czechoslovakia and Finland.

Czechoslovakia, according to conventional wisdom now, was capable of putting up a stiff resistance to Hitler in 1938 had the Czech leaders relied less on their alliance with France and Britain. Once this alliance proved worthless, the Czechoslovaks were completely demoralized and failed to use the military muscle necessary to resist aggression. As a result, Czechoslovakia was dismembered

---

* Yugoslavia permitted Soviet overflights during the Yom Kippur War and again during the Angolan crisis in 1976—both on grounds that the Russians were supplying arms to Yugoslavia's allies.

without great difficulty. The Czechoslovak situation of 1968 is taken by Yugoslav strategists as an example of how dangerous it is for a small country to entrust the army to be the sole guarantor of the nation's security. The Russians were able to "neutralize" the army by dealing directly with a few senior military men and were subsequently able to invade the country almost without firing a shot.

The Finns, on the other hand, who fought bravely against a superior enemy, had managed to retain their political independence. But the Finnish example, in the eyes of Yugoslav strategists, is instructive in another sense as well. The Finns had always counted on German-Russian rivalry in the Baltic area and had assumed that Germany would come to their aid—an assumption that was largely and suddenly invalidated by the Hitler-Stalin pact of 1939.

In urging his associates to profit from these examples, Tito repeatedly told them that the key to good foreign policy is constant reassessment and that the essence of good defense policy is the recognition of realities. So they faced up, among other things, to the fact that they could not rely on frontal defense or action by regular armed forces to defend the country against a superior enemy along a clearly defined front on the northern and eastern flatlands. They aimed at a posture clearly defensive in character which could not be interpreted as a potential threat by any of Yugoslavia's neighbors. And, at the same time, they wanted to signal to potential adversaries that the price of an attack on Yugoslavia would be high.

There are two additional aspects that seem equally important. First, the nation-in-arms concept blurs the distinction between the army and the people and hence lessens the likelihood of a military coup or sellout; and second, the character of the defense reduces reliance on sophisticated weaponry and thus reliance on the whims of outside suppliers of such equipment.* It is also, economically speaking, cheaper.

* The Yugoslavs have developed an arms industry that supplies 80 percent of their needs. Among other things, they produce fighter and ground attack jet aircraft, which are very light and use grass airstrips. Also the Yugoslavs make helicopters. Still, the backbone of the air force is Soviet-made MIG 21s. A Yugoslav-Romanian joint project is underway to produce a new jet fighter, Orao. Yugoslavia has acquired a modest quantity of Soviet-made surface-to-air missiles of SA-2, SA-3, SA-4, SA-6 and SA-7. The tanks, T-54/55 and PT-76 are also imported from the Soviet Union. According to Yugoslav sources, considerable quantities of Yugoslav-made weapons have been sold to nonaligned countries in Africa and Asia.

The Yugoslav People's Army started out as a guerrilla force, waging combat with small, dispersed units which operated in a covert fashion in Nazi-occupied Yugoslavia. But the force eventually swelled to more than 700,000 men and women in arms and employed a mixture of frontal tactics and partisan warfare.

Territorial defense as now practiced by Yugoslav strategists involves some reliance on the regular armed forces and on weapons that are normally not used in guerrilla warfare, such as tanks, aircraft and helicopters. The regular forces, which number 250,000 (including 95,000 officers and NCOs), have as one of their primary duties to slow down an enemy invasion and gradually retreat toward the mountainous part of the country. Meanwhile, total mobilization of reservists, whose number exceeds 500,000, and of the territorial defense force, which along with youth brigades numbers over 900,000, could be carried out in a day or two. Some officials told me that half of the territorial reserve force can be mobilized within a couple of hours.

From that point on, the regular and territorial forces have to operate jointly. The regular army would, partially or completely, transform itself from the holding force to the partisan form of struggle, depending on the nature of enemy attack. Simultaneously, an intensive mobilization would be carried out to prepare a citizens' army for struggle in the towns, factories, schools, cooperatives and villages.

Milan Ateljevic, secretary of the federal coordinating committee for General People's Defense, who explained details of Yugoslav territorial defense to me, emphasized the human factor. "A big power can employ modern technology, but we feel that the human factor will be crucial in any potential conflict on our soil."

Ateljevic—a tall, wiry, combative man who was born near Trebinje in Eastern Hercegovina in 1926—took part in Tito's World War II struggle and reached the rank of colonel before retiring from the army. He received me with military simplicity. Yes, he said, he heard a good deal about the United States from his father, who had spent twelve years working in Chicago.

Each community in the country, he said, has a local coordinating committee of General People's Defense, which is in charge of training and organizing local territorial defense units. In 1975 nearly one third of Yugoslavia's twenty-two million people was receiving training on how to resist an enemy invasion. The government's objective is to increase the strength of the territorial army to three million. Under the 1969 law school children receive military training, including basic weapons instruction, as part of the high school curriculum. All men go through basic training and receive subsequent refresher courses. Women are not conscripted into the regular army but can be called to serve in the territorial forces.

In addition to the regular army and the territorial forces there is civil defense, which contains about 1.4 million people; its concern is evacuation, medical care, food, and other such matters. All persons between the ages of 16 and 60 (55 for women) who do not serve in the regular and territorial forces are obliged to do civil defense duty.

Ateljevic outlined the basic defense organization with the energy and enthusiasm of a man working for a great cause that will inevitably triumph. My skeptical questions seemed to impel him to argue with even greater conviction. "No one," he said, citing the new federal constitution, "has the right to sign the capitulation of the country or of the armed forces. Nobody, whatever his position, has the right to recognize or accept the occupation of any part of the country. Nobody is entitled to take away from me my right to defend myself; neither the armed forces commanders nor any government are empowered to make a deal with an aggressor."

Theoretically, the Yugoslav concept of territorial defense seems impressive. But how would it work in practice? Will citizens fight to the bitter end? What would happen if an enemy, using Yugoslavia's internal weaknesses, managed by covert means to set one Yugoslav republic against another? Would territorial defense forces, which are practically under local control, lead the country into a civil war?

A politician with a more independent mind told me: "Frankly, this is the best and cheapest defense posture. Its basic message to a potential aggressor is that the price will be high. I believe this is well understood. We will not beg for outside help. Besides, begging doesn't do you any good when it comes down to military conflicts. We can fight, and you know the whole world will be with us if we are defending our freedom against a powerful military bloc. And the other bloc will support us, not because they love us, but because it is in their interest. No, we're not afraid of open aggression. What we are afraid of is sly infiltration and subversion of our system, exploitation of our internal weaknesses."

Behind this elaborate defense strategy, behind the policy of deliberate optimism about the resiliency of Yugoslavs and their proven capacity to exploit patriotism and mire down a modern army, there are crucial political nuances. True, the existence of an independent territorial army diminishes, at least theoretically, the role of the army and of the military chiefs.* "We cannot abdicate our rights to the army," was the way Ateljevic put it. But at the same time, by absolving the regular forces of the sole responsibility for the country's defense, the system recognized the army's crucial political role—that of guarantor of the unity of and the socialist order in Yugoslavia. The whole structure was designed for the post-Tito era.

The army, which was born out of the chaos of war and revolution, is tough, efficient and well trained. The officer corps are well indoctrinated, 95 percent of them being Communist party members. Unlike the armies of other Communist countries, the Yugoslav army has one chain of command. There is a political directorate of the armed forces, but it is under the control of the chiefs, as opposed to the structure of armed forces in the East European countries which include distinct political and military chains of command.

One thing that defines the chiefs and the entire upper echelon of the army is the fact that they all fought in World War II. This experience helped give them their practical approach and matter-of-fact tone. They are of peasant background—nine out of ten come from villages—and army experience has shaped the ideas and beliefs that frame their personal view of the world. The officers are not permitted to travel privately abroad and their knowledge of the outside world is scant; I have heard Americans who had dealings with top commanders say that their ignorance about real conditions in the West is appalling. They have a better understanding of the

---

* It also provides the fact that the general population is armed. In the mountainous areas there is a rifle or carbine in virtually every house, a good portion of those unregistered, however; most of the 1.4 million army veterans have weapons at home. According to an official report, in the Serbian republic there are areas "where one out of every seven citizens has a pistol, carbine or hunting rifle." Over 3.5 million rounds of ammunition were sold to private citizens in Serbia in 1972. Arms for territorial forces are kept in factories, public buildings and housing complexes—but under lock. In border areas these arms are given to a portion of territorial force members who keep them at home. I found the restrictive distribution of territorial forces' arms a crucial weakness in the system. Obviously, the government is nervous about the substantial number of unregistered weapons for reasons that are not hard to guess. At the same time, it wants to have an armed citizenry.

Soviet bloc; many studied in Moscow in the period preceding the Tito-Stalin feud.

The army's standing in Yugoslav society changed dramatically after 1965, for in the wake of political and economic decentralization throughout the country and especially after the demise of Rankovic's secret police establishment, the military emerged as the principal all-Yugoslav force.

Tito's style of personal rule gradually gave the generals an ever increasing political role. Tito delegated authority to individuals rather than institutions, and he began to rely increasingly on the army. The generals were sober, efficient and noncorruptible. Tito was their commander-in-chief and he commanded their loyalty.

Whenever in difficulty, Tito would turn to them. When the Yugoslav national airline JAT was involved in a corruption scandal, a career general was appointed its director general. The Ministry of Internal Security—an agency that had at one point accumulated enormous powers—is headed by a career army general; the nation's chief of intelligence is a career army general; the ministry of defense is, of course, run by career officers at all levels up to the minister himself.

Cast into the role of guardian of the country's independence and political stability, the army seems to have acquired a heightened sense of its mission. I found it fascinating to read in a Yugoslav weekly a statement by senior generals asserting that the army "would not remain in the barracks" if there was an outbreak of social unrest at some future date. The leaders and military chiefs of the Veterans Union played a crucial role in persuading Tito to crack down on the liberal-minded Communist leadership in Croatia in 1971–72.*

Another illustration of the army's crucial role in the political structure is the slow and deliberate change in the ethnic composition of the top military leadership. Traditionally, people from the backward areas of South Serbia, Montenegro, Bosnia, Hercegovina and Macedonia were attracted to a military career. Both the prewar and postwar military leadership had been dominated by the Serbs. The Croats and Slovenes, who do not hold military careers in high esteem, were sorely underrepresented in both the military and security

---

* "Our army," Tito said at the time, "is supposed—that is, it is its principal task—to defend our country against foreign enemies. But it must also protect the achievements of the revolution within the country itself, if that is necessary. This is the way it's got to be."

establishments. I frequently heard Croats complain about the Serb-dominated armed forces. Yet, while men from the backward areas still dominate lower ranks of the officer corps, the government has managed to change the top echelon of the military command in a way that reflects the overall national composition of the population. In fact, among the group of top twenty-two military commanders today, the Croats are most numerous. They comprise 38 percent of the top commanders; the Serbs hold 33 percent of these top jobs. The change in the ethnic composition was clearly designed not only to alleviate various grievances but to create a national consensus at the top level of the military.

The officers corps has been purged repeatedly since the war, and the men who have survived are undoubtedly patriotic Yugoslavs. Yet the army's political role makes many Yugoslavs, including people in responsible party positions, nervous about the generals. One Yugoslav sociologist said that one of the reasons for the development of territorial forces was to counterbalance the officer corps. By nature, background and training the officers tend to be "of authoritarian frame of mind," he continued. "They are peasant boys who like order and clarity. They are perplexed by modern complexities, and pluralistic trends in our society make them uncomfortable. Tito is a strong and forceful personality, and they like him and trust him. The problem is whether at some future date the officers may decide to act on their own. They would tend to support those who advocate Soviet-type centralism, not because of any ideological reasons but instinctively. Nobody knows what these people really think."

One of the great shortcomings of nonalignment, as far as the Yugoslav military chiefs are concerned, has been the problem of weapons procurement. During the war Tito's partisan army equipped itself first with captured German and Italian arms, later with British and American weapons as well. After the war the Russians poured in their equipment but abruptly stopped deliveries when Stalin clamped an embargo on all trade with Yugoslavia in 1948. In 1949 the United States stepped in and supplied Tito with large quantities of American arms under a military assistance program, which the Yugoslavs terminated in 1960.

Tito's decision to end the U.S. military assistance program was a part of his emerging role as a Third World leader. His public commitment to some vague idea of morality in world affairs and the

constant play for international opinion has led him to waste relationships with solid countries for ties with new, weak and often
untrustworthy nations. He had hoped to retain access to the U.S.
weapons markets, calculating that American public opinion would
be in favor of a pugnacious people standing four-square in their
little country with their fists clenched against the world. And he was
willing to pay for the arms.

This turned out to be a miscalculation. George F. Kennan, in
an account of his tour as ambassador to Yugoslavia, provided the best
written account of that phase in U.S.-Yugoslav relations.* Tito had
not counted on what Kennan described as congressional ignorance
and "sheer anti-Yugoslav sentiment" generated by anti-Tito émigrés
in the United States. Despite President Kennedy's backing, congressional critics and their allies in the Pentagon were successful in
blocking the sale of obsolete U.S. aircraft to Yugoslavia. Kennan's
valiant effort on Capitol Hill failed. Not only that. Congress adopted,
against Kennan's strenuous objections, punitive economic measures
against Yugoslavia. "I had had," Kennan wrote in his memoirs,
"some thirty-five years of experience with the affairs of Eastern
Europe," and Representative Wilbur Mills, chairman of the House
Ways and Means Committee, "so far as I knew had never been outside the United States. Yet on an important matter of foreign policy,
affecting most intimately not only the East European post at which I
was stationed but also the attitudes of surrounding countries, the
elected representatives of my country had supported his judgment
over my own."

Kennan resigned quietly a few months later. By then the Yugoslavs had realized that they would have to purchase their advanced
weapons from the Soviet Union. Kennan said he had wanted to be in
the position to reassure Tito that "in resisting Soviet pressure for a
reassociation of Yugoslavia with the Soviet bloc he could always be
confident of an alternative." But, disarmed, he could only remain
silent. "The Yugoslavs would have to fight their own battles as
though we did not exist," Kennan added.

The Yugoslavs in the seventies again attempted to "resume military cooperation with the United States," as a secretary of the central committee of the Yugoslav Communist party privately described

* George F. Kennan, *Memoirs, 1950–1963*. Boston, 1970.

the decision to me. The matter was first raised in a meeting between Tito and Kissinger in 1974. Two American ambassadors, Malcolm Toon and Laurence Silberman, both vigorously advocated affirmative action. Kissinger agreed. In a meeting with Milos Minic, the Yugoslav foreign minister, in October 1975, Kissinger promised to give a formal reply "within two weeks" to the Yugoslavs, who had already presented their shopping list. But weeks extended into months without any U.S. reply. When an affirmative answer finally came in January 1976, the accompanying publicity in the United States and elsewhere made Yugoslav political leaders so jittery that Tito decided to quietly postpone the whole deal.

The affair revealed Yugoslavia's vulnerability and her susceptibility to Soviet pressures. The military chiefs clearly wanted to diversify their sources of arms and to acquire American equipment.

An extraordinarily frank interview with three Yugoslav generals, published in the weekly *NIN* in December 1975, revealed an aspect of the military's thinking. The generals, quoted collectively, made it abundantly clear that the potential enemy was Russia.

The enemy, they said, would try to mount a "swift" tank and paratroop attack to take "a part of our territory and dream up a Quisling-type government, which would then ask for assistance from abroad." Yugoslav forces, they said, would have to destroy "at least two thousand tanks" during the first few days. Although they never named the enemy, the reference to the two thousand tanks deployed in a swift attack left no doubt in anybody's mind as to whom they were talking about. The most vulnerable part of Yugoslavia is that adjacent to the Hungarian and Romanian border. It is natural tank country and the only area of Yugoslavia where such an operation could be mounted. Moreover, the scenario resembles Russia's invasions of Hungary and Czechoslovakia in its political aspects, namely the setting up of puppet governments who then invite Soviet help. (It is worth pointing out that one of the main items on the Yugoslav shopping list was the wire-guided antitank missile TOW.) While the military leaders clearly wanted to acquire sophisticated antitank and electronics equipment in the United States, Tito and his closest advisers drew back from the deal once it became a subject of discussion in the U.S. press. "Couldn't we buy the arms without anybody knowing about it?" General Ljubicic, the defense minister, asked a senior American official. Underlying this reaction was Belgrade's perception of the relative increase of Soviet power in Europe and its impact on Yugoslavia's neutrality and independence. Tito's radius of independent action has been narrowed to a point where even Yugoslav purchases of relatively small amounts of U.S. arms are viewed by the Yugoslavs as entailing grave political risks for their relations with the Eastern bloc.

The diplomatic game is very subtle and intricate. Yugoslavia's ingenious combination of nonalignment and territorial defense can in the final analysis ensure the country's autonomy as long as it is not put to a severe test. In a changing international environment a small country must constantly seek to avoid conflict with a big power, on one hand, by making cautious adjustments to defuse tension and, on the other, by projecting its determination that the possibility of conflict is preferable to simple capitulation.

This is Yugoslavia's quandary: while trying to reduce the intensity of ideological disagreements and perhaps make meaningful and concrete concessions to a great power, the Yugoslav Communists have to hold out the prospect of military struggle against that very power. The success of this approach depends on Yugoslavia's ability to manage her ideological and political conflict with the Kremlin and a continued assessment of her relationships among major global powers. In short, it requires leadership with diplomatic talents of the highest order. Tito has been exceptionally successful at this game, but among those who are cited as his obvious successors no one has thus far demonstrated similar skills.

What the Yugoslavs have done in the seventies has been to institutionalize Tito's policies and concepts. But will the Russians tolerate Yugoslavia's nonalignment after Tito? Many Yugoslav Sovietologists profess to see positive changes in the Kremlin. "Russia," one expert told me, "is still an old-fashioned empire. It seeks military control over areas under its control or influence. But the Russians are becoming more sophisticated. Once they gain sufficient economic strength, their behavior in Eastern Europe will change. But this, of course, is going to take some time." Another expert, who is a member of the executive secretariat of the Yugoslav party, echoed this view. He illustrated it by citing Yugoslav experiences: for many years after World War II the Tito regime pursued Soviet-type policies because of the country's feeble economy. "We kept the borders shut and we feared what is now called a free flow of information as long as our people could not buy basic consumer goods here.

The West seemed tremendously attractive to them. They had to go to Italy or Austria to buy a silk scarf or nylon stockings and such things. Once we gained economic strength we realized we had nothing to fear in that respect. People now travel wherever they want to and they come back. We had more people vacationing in Greece and Spain last year than on our own Dalmatian coast."

But these are long-term assessments. As far as the immediate future is concerned, the Yugoslavs remain extremely suspicious of the Kremlin. Its self-proclaimed right to intervene in internal affairs of other socialist countries—"if the basis of socialism" and "the basis of our ties and the security of the commonwealth of our countries are threatened"—has ominous implications. Yugoslavia is a socialist country but not a bloc member. But the Brezhnev doctrine refers to the "socialist commonwealth," whose extent has never been specifically defined. It was Brezhnev who during a visit to Yugoslavia in 1976 tried to project himself as "Little Red Ridinghood" to assure his hosts that the Kremlin is not a Big Bad Wolf. It would be hard to find Yugoslavs who believed him.

This leitmotif echoed and re-echoed in numerous Balkan conversations. In public pronouncements and official interviews, however, the Yugoslavs have all along insisted with near paranoid determination that both military blocs pose a threat to their country.

There is a speculative verve in South Slavs, a shade of Byzantium and Greece. At first I was prey to the natural delusion to which many a foreign visitor falls victim; for many spokesmen, when talking privately to Westerners, emphasize Yugoslavia's resistance to Soviet pressures and all its sinister implications. But then I realized that in their discussions with Russians, these same spokesmen would emphasize different aspects of the country's policy, such as the Communist character of the system despite impulses toward pluralism. I came to admire the diplomatic skill of Yugoslavs. They carefully chipped and pared at an argument to achieve the desired impact. This, in my experience, rarely involved outright lies; deceptions yes, forgeries no. It is only as if different sides of the coin are shown to different audiences.

But beneath the rhetoric and fragments of information one could distinguish the long-range direction of policy. Tito apparently had reached the conclusion that the Russians would not resort to outright military aggression against Yugoslavia, and that this regime must seek to reduce ideological and political differences with Moscow without compromising Yugoslavia's independence. In a variety of ways—some subtle and symbolic, others of concrete practical value to Moscow—Tito has moved his country into a closer relationship with the Soviet bloc.* In addition to expanded economic cooperation, the Yugoslavs have muted their public criticism of the Kremlin and have taken precautions to eliminate even a whiff of anti-Sovietism in the press. A somewhat more repressive line was taken against certain intellectuals, apparently to engender Soviet confidence in the Communist character of the Yugoslav society. One victim of this policy was a dissident publicist, Mihajlo Mihajlov, who was sentenced to seven years in prison in 1974 for articles he published in the Russian émigré press and in the *New York Times* over the preceding three years.† This is an example of Tito's regime at its worst, trying a man whose views and activities were of no consequence whatsoever as far as Yugoslav internal affairs were concerned. Likewise, a few weeks before the expulsion from Russia of Alexander Solzhenitsyn, the Yugoslav press for the first time attacked the dissident Soviet writer who, up to that point, had been lionized in the Yugoslav media.

Another thing that has attracted the attention of foreign observers is the increased use by Soviet naval ships of a new major Yugoslav naval dockyard at Tivat, in Kotor Bay. The Russians have been urging Tito to provide them with an unrestricted base for the Soviet Mediterranean fleet, something the Yugoslavs have steadfastly refused. But the Russians have made use of a Yugoslav law permitting any nation to berth not more than two warships at a time in Yugoslav docks. The law permits a single ship to remain up to six months and the Soviet fleet has been using the Tivat facility up to the maximum allowed.

I have heard Yugoslavs say that all these changes were merely Belgrade's insurance policy for the future. There is no doubt that this is the intent. The Yugoslavs have pushed the development of a strong, self-reliant defense force, with the territorial army serving as a deterrent against foreign intervention and the regular army taking on the role of guardian of political stability.

---

* This was Tito's personal decision. The Yugoslav Foreign Ministry advocated a different line. As Jure Bilic, one of the party secretaries, acknowledged publicly, the Foreign Ministry advocated a move toward "an Austrian- or Swiss-type neutrality."

† Mihajlov was released from jail in November 1977.

Is Tito's assessment correct? What if his concessions only whet the bear's appetite? I was present at an extraordinary discussion with a senior government figure in the summer of 1976 when this question was raised. The Yugoslav official, who was in his late fifties, joined U.S. Ambassador Laurence Silberman and two other NATO ambassadors for a chat at a diplomatic function. He spoke gloomily about American intentions in Europe in the context of the "Sonnenfeldt doctrine." Helmut Sonnenfeldt, a senior State Department official, had given a private briefing to U.S. ambassadors in Europe at a meeting in London the previous December. The gist of his remarks, as reported later by columnists Robert Novak and Rowland Evans, was that American diplomacy should not only refrain from opposing Soviet objectives in Eastern Europe but passively allow the Russians to consolidate their hold on the region .The Yugoslavs interpreted the leak as a reflection of a secret understanding between Washington and Moscow.

Yes, the official said, there is a possibility of Russian intervention in internal Yugoslav affairs at a future date. "We will fight them," he said, "but that will not remain a local war. Don't think that for a moment. We will involve all of Europe in it." The striking thing about his statement was its logic as well as the vehemence with which it was uttered. "But how?" Silberman inquired. The official responded with even greater emphasis and anger: "We will see to it. It's not going to be all the world cheering the brave Yugoslavs as though we are on the stage." He abruptly cut off further discussion.

I was startled by the simplicity and directness of the man's statements. Was this a bluff? An official view? Or only the spontaneous reaction of an old Communist guerrilla fighter who sensed the difficulty in maintaining an independent Communist state in a geographically and politically exposed position such as the one occupied by Yugoslavia? I don't know. But his remarks provided a hint about the thinking of top Yugoslav officials, demonstrating as well those attitudes of Yugoslavs that have become their weapons for survival—unpredictability, reckless courage and anarchic disregard for the consequences of their actions.

In the cold light of analytical research, Yugoslavia's security appears to me tragically precarious; and the Yugoslav Communists, like the heroes in ancient Greek tragedies, seem condemned to an inevitable fate they cannot escape. But there is the "human element" one cannot discount. There is a word that applies to the

Yugoslavs and that is not easily translated. The word *inat* means spitefulness to the point where one is prepared to cut off his nose to spite his face. It is a quality that makes the life in a multinational country more difficult; at the same time it makes the Yugoslavs ignore the pedestrian rules of logic when it comes to foreign enemies.

Even when ethnic hatreds run high and national Communist factions are most antagonistic among the Yugoslav republics, the prospect of a Russian threat can almost overnight rekindle a spirit of unity and patriotism that no amount of rational reasoning could ever generate. The Czechoslovak invasion ignited such sentiments from sleepy mountain villages to major urban areas. J. F. Balvany, a Swiss reporter who was in Yugoslavia at that time, told me about this sudden transformation. "I talked to many people—Serbs, Croats, Slovenes, Macedonians, what have you. That summer they were Yugoslavs, ready to wage a patriotic war against the Russians. I will never forget it. Mind you, that was spontaneous, not organized by the government. Even officials were patriots first, Communists second. A few years later, when the memory of the Prague invasion faded, they went back to their old quarrels and officials became nasty again."

And yet, the Yugoslavs' attitude toward Russia is ambivalent. They do not hate the Russians. Even among the Roman Catholic Croats and Slovenes I didn't hear anti-Russian jokes that included vicious ethnic slurs of the kind one hears elsewhere in Eastern Europe. Among the Serbs and other Orthodox population there is a measure of active sympathy for Russia, the ancient defender of the faith. Russia had a place in the old Orthodox mythology that had framed the Serbs' view of the world. The Yugoslavs, in general, see a Russian threat not in ethnic or racial terms, but in the context of reimposition of Soviet-style centralism and curtailment of the personal freedom and national independence that they have gained with Tito. They experienced the Soviet system in the immediate postwar years and to them Tito's communism is not only a lesser of two evils, but also the hope of greater democratization for the future.

As I listened to popular sentiments I discovered that in a strange way the Yugoslavs don't seem afraid of the Russians. Most frequently expressed was a confidence that all potential invaders would share the fate of the former conquerors whose empires had vanished long ago. "Let them come," they warned with what seemed to be a zest for a good fight. "We'll fight them."

A Slovene sociologist explained Yugoslavia's attitude by quoting the Russian poet Nekrasov's verse, *Ty bessylnaya to moguchaya, Matushka Rosiya* ("You are powerless and the most powerful, Mother Russia"). "Russia is powerful in the sense that you can't conquer her, but she is vulnerable from within. They know that, we know that. Today, freedom is an essential measure of power. The Russians don't want to fight abroad. If they were to march in, they would have to fight, for we know how to fight. So they are more likely to use covert methods. But the way we have set up our system, it will be very hard to take over this country by using a few traitors, as they did in Czechoslovakia. At least we believe that."

This view was echoed among Western military specialists on Balkan affairs. An American general, who at one time headed the U.S. military assistance program to Yugoslavia, put it this way: "The Yugoslavs are tough as hell. They are going to fight whether you give them a wooden club or a TOW. The Russians can't make a quick grab there, nor can they act by proxy, say by using the Bulgarians and the Hungarians. They would have to go in themselves and that would be a very protracted thing. That's the last thing the Russians want."

10

Dissent and Opposition

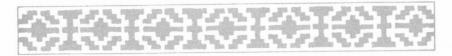

For our country, freedom is not a great tradition, but rather an unfulfilled dream. We've exhausted our passion for freedom in the struggle to get it.

There are theoreticians who maintain that too much knowledge, too much beauty, too much justice, too much freedom threaten the former great freedom that kept us warm for so many years.

They prefer the fight for freedom to being free. The fight for freedom is always easier than the practice of freedom.

MATIJA BECKOVIC

MY OFFICE WAS LOCATED IN THE HEART OF BELGRADE IN A DISTRICT with many restaurants, sidewalk cafés, taverns and simple bistros. I frequented two sidewalk cafés whose patrons were intellectuals—students, actors, writers, journalists—predominantly younger people, many of them bearded and shaggy-haired, with time to idle in the sunlight and talk endlessly. Listening to them, I was introduced to the curious ways of Yugoslav dissent. Men from the nearby Belgrade TV headquarters came down at noon, ordered a small bottle of aromatic, yellowish *rakija* and a plate of feta cheese and olives and talked sometimes bitterly, sometimes excitedly about cuts they had been forced to make in their films. Journalists from various newspapers traded gossip, and students complained about a hopelessly tangled labor situation that dimmed the prospects for employment. In the buzz of oaths and shouts, there was a thread of disaffection with the authoritarian strain in the Yugoslav political system. I recall one mid-morning conversation with a group of younger intellectuals whose free discussions, it seemed to me, stood in sharp contrast to the comparative timorousness of other East Europeans. It was this contrast that I advanced in the debate, adding as a clincher to my argument the fact that Yugoslavs are permitted to travel ouside the borders of the country, something that East Europeans are not allowed to do. "But I don't want to travel anywhere," a young writer shot back in a sardonic tone, leaning on the table and making it creak. "I want to be free here. This is my country. Let them travel if they want to . . ."

The inexorable logic of his statement merely defined my bias: I was evaluating Yugoslavia in terms of my experiences in Russia and Eastern Europe and saw Yugoslavs enjoying greater personal freedom than their Communist neighbors. My interlocutors were on a different vector, viewing the gap between their freedoms and those enjoyed by citizens of West European democracies. "Even our *Gastarbeiter* in Sweden," another intellectual said, "can vote in Swedish elections. In Sweden you have real communism," he added in a humorous vein. His statement came as a surprise, for I knew that he was a party member in a responsible middle-level position.

All this was an accepted part of café talk as long as the voices were kept at the conversational level. The *kafana* is a proper setting for grumbling, for antiregime jokes and stories and I was able to gossip with the habitués about all sorts of things. By decree, the government tried in 1974 to put a stop to ethnic and political jokes, prescribing severe penalties. But this did not seem to affect café conversations at all, as if the setting provided a special immunity. In a different setting the people seemed more cautious. At a cocktail party, I once met a medium-level official with whom I had traded jokes in the *kafana*. Since I knew that he delighted in hearing a good joke, I was about to tell him one when he cut me off sternly by saying, "I'm not going to listen to any jokes here. You know who built the banks of the Moscow River in Moscow? The left bank was built by people who told jokes, the right by those who listened to them."

Dissent at the *kafana* level, I was told by many Yugoslavs, is a tradition of sorts. It makes the absence of genuine political life endurable. Years of foreign rule have made Yugoslavs vacillate between submission to authority and rebellion against it. The relationship between rulers and the ruled provides for outbursts of mischievous disobedience. At the same time the ruled seem to accept occasional gross injustices as something inevitable. This was made painfully evident to me during a long conversation with Lev Znidarcic, an elderly Croat lawyer who with three colleagues was arrested in late 1975 and held in jail for nearly four months. The

four Zagreb attorneys had earlier acted as defense counsel to a group
of imprisoned Croat nationalists. No charges were filed against the
attorneys, and they were released without an explanation. "Imagine," Znidarcic recalled ruefully, "they didn't even apologize! Or say
at least there has been a mistake!"

Repression in Yugoslavia often depends on the idiosyncrasies of
provincial chieftains, or even of law enforcement officers. There are
matters that have nothing to do with communism or democracy but
are simply Balkan traditions. More often than not such repression is
not sponsored by the party.

I was told a story involving the Argentine ambassador to
Switzerland, who in 1974 was motoring through Yugoslavia on vacation and who had a highly unpleasant confrontation with two Yugoslav policemen on a lonely road in Montenegro. The policemen
stopped the ambassador for speeding and tried to collect a fine
equivalent to about two dollars. The Argentinean invoked diplomatic immunity. Since they had no common language to communicate, the policemen grasped the fact that the foreigner did not
want to pay the fine and was seemingly condescending toward them.
Both sides had invested a great deal of face in the irrational dispute,
and when push came to shove, the policemen drew their nightsticks
and beat up the diplomat so badly that he had to be hospitalized.
The president of Montenegro, who related this story to me, said he
and Foreign Minister Minic had to call on the envoy at the hospital
and formally apologize for the incident.

The lack of logic, of course, doesn't make the capriciousness of
the authorities more tolerable. The regime has been consistent in
applying repressive measures against potential political opposition
groups. Dissent, one official told me privately, "is not a real problem
here. In Russia you have a couple of hundred dissidents who talk,
complain and criticize but who are not representative of the Soviet
society. In Yugoslavia, all Yugoslavs are dissidents to a varying degree; they have to criticize, complain, talk incessantly about what's
wrong. Just go down to the *kafana* and you'll hear it. But that's not a
problem. Our problem is organized political action."

Since oppositionist forces tend to coalesce around nationalist
grievances, the regime has been particularly hard on the Croats and
Kosovo Albanians. But even here repression is used sparingly to
avoid overkill. The Croatian Roman Catholic Church, for instance,
has its own press that conducts running dialogues with Croatian

Communists. Because of the fragmented nature of the country and old ethnic suspicions, the Croatian clergy find it impossible to make common cause with the Serbian Orthodox Church for greater religious freedom. The sentiment is reciprocal. Why, I asked a Croat Church official, don't you get together with the Serbs and wage common struggle for greater religious liberties? "Oh, we can't do that," he replied as though he were articulating a self-evident truth. I received an identical reply from a Serbian Church official.

Paradoxically, the real and most serious opposition to the regime is on the left, among the people who had accepted the idea of socialism but who have become disillusioned with the way it is applied. The Communist party, for better or for worse, has been the prime mover of political innovation. Nowhere else in the Communist world has the challenge of freedom been tested as seriously as in Yugoslavia. The country's early and wide opening to the influence and example of Western technology, thoughts and institutions has helped its entry into the modern age in which ideological positions are increasingly irrelevant to the complex decision-making processes. Lacking doctrinaire belief in the sanctity of Marxism, Tito and his colleagues recognized the pluralistic nature of modern society. They realized for the good of Yugoslavia's socialism and their careers that ideology had to be pared and twisted. In contrast to Russia's one-party system, the Yugoslavs advanced the idea of a nonparty, self-managerial democratic socialism. The party's name was changed to the "League of Communists" and its function was to guide and manage the competition of institutions and various interest groups within the league's framework. The change introduced a greater degree of permissiveness and candor in public life.

But while the regime recognized pluralism within the party, it was never willing to permit the kind of political pluralism that could challenge the ruling group's monopoly on power. The measure of freedom, never clearly defined, became the main issue between the regime and its critics. Government spokesmen defended their policy, holding as equally irrational and incompetent those who advocated greater freedoms with Orthodox Communist elements who preferred Soviet-style centralism.

Typical of criticism aimed at the government was an article written by novelist Dobrica Cosic, an old Communist who until 1968 served as a member of the Central Committee of the Serbian party. After describing the Tito regime as a "group of spiritual

nihilists" who have stifled intellectual freedom and thus undermined the essence of socialism, Cosic said the bureaucracy and the
corrupted intellectuals have formed a "privileged elite in the midst
of the poverty and spiritual misery of the ordinary people." He
continued:

> The traditional historical optimism, the belief that progress is a
> function of natural law—which is the most cunning form of con-
> formism—must be left to the ideologists and hedonists if one wants
> to retain belief in socialism and a possible society of freedom and
> justice.
> From such a conviction the following confession must flow: We
> have been deceived but we are also swindlers.
> Misuse of freedom is certainly possible, but not in the creative
> sphere. In the history of the world and of this country, the greatest
> misuse of freedom has always been perpetrated by those in power
> and by political passions. Thus today the frequent and fatal misuse
> of freedom for socialist ends is the fault of those in power rather
> than those working in science, the arts and philosophy. It must be
> emphasized again that deprivation of freedom is the worst crime.

The article was published in the bimonthly magazine *Praxis*, in
Zagreb in 1975, and it provides an insight into the kind of debate
that was under way at the time. Cosic's career as a highly successful
novelist was not affected by the article. But another relatively unknown writer, Dragoljub Ignjatovic, was imprisoned for saying
roughly the same thing at a philosophical gathering. He was tried
and convicted of "spreading false information," then was released
following an international uproar over the incident. But then the
authorities brought charges against Ignjatovic's defense counsel,
Srdja Popovic, who was accused of "spreading false news" while trying in the course of the Ignjatovic trial to prove from official sources
that his client's statements about Yugoslavia's social and economic
situation were accurate.*
There is something symbolic about the cases of these two writers. They epitomize the regime's willingness to tolerate freedom of

---

* Popovic, who is a member of his family's prosperous law firm, traveled
throughout Western Europe trying to drum up international support for his
case. He was tried and given a suspended one year sentence. Lost in the unfold-
ing sensation of Yugoslavia's trampling on the basic right of a lawyer to speak
in defense of his client was the fact that that right never existed in Communist
countries, including Yugoslavia, whenever political offenses were at stake.

expression and its instinctive lurch toward repression and curtailment of personal liberties. There has been a lack of consistency in the swings between the two extremes, an unpredictability that makes one think of Tito's regime as mild despotism tempered by Balkan inefficiency.

But in nearly all the cases of repression I heard about during my tour, the authorities invariably sought to create an area of agreement with dissident elements, to seduce them with offers of positions and privileges. Repression was resorted to reluctantly, against the most militant and unyielding when other means of persuasion failed.

I had conversations—in Belgrade, Zagreb and other cities—with various opposition figures. I have drawn profiles of two men not because they are leading oppositionists—they are not—but because of their remarkable personal courage and willingness to talk frankly about their careers. Jovan Barovic is the country's leading civil rights lawyer; Ljubomir Tadic is a Marxist philosopher and sociologist who until 1975 was a professor at the University of Belgrade. Both became Communists before Hitler's attack on Yugoslavia; both were members of Tito's first regular military unit; both were eventually expelled from the party.

Barovic is a short, bull-chested man who looks like James Cagney. Although he is engaged in an uneven struggle, his fearlessness and conviction of the rightness of his purpose give him a kind of skeptical good humor. No Communist court has ever acquitted a political offender; indeed, their guilt is often announced in advance by prominent government figures as was the case with one of Barovic's clients, the writer Mihajlo Mihajlov, who was publicly condemned by Tito a few days before his trial. And yet Barovic enacts each of his cases as though it were an act of love, trying to construct a defense that would demonstrate the injustice of the foreordained proceedings and at the same time appeal to the basic decency of those who sit in judgment.

An attorney such as Barovic lives in a dangerous world beset by conflicts between expediency and principle. The government invariably chooses expediency to silence troublesome opponents; Barovic and his colleagues stand on principles, trying to create out of the Socialist tradition a forum strong enough to withstand tyrannical impulses of the ruling elite. The government always wins. And yet those persecuted on political grounds—Croatian nationalists, Al-

banian separatists, pro-Soviet conspirators, maverick intellectuals—
seek Barovic's help. Barovic has been defense counsel in nearly every
important political trial in recent years.

Why do they select him? I once asked Barovic why he gets more
"political cases" than any other attorney.

"Why?" He pouted his lips and looked heavenward before turning his eyes on me. "I don't know. I think people want to hear the
truth and they believe I am not afraid to defend them honestly."

He related a story of an Albanian civil rights riot in Tetovo, a
town of seven thousand in Macedonia. For a day and a night the
Albanian demonstrators paralyzed all authority in Tetovo in protest
against discrimination at the hands of the Macedonians. Police rein-
forcements were brought, the town was blocked off, and mass arrests
followed. Nearly one hundred persons were charged. Barovic was
called in by the Albanian community. "I spent more than two
months on the case and I defended them as best I could. After my
final appeal, mothers and wives of the men on trial came up to me
and started kissing me, something very unusual for Moslem women
to do. One old woman told me, 'Doctor'—they call all educated men
that way—'Doctor, you told the truth, it's not important what hap-
pens now.' Anyway, most of the men were sentenced. Almost a year
later, one day early in the morning I get a call. A group of fifty
Albanians from Tetovo had just arrived at the Belgrade railroad
station and they were asking me to take them to the prime minister.
More than forty of their relatives were still in jail. I went to the
railroad station and led them to the government building. It was a
splendid march, old men clad in baggy Turkish trousers and tall
black boots and old women wearing colorful native costumes. When
we reached the government building, my clients sat down in the
hall. Marble floors, you know. We got to see the minister of justice
and I presented their grievances—repression, police brutality and all.
When I'd finished, the minister asked them, 'Is all this true?' and
they replied, 'Yes, except that all was even worse.' Most of the arrested were released soon afterwards and the problems in Tetovo
were settled. Another thing. When I was in Tetovo last, I was not
permitted to pay for my food or anything. Albanians run small shops
and restaurants and their community leaders have decided that I
shall not be allowed to pay for anything."

The Tetovo Albanians were tried under Article 118 of the
Penal Code—an omnibus provision dealing with "hostile propa-

ganda," "counterrevolutionary activities" and other actions against the social order. It is worded imprecisely, without defining the terms, and this permits the authorities to prosecute anyone. Other clients of Barovic were tried under the same provision: Professor Mihajlo Djuric, a sociologist, for making a critical remark in class about the regime; Davor Aras, a historian and representative of the Yugoslav Academy of Sciences in Zadar, for joining a group of Croat nationalists who allegedly planned to organize an IRA-type organization; a group of Albanian intellectuals in Kosovo for advocating secession of the province; Milivoj Stefanovic, one-time editor in chief of the government news agency Tanjug, for his pro-Soviet sentiments and activities; Vlado Dapcevic, an émigré politician of Stalinist persuasion who was kidnapped from Romania by Yugoslav agents and brought to Yugoslavia to stand trial. The list is long.

"Our state is constantly struggling to create a legal framework to protect itself," Barovic said. "But there is a tendency to turn political expediency into law. That's why you have political interventions in courts, especially in the area of political offenses and also economic crimes. When crime is determined by political decision the whole concept of legality gets lost."

Of all intellectuals with an interest in civil liberties, Barovic personifies the most trenchant and uninhibited drive for justice. His personal commitment to socialism is tempered by a respect for rights of each individual. He could say "we"—meaning Tito's Yugoslavia—in a way that would be hardly possible for most of his colleagues. In 1940, when he was seventeen years old, he became a member of the Communist party and was expelled from high school; the next year he was a soldier, party secretary in his unit; by the end of the war he was political commissar of an armored division with the rank of lieutenant colonel. And then, in 1954, the man who spent years trying to instill Marxist ideas into the heads of illiterate peasants found himself at odds with the dogma. He was ousted from the party and army. So direct and so clear have all his subsequent steps been that it seemed inevitable that he should become a civil rights lawyer. Enduring great personal sacrifices as he tried to support his wife and two small children, Barovic entered the University of Belgrade Law School in 1955. He was graduated in 1958 but could not find a job. Nothing had gone easily. He was finally hired as an apprentice by two prominent liberal attorneys, Veljko Kovacevic and Slavko Kirsner. Kovacevic, a Hercegovinian who was an active Social

Democrat before World War II, was defense attorney for Milovan Djilas. Kirsner, a member of an established Serbian Jewish family, was one of the most respected legal minds in the city. The partners have had difficulties with the Tito regime (Kovacevic, in fact, was sentenced to three months in jail in 1953 for having vigorously defended a pro-Soviet Yugoslav). But, as Kirsner said in hiring Barovic, "Everyone has the right to a chance." He passed the bar examination in 1964, earlier attempts having been blocked by "higher authority," as one member of the commission recalled. He was forty-two years old when he began practicing law on his own.

It would be hard to view Joro, as his friends call Barovic, as a regular attorney. His faith in legality seems to have qualities of a natural force. You wouldn't want him to represent you in a civil suit, unless you are absolutely in the right. I know a Belgrade journalist, Dragoljub Golubovic, who engaged Barovic in his divorce case. Although Golubovic's position was somewhat ambiguous, the case was settled to his satisfaction. At the last moment, as the judge was about to award most of the joint property to Golubovic, Barovic without any consultations with his client told the judge that the Golubovics' apartment should be given to the wife. "Imagine, the SOB felt sorry for her," Golubovic said later, after the judge ruled that the apartment be awarded to Mrs. Golubovic.

When it comes to defending political offenders, Joro is the man to turn to. His determination, in spite of certain aspects of utopianism, has a solid relation to realities. He fights losing battles but along every step of the way he makes the arbitrariness of the government's injustices ring with clarity.

What had made him turn from a political commissar into a civil rights lawyer, I asked him once. We were sitting in the garden of his home on a warm spring afternoon amid the fragrance of blossoming peach trees. His lengthy and vivid recollections opened up an entirely new world for me.

He became involved in politics while attending high school. "It was then that I first heard about the rich and poor, about communism, and about Soviet Russia. The very notion of Russia involved mysticism. Everything was better there. We would daydream about Russia the way religious rural youth daydream about paradise. I established contact with a party member who worked in a bookstore, obtaining books about Russia. I also read Jack London and party literature. I was attracted by the secretiveness of the movement. I was a member of a band that possessed the knowledge of the future."

The war made life dangerous and dramatic. Everything he did in the party was intensified and lived with a special kind of awareness. In addition to fighting with a rifle in his hands, his principal job was political work. "I was to initiate my brave peasants into Marxism-Leninism. We had Stalin's booklet, *History of the Soviet Communist Party*, about fifty pages, and I had to work with them through and through. The fourth chapter on dialectical materialism bedeviled our evening sessions. That chapter was beyond their comprehension. So they would learn it by heart."

Organization was the most important part of the party life. Everything was subjected to it. There was no independent existence outside the party. "That's how you get the terrific cohesion. In my unit I had to observe and grade each party member. How does he behave in battle? In other situations? The greatest personal reward was a commendation for your work by the party; and, conversely, criticism was painful, for you felt sinful, as though God had refused to accept your prayers."

After the war, at age twenty-three, Barovic found himself in the post of political commissar of several divisions. "We had to educate and civilize our peasant officers. Ironically, I and people like myself with some high school education were regarded as 'intellectuals' in the corps. As commissar I had to clean out politically undesirable personnel from the armed forces, approve marriages of lower ranking officers.

"But now that the crescendo had ceased I found myself in the role of a gendarme. How senseless, how empty, how sick everything suddenly seemed. We were left flat with our poverty and humiliating life that the struggle against the enemy kept out of our minds. My comrades, my heroes, were now interested in women, clothes, whoring, privileges, the good life. They went as far as to steal supplies. Perhaps I am an incurable romantic, but I felt superfluous. Then in 1948 the conflict with Stalin crept up on us. That was another great challenge and all my doubts drowned in it.

"There is something in my nature that urges me to support the national government which resists a great power. Most Yugoslavs are like that. I never weighed rational aspects of the conflict, the imbalance of forces. As far as I was concerned our resistance was a beautiful moment in history. I threw myself with all my heart into the struggle against the Russians. I had idolized them. I had worked for years to create an illusion about Russia in the minds of my soldiers. Now I had to destroy this illusion. We had adored Stalin so long and so uncritically that 1948 was another revolution, a moment of truth. As a political commissar of a division, I had to be told what to do: we had to create ideological differences with the Russians, we criticized their huge bureaucracy, their police state and the absence of freedom. We survived, but our world of rhetoric was damaged beyond repair. Even within the party a feeling of bewilderment and disgust produced a drive for change.

"In 1952, when I was assigned to attend the High Military Academy in Belgrade, I began to question our party's position. All the faults we attributed to the Soviet system were in existence in our system. Then came the death of Stalin. Suddenly, the leaders told us that the struggle against Moscow should be regarded as completed. Just like that. Then, just as suddenly, Djilas started a series of articles calling for greater democratization.

"For us, Djilas was an exciting figure, young, good-looking, most articulate among the top leaders; we were mesmerized by his inexhaustible flow of pungent rhetoric. He spoke about humanist revolution, a movement toward pluralism but avoiding errors of both capitalism and communism. He had sensed the mood and desires of the people and the party. We, of course, thought this was a new party line, for Djilas was the chief ideologue and Tito's heir apparent. We were excited about his ideas, we saw a new revolution in the society. I accepted the ideas wholeheartedly for they represented what I thought socialism was all about. Then, without forewarning, Djilas was ousted and disgraced. I told my comrades I thought this was a setback. Many of them, who until yesterday supported Djilas's ideas, suddenly switched saying they would go along with the majority on the Central Committee.

"A few weeks later, when I was subjected to an investigation as a supporter of Djilas, I realized that some of my closest comrades had already made written denunciations of me. I remember that one man, Colonel Asim Pervan, stood up during the meeting trying to say that I was not a traitor but that I merely had a different point of view. But others attacked him, trying to have him expelled from the party as well. The moment I was expelled from the party, I became a nonperson, thin air for my friends and colleagues. It was only a matter of days before I was to be forced out of the academy and the army. For me as a Communist, this was a source of enormous torment and humiliation. Old war buddies turning their heads away, my classmates looking through me as though I didn't have physical existence. And I was disappointed. What had happened to these heroes?"

Courage has been the hallmark of Barovic's subsequent legal career. He was denied work. After his discharge from the military he worked briefly for a foreign radio monitoring bureau. But then he met Djilas for the first time and struck up a friendship with him. Old comrades in the security police tried to reason with Barovic, to threaten him. I have met some of his friends who told me that the Barovic family lived on bread and milk for years. Only after he passed the bar did Barovic's life become easier. At the same time, Tito's reforms diluted the authoritarian strain of his regime.

"In my career, the ethical question has been important for me. I felt it would be shameful to do things against my deep conviction. Then there is a question of honor. I didn't want to appear a coward. When the authorities put on pressure I refused to compromise. You make just one compromise on matters regarding your personal integrity and you are through. I have one life, I said, and you can take it away but that's all you can do.

"I prospered as a lawyer, not in a financial sense. But in legal circles and in court I never had any professional difficulties. By our criminal code, we have become a civilized nation. I can tell you that our legal system has improved tremendously, in all respects but one. We still remain similar to totalitarian regimes of Eastern Europe in the sense that political repression of individuals is possible. And you've got to struggle against that in the courts."

Barovic, who is of a tough and vigorous rural stock, spoke with the kind of intensity in which feeling and intellect blend. There is a strong attachment to the old values, yet he has the instinct of a political commissar who knows how to plead the case in a Marxist context.

He turned to law because, once outside the party he helped build, he wanted to determine his fate and future himself. He had done nothing wrong, and that ferocious Montenegrin pride would not permit him to compromise his honor. And yet he had been cast in a mold, bringing his attitudes with him—above all, his belief in the ideals of socialism. All he was trying to do was ask the Establishment to live up to its promises.

Barovic can do this with far greater irreverence than lawyers who belong, at least spiritually, to the old bourgeois world. Barovic's partner, Veljko Kovacevic, is an elderly gentleman of great personal courage and integrity. His knowledge of the law is probably greater than Barovic's, but Kovacevic belongs to a different world. He and people like him build legalistic, procedural defenses. Barovic, on the other hand, is spiritually a part of Tito's Yugoslavia. He is a member of the so-called "Club '41," the name of the dwindling band of prewar Communists who helped Tito organize the revolutionary war. Fewer than three thousand club members are still around, most of whom occupy key positions in the country. Joro Barovic's main concerns in court are the written laws and personal and ideological commitments of the old Communists to equality, justice and freedom. Who can argue against these? Weren't they the proclaimed goals of the revolution?

Nor does Barovic let false assertions of the prosecutions pass without challenge. The trial of Vlado Dapcevic is typical. Dapcevic was captured by Yugoslav agents in Bucharest on the evening of August 7, 1975, and forcibly hauled to Yugoslavia the next day. In the struggle that accompanied his capture, the agents broke several of Dapcevic's ribs, and on August 8 he was treated by doctors in Belgrade. However, the indictment and a public announcement asserted that Dapcevic was captured on December 21, 1975, while trying to illegally enter into Yugoslavia. "Comrades," Barovic told the judges, "I move for a dismissal of the charges. You've got the wrong man here. My client has been in Yugoslavia since August 8. I have witnesses to prove this. You say the man on trial entered on December 21. That must be another man. I want to call the following witnesses....."

After protracted discussion the judge ruled against Barovic. He was not permitted to call his witnesses, but he continued to challenge the prosecution. I recall a trial in Moscow of dissident Anatoly Marchenko, which I attended in August 1968. The atmosphere was entirely different and a timorous defense council appeared to be a part of the prosecuting team. By comparison there was a real struggle in the Yugoslav courts. I talked to several seasoned observers of Communist affairs who were astonished at the degree of legality within the Yugoslav system compared to that in the Soviet bloc. This is also the argument made by Barovic. "Patiently," he said, "you have to work on changes within the system. It may take a long time, I know. But what is the alternative?"

Professor Ljuba Tadic, by temperament a soft-spoken and introspective man, is, like Barovic, a veteran of the partisan struggle.

Also like Barovic, Tadic first saw the world through the window of the patriarchal society. But where Barovic's was a rebellion of the heart, Tadic's rebellion is of the mind; where Barovic works within the system to establish respect for basic liberties, Tadic has boldly confronted power by challenging the entire political establishment; and where Barovic is one of a few civil rights lawyers, Tadic belongs to a large group of Marxist intellectuals who come into conflict with a Marxist government.

There is a special irony in the fact that the most serious challenge to the Establishment had come from within that elite group, indeed from the people who were supposed to be high priests of the dogma—the Marxist philosophers. The opposition is not confined to a group of individual philosophers and teachers but is solidly established in universities and professional organizations, both of which are supposed to be under party control.

Stripped to its essentials, the conflict between Marxist thinkers and the Tito regime is political. The thinkers argue that the country is ruled by a political-bureaucratic elite which enjoys a monopoly of power and privilege and which is heading toward authoritarianism; that its economic policy and the trend toward a consumer society have created class distinctions in the country and have failed to provide "equal social conditions" for all citizens; that the position of workers remains the same whether conditions of production are determined by the state or by a private proprietor; that the regime has mismanaged the economy and introduced the "two basic evils of every class society, poverty and unemployment"; that individual freedoms proclaimed in the constitution are a privilege enjoyed by "the new bourgeoisie" while the average citizen is powerless to influence policies or "the legal basis of the system"; that the arbitrariness of the government—here Article 118 of the Criminal Code is cited—has made individuals feel insecure since each can be "crushed should he venture to taste a little more freedom"; that, in short, Tito's socialism is a failure. The Yugoslav model, they argue, is "better" than the Soviet model, because the latter had totally "suppressed the original ideas of socialism"; a new vision of socialism must be based on new premises which are only partly, and insufficiently, reflected in Yugoslav socialism.

The fact that such ideas could be openly expressed by Marxist philosophers and sociologists at the universities of Belgrade, Zagreb and Ljubljana is in itself remarkable. Such defiance is unimaginable in the Soviet bloc countries.

The focus of dissident views was the bimonthly journal, *Praxis*, founded in 1964 in Zagreb and edited by an exceptionally able sociologist, Rudi Supek, and his colleagues at the Faculty of Philosophy of the University of Zagreb. Other scholarly journals, such as *Filozofija*, published in Belgrade, pursued identical editorial policies, but *Praxis* became the flagship of critical Marxist thought. Among *Praxis* contributors and editorial board members were some well-known international figures such as Herbert Marcuse, Henri Lefebvre, Noam Chomsky, Jurgen Habermas, Erich Fromm, Zygmund Baumann, Ernst Bloch, Enzo Paci, and Leszek Kolakowski. The *Praxis* group also started seminars on the Adriatic island of Korcula, where Marxist scholars from East and West gathered each summer for discussions and exchanges of views.*

Until the outbreak of student unrest in 1968, Marxist eggheads of the *Praxis* group were accorded the regime's benign neglect. All Communist governments feel compelled to have theoreticians elaborate on their policies. But the rebellious students who took over the campuses of Belgrade and Zagreb universities in June of 1968 demanded abolition of bureaucratic privileges, greater democratization of the country's life, abolition of social differences, the end to mass unemployment, and university reforms. Later, after the student unrest was over and after the impact of Czechoslovak invasion had receded, the Yugoslav regime decided that Marxist professors had "corrupted their students" and "poisoned their minds with wrong ideas." Then, in 1973, the *Praxis* intellectuals began to feel the orchestrated wrath of the ruling elite.

Ljuba Tadic has been in the midst of the *Praxis* opposition. Born in the highlands above the Piva River in 1925, he joined Tito's partisans at age seventeen, following his older brother, who was a Communist party member. As sons of an impoverished former captain in the pre-World War I Montenegrin army, they had come to the movement because they were offended by the injustice and the underdevelopment they found in royalist Yugoslavia. Ljuba Tadic's commitment to the cause was not shaken when his brother was court-martialed and executed by Communist authorities on false charges.

* Philosopher Karel Kosik, one of the architects of the Prague Spring and member of Dubcek's central committee, and other Czech liberals attended the Korcula sessions in the years prior to the Soviet invasion of 1968.

Unlike most of his war comrades, he opted for an academic life after the war, finished high school, then took a law degree from the University of Belgrade in 1952. While studying law he also took a degree in philosophy and political science. In 1959 he got his doctorate in theory of law at the University of Ljubljana.

When I met Tadic, he was a full professor of philosophy at the University of Belgrade. He had a skeptical, analytical mind and an agreeable disdain for theatrical, emotional arguments. The titles of his books provided a hint as to his theoretical and practical interests: the first, *Order and Freedom*, published in 1967, was followed by *Tradition and Revolution*, which came out in 1972, and *Authority and Dissent* and *Philosophy of Law*, both published but not distributed for sale. Behind horn-rimmed glasses his eyes were sad. He and his colleagues at the Faculty of Philosophy were subjected to savage criticism in the mass media.*

It was an unequal polemical struggle. The government had at its disposal all the means of communications. In the traditional Balkan manner, regime ideologists turned toward demonology and scapegoating. Members of the *Praxis* group were branded as "utopians," "anarcho-liberals," "revisionists," "new leftists," "extreme leftists," and "abstract humanists." Nothing in my experience demonstrated the irrelevancy of the official ideology as vividly as the daily barrage of abuse heaped on the *Praxis* group; in the ranks of regime propagandists there was nobody to match the theoretical knowledge of Marxism of a Tadic or a Mihajlo Markovic.

The *Praxis* intellectuals seem to have retained illusions about the ultimate utopia of socialism. They are convinced that socialism is capable of providing answers to the increasingly numerous problems of man on this planet; socialism, they say, can resolve the problems of the technological age; but, they say, the ideas of socialism must not be confused and identified with the existing socialist systems. The Russian system is a clear perversion of socialism because of its totalitarian nature; the Yugoslav model has moved away from the Soviet system but the Yugoslav party remains an authoritarian Leninist party. How can you have socialism without legal guarantees of individual rights and freedoms? What sort of socialist system is it

---

* Other Marxist scholars under attack were Mihajlo Markovic, Zaga Pesic-Golubovic, Svetozar Stojanovic, Miladin Zivotic, Nebojsa Popov, Triva Indjic, and Dragoljub Micunovic.

when a small ruling group promotes its will "to the level of law"? Why are Marxist regimes afraid of critical Marxist thoughts? Marx's fundamental position is to criticize existing things in the name of what they could become. As Tadic put it, "For Marx, the future is a dynamic potential and we are pointing out the future. But for a dogmatic, conservative regime, the future is far away and revolution is only a political act (of taking power), not a spiritual change."

Underlying the long dispute was a *Praxis* demand for freedom of speech and the regime's unwillingness to tolerate ideological pluralism within the Marxist elite.

In the West, Yugoslav dissent is associated with the names of Djilas, Mihajlov and with occasional capricious arrests of various nationalists, primarily Croats. But the first long political discourse in postwar Yugoslavia was generated by *Praxis* and its supporters. They found support not only among the students and faculty of the principal universities but also among professional organizations such as the Yugoslav Union of Philosophers, the Croatian Philosophical Society, the Yugoslav Sociological Association, the Serbian Philosophical Society, and various other state-supported institutions. What is even more remarkable, party organizations within these institutions took the side of the dissidents even after Tito himself publicly demanded they be silenced and prevented from "corrupting the youth."

Behind ideological disputes of this nature stand practical realities and political rivalries. One of Tito's closest associates, Vladimir Bakaric, already in 1968 accused some *Praxis* associates of being "American agents." But younger men who had taken charge of Croatia and Serbia displayed a healthy detachment from the ritual demonology of Communist politics. Miko Tripalo in Croatia and Marko Nikezic in Serbia represented a new breed of Communists; they were more sophisticated, better educated. And while their views differed from those of the *Praxis* group, they shared the overriding interest in greater democratization of Yugoslav life. Only after Tripalo and Nikezic were ousted from power in 1972 did the regime turn its fury on the Marxist dissidents.

Tito's technology of repression, however, differs substantially from the kind practiced in the Soviet Union. Tito's is "repression with a human face." First, the authories try to reach a compromise with a dissident group; if that fails a combination of threats and attractive financial inducements is advanced to break the impasse; if this fails to achieve a desired effect, the authorities try to break up the unity of the group by offering lucrative positions to some of its members; finally, raw force is used. The application of force is calibrated to inhibit heretics but tries to avoid incurring the permanent displeasure of Western liberals and leftists. The *Praxis* conflict had come at a time when Western European Communists were accepting the idea of political pluralism and freedom of speech.

In the face of regime pressures, *Praxis* intellectuals in Zagreb, Belgrade and Ljubljana showed a remarkable degree of cohesion. This in turn had only sharpened the confrontation. First, the authorities moved in 1974 to shut down the journal by withdrawing annual subsidies to the Croatian Philosophical Association and the Yugoslav Union of Philosophers, who were the publishers of *Praxis*. The journal, however, continued to appear. Its editorial staff and contributors refused to accept fees for their work, and they collected money to cover printer's bills. Faced with such determination, the party in early 1975 passed the word through various printing establishments that *Praxis* was not to be printed any more. Printers consequently refused to handle *Praxis* copy, and the journal was effectively banned without the government going on the record as suppressing a Marxist theoretical publication.

But government actions against individual intellectuals proved more difficult. On this plane, the government focused its efforts on ousting Tadic, Markovic and six other University of Belgrade professors from the faculty. After the eight refused to compromise, the authorities offered them well-paying research jobs outside the university. They refused. The authorities then moved to have the university council expel the eight. The council refused. Liberal arts students in Belgrade held a meeting and threatened a strike if the eight professors were ousted. Security police entered the picture: a number of students were arrested and tried for supporting their teachers; twelve were sent to prison for terms of up to six months. University student at Ljubljana and Zagreb expressed their solidarity with their Belgrade colleagues. Eventually, with students and faculty supporting the dissident professors, the authorities changed the law so that the eight could be expelled from their jobs in March 1975.

Even then, the regime's repression-with-a-human-face provided for good jobs for the professors. Tadic and two other colleagues were given positions at the Institute for the Study of International Labor Movement; Markovic was allowed to travel to the United States to take up a year's fellowship at the Woodrow Wilson International Center for Scholars in Washington; Mrs. Pesic-Golubovic went to England and Sweden on a lecture tour. But when Tadic and two of his associates were elected to the institute's ruling council by secret ballot, the authorities ordered the institute's director, Andrija Kresic, to fire them. Kresic refused and quit his job. Another act of defiance came when the Serbian Philosophical Society reelected the professors to the editorial board of the journal *Filozofija* with Tadic as editor-in-chief. The government, using an obscure regulation, refused to confirm the appointments. Rudi Supek, in the midst of the controversy, was reelected president of the Yugoslav Sociological Association, but the regime prohibited the group from holding its annual meeting.

Gradually but carefully, the regime moved to ban the books of various oppositionists, to eliminate their names wherever possible. Even Tadic's translation of Marx's *Critique of Hegel's Philosophy of Law* was blacklisted.

One of the banned books was Predrag Vranjicki's iconoclastic *History of Marxism*. In a seminar discussion Vranjicki, of Zagreb University, argued that the Soviet bloc countries "are not socialist at all." In the countries with socialist rule, the system oppresses and manipulates people without even giving them the basic freedoms which exist in bourgeois states. "The inhumane situation into which working people have been brought must necessarily be a fallow ground for many other inhuman acts, such as the oppression of individuals or even entire nations, as for instance is the case with Czechoslovakia," he added.

A writer of independent intelligence, who seemed constantly tempted to make light of Marxists and their squabbles, drew a curious parallel for me. "We are in the period of Communist Reformation. In the sixteenth century you had different ways of interpreting the Bible. Now they have different ways of interpreting Marx. The regime, of course, uses Marx as a convenient tool. For the men in power, the risks always outweigh the opportunities. The regime remains authoritarian, there's no doubt about it. But it took Tito more than five years to close down *Praxis* and to oust the professors from their jobs. This is an important qualitative difference. In Russia, they could have done this in a few days, without any fuss. What I see as important in the whole thing is that among the Communists there are differences of opinion, that younger men would like to see a pluralistic society in Yugoslavia. As long as the old partisans are in power, nothing like that will happen. But eventually we will evolve into a pluralistic society."

I spoke about this to Leo Mates, formerly Tito's ambassador in Washington and for many years his private secretary. His view was that Yugoslav socialism will eventually evolve into a pluralistic system, but that time is needed to generate a feeling of civic responsibility among the population and create institutions for coping with problems of the modern age. You can't do this overnight, was the thrust of Mates's remarks; our people have not had much solid democractic experience.

11

Conversations with Djilas

IT IS NOT READILY APPARENT WHETHER THE GOVERNMENT REGARDS
Milovan Djilas as the leading oppositionist or whether its repressive
measures against him reflect Marshal Tito's strong personal animus
toward his former right-hand man. Whatever the reasons, Djilas has
been living under police surveillance and has been the target of
much hatred in the official press ever since his fall from power in
1954. He has been jailed for a total of more than nine years, in the
same prison where he had served a term for being a Marxist revolutionary before World War II.

I had read his *Conversations with Stalin* and *The New Class* in
my college days. In an antiheroic age, he seemed to me the prototype
of the romantic hero who had enlarged his own legend through
intelligence and courage. But the reason I went to see Djilas four
days after I arrived in Yugoslavia was a selfish one.

Just before we had left Washington, Karin and I attended a
dinner at the residence of the Yugoslav ambassador. During the evening a member of the Yugoslav embassy took me aside and offered
what he described as a "friendly" counsel. "Don't visit Djilas right
away," the diplomat said. "He is being watched and you shouldn't
spoil your relations with people in the government."

Had I not been told this, I probably would have waited for a
suitable opportunity to look Djilas up. But the diplomat's unsolic-
ited advice—given in the midst of the Watergate crisis in May of
1973—produced the opposite effect. I will have to make a call on
Djilas during my first week there, I told the diplomat.

On a sultry summer afternoon, my *Post* colleague Dan Morgan
and I went to the Djilas apartment, walking past the Federal Parliament and then down a quiet side street where linden trees arched
to form a tunnel of shade. As we passed through a large vaulted
entrance, I wondered where the surveillance men were located. The
street was empty.

Djilas came to the door, dressed in a red polo shirt and light-brown jersey slacks. I had not expected to find him so youthful and vigorous. His hair had grown more white but his quizzical and sad face looked just like the photographs one sees on the glossy jackets of his books published in the United States. He received us with studied courtesy and simplicity, without the hautiness of reputation. He was obviously accustomed to such visits and extended his hospitality in an unobtrusive manner. But for all his easy informality he had the inner toughness of a sage whose courageous insistence to speak the truth had earned him a world reputation.

I realized during that first meeting that Djilas's interest in and accessibility to foreign journalists was his principal line of defense against the repressive impulses of Tito. My colleagues and I represented the means which he could use to fight back. He has suffered a great deal—both physically and spiritually—but his struggle has given a meaning to his life. He never lapsed into nihilism, pessimism or boredom.

Despite a certain considered reserve in conversations, we established the right connection during the first meeting. Perhaps the language was the key for instant rapport. I don't know. But for the following three years Djilas and his wife Stefica became frequent guests at our home. And was it a strange coincidence—or fitting irony—that I came to feel pleasantly at ease in Djilas's cavernous dark living room, whose sole source of light was from the window in the tiny adjacent dining room?

The entire apartment was crammed with paintings by modern Yugoslav artists and Russian ikons; Stefica had assembled a collection of antique oil lamps and nineteenth-century Chinese pottery. And there were books, all sorts of books, and Stefica's potted plants to give the apartment a sense of snugness. In this self-contained world the faces of my friends glowed and our conversations sparkled. We talked about Dostoyevski, his Raskolnikov, about Stalin, Alexander Solzhenitsyn, Watergate, Princeton historians and politcal scientists whom Djilas met during his brief visit to the United States in 1968. He analyzed Robert Tucker's latest book and spoke about Karl Popper. Watergate fascinated him. "It shows the tremendous vitality of America," he would say. "There are Watergates all over Europe, but only in America can you have such an open and sustained challenge to the presidency."

My son occasionally accompanied me for Sunday morning

coffee at the Djilases', where he learned at an early age how to handle a 45-caliber Mauser, which had embossed on its handle: "To Lt. Gen. Milovan Djilas from Marshal I. S. Konev"; the souvenir was hidden in the drawer of Milovan's desk, but another weapon, an antique Montenegrin *kubura*, was positioned on top of a living-room chest and my son would speed toward it even before we greeted our hosts.

Occasionally I spoke openly, although I knew that we were under electronic surveillance. More often we would go for a walk, through the maze of old streets in the old city, where we could talk freely.*

These walks were of enormous value to me, being in a sense history lessons. Once, as we walked by the tiny Russian church located in back of the huge Church of St. Mark, he suddenly recalled that the White Russian leader, Admiral Wrangel, was buried in the small crypt under the blue, Russian onion dome. Wrangel had died in Paris, and King Alexander of Yugoslavia brought his body here "to be buried on Slav soil," Djilas said. "When we Communists took Belgrade we told the Russians we wanted to throw Wrangel's body out of here. This was a result of our naïveté: we didn't want a counterrevolutionary leader buried in the heart of liberated Belgrade. But the Russians said, 'Well, you'd better leave the body in peace. It doesn't do any harm.' "

Another time he pointed out a dilapidated villa in my neighborhood and related a story about King Peter I, who had ruled Serbia in the first two decades of the century and who had died in that villa. "Imagine, the old king had translated John Stuart Mill's essay 'On Liberty' into Serbo-Croatian." This remark was followed by a discourse on the legal system in the old Serbian kingdom that he delivered with a vividness I cannot reproduce. Down the road was a modest palace of Prince Milos, an illiterate Serbian merchant who realized at the time of the collapse of the Serbian insurrection against Turkey in 1813 that the achievements of the preceding nine years of bloody fighting were about to disintegrate unless a compromise with the Sultan was reached. "Milos was a man of genius.

---

* Sometimes we would walk down to the Tasmajdan Park, then turn onto the Svetozara Markovica Street. Only after I returned to Washington and had a chance to look at some old Belgrade maps did I realize that that street was called the Milovan Djilas Street before his fall from power. It was typical of Djilas never to mention that fact to me.

He seized the moment and won internal autonomy for Serbia,"
Djilas said.

He was an exceptional guide, fantastically erudite without
being bookish. His stories were engaging and subtle. Walking with
him, I began to experience the drama of history. I caught a glimpse
of the Yugoslavs not only as they are today, but also as they struggled
through their unfortunate history. He loved to tell jokes.*

From fragments of conversations and casual remarks I also
began to understand his mind. But my view of Djilas kept changing.
Within the first weeks I had discovered a certain thoughtful reserve
with which he shielded his privacy. As far as I could determine he
had no intimates outside his immediate family. After about six
months or so I started to feel as if I had begun to understand the
tangled emotions and thoughts which underlay his cool and un-
ruffled exterior. In the end, after three years of friendship, I told him
of my decision to write a book about Yugoslavia; he graciously subjected himself to lengthy interviews, some of them tape recorded.
Yet, I was left with the uncomfortable feeling that all this wealth of
detail did not bring me any closer to an understanding of Djilas the
man.

Later I read my notes and listened to the tapes, then discarded
both. The man was hidden behind all these facts. Besides, he had
already written his life story up to the point when he rose to power
in 1945.†

Djilas was born into a family that was large and rebellious. His
father was an officer and farmer, who built a stone house in the
village of Podbisce, near Kolasin, on land given to him by the prince.

---

* Khrushchev, who dictated his memoirs in the late sixties, recalled in detail a joke Djilas told him in 1944. Djilas is an exquisite storyteller when he
communicates in his native tongue, or in Russian, which he speaks fluently. But
when using English, which he speaks haltingly, he manages to destroy the best
anecdotes.

† His *Land Without Justice*, an account of his childhood, came out in 1958;
Memoir of a Revolutionary, the account of his youth, up to the outbreak of
World War II, came out in 1973; *Wartime*, his portrayal of the Communist struggle during the war and their eventual triumph, was published in 1977. Other
books include *Montenegro*, in 1963; *The Leper and Other Stories*, in 1964;
Njegos, in 1966; *The Unperfect Society*, in 1969; *Under the Colors*, a novel, in
1971; and *The Stone and the Violets*, a collection of short stories, in 1972. All
these books were first published by Djilas's friend and publisher William
Jovanovich, of Harcourt Brace Jovanovich. He also published Djilas's translation into Serbo-Croatian of Milton's *Paradise Lost*.

The Djilas clan comes from a section of Montenegro that had been under loose Turkish rule up to the nineteenth century. But Milovan grew up a Montenegrin, and I believe it is impossible to understand the man without understanding his Montenegrin background.

Montenegro, as Crna Gora (Black Mountain) is known, is located in a small area of majestic mountain ranges that rise above the southern portion of the Yugoslav Adriatic coast. The Croats of the city-republic of Dubrovnik and the Serbs of Montenegro were the only Yugoslavs who managed to retain political independence after the Turkish conquest of the Balkans.* After the collapse of the medieval Serbian State, many Serbs moved into the mountains of the Dinaric Range to escape persecution and to preserve their religion. But even those who moved well above the timber line were subjected to Turkish rule. Only in the Old Montenegro did Serbian tribes refuse to acknowledge Turkish authority, and they established their own state. Montenegro's independence was forged by a constant struggle with the Turks. In the course of this centuries-long struggle, the Montenegrins have developed certain peculiar characteristics.

They lived in Spartan simplicity. The land, which was very poor, was cultivated mostly by women. Each family had a few sheep. Most of the men practiced only one occupation—they were warriors. Deeply ingrained in the consciousness of Montenegrin tribes were the ideas of freedom and physical courage—the highest virtues by which a man's honor was measured. And until well into the twentieth century, the principality's social organization was based on the clan.

There are echoes of the Homeric world in Montenegro. The concept of civic responsibility was alien to its citizens. Only when fighting the Turks to ensure their own survival did the Montenegrins willingly obey their ruler. Otherwise a man's allegiance was to his clan and his ultimate goal was to live an honorable life. The poet Njegos, who was the prince-bishop of Montenegro from 1830 to 1851, gave the common wisdom a poetic form when he wrote:

---

* Dubrovnik, which maintained its position through skillful diplomatic maneuvering between Turkey and Venice, lost its independence in the early nineteenth century during the Napoleonic thrust into the Balkans. It was subsequently incorporated in the Austro-Hungarian empire. Montenegro, however, remained an independent principality until the end of the Great War, when the Montenegrin Assembly voted to join the new Yugoslav State.

Everything doth perish saving honor
This lives on through everlasting ages
Life eternal marks the honored grave
A life of shame leads to eternal death.

There is a thin line between freedom and anarchy, as there is between the heroic and the bizarre. For some, as for Lord Tennyson, Montenegro was a "rough rock-throne of Freedom." Others, mostly in the German-speaking world, regarded the Montenegrins as curious savages and headhunters. Late into the nineteenth century the Montenegrins would come back from battling the Turks carrying heads of their victims. These heads were proof of a man's valor and victory over the infidels. Clans were in fierce competition to collect Turkish heads, which were to be displayed as trophies in the capital and in various villages.*

The Montenegrins' love of freedom, their ferociousness in battle and their reckless bravery were simply a response to a beleaguered form of life. But the root of their heroism lay in the oral tradition. Exploits of their ancestors were passed down through the generations as richly embroidered stories and legends. Their proclivity for storytelling is an integral part of the Montenegrin psyche. Against their primitive existence and excruciating poverty, the stories of ancestral valor and honor have been the only things they could hang onto. As the poet Njegos put it, "stories are the soul's delight."

As a result of their traditions, the Montenegrins are born poets and soldiers, with the highlander's swagger and quick temper, and with an immense sense of pride in their family and clan traditions. They are capable of singleminded commitments, which, if made publicly, are exclusivist in character. Pragmatism is an alien concept equated with cowardice.

Although Djilas grew up in a Montenegro in which the clan structure was dissolving to make way for a modern political system, remnants of the collective concepts of an ancient, agricultural and

* Foreign visitors to Cetinje, the capital, invariably recorded their shock at seeing Turkish heads lined up behind the monastery and the prince's palace. Prince Nikola, sensitive to the derisive description of his country in the West European press, prohibited the custom in 1876. But his order was secretly ignored and Montenegrin warriors in subsequent military campaigns would cut off noses and ears of their Turkish victims to demonstrate their valor before other clansmen.

largely tribal world was still strong. He, as all Montenegrins, was fed family and clan legends and stories before he started school.

Explaining a man in terms of supposed ethnic traits, I believe, is one of the most perilous endeavors.* As far as I could see, he was far removed from the Montenegrin stereotype; he seemed much closer to an urbane, sophisticated and reserved Western intellectual than to his ancestors. And yet his Montenegrin heritage was a vital element of his makeup, detectible in his enthusiasm for story-telling, his wit, his love of language, his admiration for physical courage, his determination to keep his integrity intact, and, above all, in his system of values. In some respect he resembled the nineteenth-century Montenegrin military chieftain and writer Marko Miljanov, who regarded the concept of *cojstvo*, or manliness, as the ultimate standard of behavior. *Cojstvo* involved the notions of uncompromising honesty, physical courage and honor.

When the writer Mihajlo Mihajlov was arrested in 1974, Djilas wrote an article in his defense that was published in the *New York Times*. I read the article in Greece, where I was on an assignment at the time, and was struck by its sharp attack on the Tito regime. Upon my return to Belgrade, I asked Djilas about the article. "I had to say something," he said, "I had to speak up against injustice."

Was he afraid, I asked, thinking about Djilas's own problems with the regime. "Of course I am afraid," he said, "but I know that I mustn't show it."

As a youth Djilas was drawn to literature. He wanted to write and started studying literature at the University of Belgrade in 1929. It was the beginning of a great internal political turmoil and of the Great Depression. In 1932, when he was twenty-one, Djilas joined the clandestine Communist party. He had already been an active student organizer and in the last semester of his studies he had been arrested, and in April 1933 he was sentenced to three years in jail for his revolutionary activities. While in jail he completed his Marxist education and made friends with other Communists, among them Rankovic. Once out of jail he became a full-time revolutionary and part-time writer. Among other things, he translated Maxim Gorki's

* Indeed, when Djilas was put on trial by his former comrades in 1956, the prosecutor described him as being Montenegrin, clearly suggesting that his "aberrant" behavior stemmed from his heritage. Djilas objected, saying the record should show that he regarded himself as being a Yugoslav.

The Life of Klim Samkin from Russian into Serbo-Croatian. When
Tito took over the party's leadership, he selected Djilas along with
Kardelj and Rankovic as his top lieutenants. He remained a member
of the ruling quartet until 1954, when he was ousted after a dispute
with Tito.

I have heard many Yugoslavs—including political enemies of
Djilas—say that he more than any other man had shaped the Yugoslav party. He was a relentless man who drove himself and all others
with the same severity and demanded, above all other qualities,
absolute loyalty to the cause. He was a believer. The absolute commitment was a source of identity and of power.

An incident that turned Djilas into a man of Cromwellian recti-
tude (a quality he subsequently forced upon the party) involved
his relations with his first wife, Mitra Mitrovic. She was of a petit
bourgeois background; they met at the university and eventually
were married. Both were passionately in love. But Milovan was also
in love with communism, and he tried to bring Mitra into the movement. Given her patriarchal upbringing, Mitra initially brushed
aside Milovan's theories and his explanations about the new "Communist" relations between men and women. Sex, he had argued, has
been mystified by the bourgeois society "to turn women into slaves"
and was an outgrowth of property relations. That was a period of
considerable sexual promiscuity among left-wing intellectuals;
young Communists of the period argued that the sexual act is equal
to any of the numerous physiological needs of men and women and
should be treated accordingly.

After Djilas was sentenced to three years in prison, Mitra gradually joined the Communists; she also started having sexual relations
with other men, presumably having accepted the Communist view
of sex, while remaining in love with Milovan.

The word of Mitra's infidelity reached Djilas in prison. It must
have been a shattering blow to the proud Montenegrin. There was
an element of the Byronic egotist about Djilas at the time. He was a
young leftish writer, a fashionable thing to be, and he was deeply
committed to the Communist cause. But while driven by a dark
compulsion to seek social justice, he saw this struggle in terms of an
historical drama in which he played a part. Mitra's affairs, which
became the subject of party gossip, not only wounded his innermost
feelings but also raised the question of his manly honor within the
party itself. He felt betrayed. How could he blame Mitra? Didn't *he*

urge concepts of the new Communist morality upon her? How often had he made fun of her "bourgeois" morality?

He had to summon forth his fierce inner determination in order to hide his wounds. Mitra's actions had destroyed his privately cherished dreams. Now, nothing existed for him but the party.* In early 1937, less than a year after he came out of jail, he introduced a new moral code for the party with chastity and loyalty becoming the cornerstone in relations between the sexes and with sexual promiscuity becoming a cardinal sin. Those who violated the code could be punished, even expelled; once the Communists started the military struggle against Nazi Germany and Italy, the violators were executed.†

His pull toward Puritanism reflected his desire to salvage the honor of his old ideals. But what he did was of exceptional practical importance. It produced a sharp increase in the power of the leadership in the personal life of party members and created the basis for a centralized disciplined Leninist party among quarrelsome South Slav Communists who had a proclivity toward factionalism.

Djilas' power as the chief ideologist and interpreter of the dogma increased as well. Tito was largely disinterested in theory and knew little about it; Kardelj, a Slovene school teacher, was by nature an insider and lacked assertiveness; and Rankovic, the least educated among the four, saw dogma only as a practical organizational tool. Among the four, Djilas was the most articulate. He was brash and imbued with a passion for revolution.

The war gave Djilas a particular slant on socialism, and it brought out his preoccupation with physical courage and honor. The Marxist assumptions he had adopted as a guide to the contemporary world now blended neatly with old Montenegrin traditions.

---

* He divorced Mitra after the war. "It was only a party marriage as far as I was concerned," he told me, trying to explain his action in terms of his rebellion against bureaucratic communism. "Women in my life never deflected me away from my party and social obligations. Political matters were always more important to me."

† Incidentally, Rankovic's wife Andja was involved in experiences similar to Mitra's. Djilas and Rankovic—both seen as "betrayed" men by their colleagues —controlled two most important aspects of the Yugoslav Communist party (Djilas ideology and propaganda; Rankovic, party personnel and later, during the war, the Communist secret police). Both enforced the new morality with exceptional vigor. The only exception to the rule was Tito.

The partisans were fighting for freedom against foreign enemies and at the same time conducting a revolution for a new social order.

"Making revolution is a beautiful experience," Djilas once told me, "more beautiful than writing about it." He was thirty-four years old when, after the Communist victory in 1945, he tasted what he calls the "unforgettable, majestic and demonic pleasures of power."

A new wind was blowing: there was the release of energy that comes in a revolution when new people with different ideas take over old institutions. His job was to shape the minds of the people. His belief in the Soviet Union as a force working for international socialism was absolute, but problems were emerging. His ascetic core was offended by the behavior of Russian officers and advisers, who engaged in drunkenness, violence, looting and rape. Moreover, the Soviets wanted to take over Yugoslav airports and assume control over natural resources; above all, they tried to bend to their purposes the two principal tools of any totalitarian regime—information and internal security. In foreign affairs Stalin would not support Yugoslavia's claim on Trieste.* And yet, he remained a believer. He told me a story of his talks with Molotov after the announcement of the Marshall Plan proposal. "We were in Paris and Molotov came to my room to ask about the attitude of the Yugoslav party toward the American proposal. Knowing our leadership, I could tell him with confidence that we would be against it. Later that same day he came up to me and said he had had a chance to communicate with Stalin and that Stalin shared my view. I was delighted by the thought that I had correctly anticipated Stalin's position."

But how could he maintain his blind faith in Russia and communism in the face of repeated warning signals? Djilas chuckled as he paraphrased Malraux. To be a Marxist revolutionary in its true sense is a state of mind—like being in love, he said. "It is not possible for you to see the woman you love. Only after it's all over can you see her in her true colors."

He acknowledged, just a trifle grudgingly, that there were other reasons he didn't repudiate Russia at this time. For a while he was intoxicated by power; he entered the world of chauffeur-driven limousines, special privileges, secret documents, special telephones;

* "We had to pull our troops out of Trieste when the Russians told us they were not about to go into another war for the sake of Yugoslav claims on the city," Djilas said.

he lived in an elegant villa which once belonged to a bourgeois politician; he met privately with Stalin, Molotov, Georgi Dimitrov and other luminaries of the Communist world. Stalin, in particular, was cordial to the young Montenegrin and spent more time with him in private than with any other Yugoslav leader. "I always felt Stalin tried to win me over to his side," Djilas told me. The gambit was a natural; Tito, as a Croat with imperfect command of the Serbo-Croatian language,* still felt insecure about his acceptance by the Serbs, the largest Yugoslav nationality; Kardelj, as a Slovene suffering from the same anxieties except that his command of the language was even less perfect, was bookish and reticent; Djilas in contrast was unabashedly proud and sure of himself, and he was a Serb from Montenegro, where pro-Russian sentiments were a tradition of sorts.

However, once the conflict with Stalin broke out, Djilas used the full force of his intellectual powers to defend the Yugoslav position. His job as the chief ideologue and man in charge of propaganda was to "turn the brains" of party members toward the new Yugoslav line, while at the same time conducting a war of words with the Russians and other East Europeans. He drafted the key Yugoslav documents during the conflict.† He was the "idea man," searching for theoretical justifications for Yugoslavia's stand. This was a period when Marxism still had some of its prestige and when Stalin's supremacy in the world Communist movement was unchallengeable. Since Communist regime was thought possible without a solid basis in Marxist-Leninist theories, Djilas and Kardelj perused the works of Marx, Engels and Lenin, looking for formulations which supported Yugoslavia's new course. "For the first time we began to think about the role of ideology and about socialism in general," Djilas said.

What followed was a "great liberation from illusions." For nearly three years he was preoccupied largely with the tactics of ideological struggle. For a Marxist regime that was excommunicated

---

* Tito speaks Serbo-Croatian with a strange accent, which, I was told, is peculiar to a small area of Zagorje near the Slovenian border where he was born.

† In 1975 the Yugoslav press reproduced these documents claiming that their authors were Tito and Kardelj. I asked Djilas about this and he slapped his knee delightedly as he laughed. He pointed out to me that the draft had been typed in the Cyrillic alphabet—"on my typewriter"—and that some handwritten changes were written in Latin script—"that is Kardelj's handwriting"—and some in Cyrillic script that was unmistakably in Djilas' own handwriting.

by the Kremlin from the world Communist movement, this meant the struggle for survival. The Yugoslav Communists sought to establish their system as truly Marxist and to portray Stalin's as a betrayal of socialism. This was essential for Tito and his colleagues if they hoped to maintain their power. Djilas in the process also tried to develop a specific direction for Yugoslavia's road to socialism. In 1950 the basic concepts of workers' self-management and political nonalignment were first put into practice. The conflict with Stalin, Djilas said, was "the most interesting and exciting period" of his political career.

The precise moment he moved away from communism is unclear. The process was gradual. At one point in 1952, he told me, it dawned on him that the working class was the weakest of all classes in a society, although it was one of the most important ones. "I realized that the working class is weak in the sense that each of its members wants to get out of it and certainly hopes that his son will not become a worker but rather an engineer or a white-collar worker." The Communist party, which exercised its power in the name of the working class, was creating a society which was as unjust as the one it had destroyed.

There were other things that influenced his thinking. He traveled widely, visiting Great Britain, the United States, India and other countries; he established close personal relations with left-wing members of the British Labour Party, especially with Aneurin Bevan and Jenny Lee; and he wanted to study Scandinavian socialism.

In his mind Djilas took the rift with Russia to its logical conclusion—the establishment of democratic socialism in Yugoslavia. The rhetoric of Tito's brand of socialism elicited clear moral and political judgments which steered Djilas away from communism. "I looked at America," he said, "its huge industry and working class, and wondered why communism didn't take hold there. Why were the American workers against socialism? I felt we had to ask these questions."

Franklin Roosevelt's social legislation fascinated him. When James Riddleberger, who was appointed U.S. ambassador to Belgrade in mid-1953, paid his first formal call on Djilas he spent two hours with Tito's top ideologist answering questions about New Deal measures. "Djilas wanted to know details about FDR's social reforms, minimum wages, working conditions," Riddleberger recalled later. "When I returned to the embassy and told my boys about the meeting, they were flabbergasted. What in the world is going on, they asked."

With the fervor with which he once embraced Marxism, Djilas accepted the idea of democratic socialism. Tito encouraged him to move in that direction in order to establish an ideological counterweight to the Soviet ideology. But the death of Stalin in the spring of 1953 brought about a sharp change in Tito's views and plans. Tito saw in it an opportunity to repair relations with the Soviet bloc; his feud with Stalin had won Tito a good measure of personal popularity in Yugoslavia and he was confidently establishing himself as an autocrat. Djilas, on the other hand, saw no possibility of going back.

Within a period of five to six weeks in late 1953 Djilas took his case before the party and the country. Since he controlled the nation's press and media, he published a series of articles criticizing the totalitarian strain in the Communist establishment of which he was such a prominent member. He diagnosed the problem as one of the ruling oligarchy becoming a "new class" which monopolized power, privileges and the entire life of the country. The cure, he said, lay in continued democratization of the party's and of the nation's life.

Party membership, believing that Djilas as usual was announcing a change in the party line, responded enthusiastically to his articles. But the upper tier of the ruling group, and Tito in particular, became obsessed by fears of crossing a point of no return. Tito sensed that if not stopped, Djilas would soon dominate the situation. An expert manipulator, Tito moved behind the scenes to torpedo his former favorite. In January of 1954, in a meeting of the central committee which Tito controlled, Djilas was ousted from the leadership. Some months later Djilas turned in his party card, "I resigned from the party," he said with a smile. "I was not expelled."

He knew that he was going to lose out, yet he precipitated the showdown by means of his iconoclastic writing. He could not accept Tito's decisions to halt liberalization and to seek rapprochement with the Soviet Union. He also resented Tito's growing personal authority. "Why are we arguing against Stalin and Stalinism while retaining a similar political structure [in Yugoslavia]?" he asked. "Even today our system has not changed very much from Russia's. It is not identical, but there are basic characteristics common to both. I told Kardelj that I could not accept the new course. I could not work against my convictions. Earlier I often did things that were against my deep convictions but they fitted into the general picture of my world. Kardelj agreed with me, but later he went to Tito and warned him that I posed a threat to the party. Rankovic was open. We were close friends. But he told me, 'I hope I'll never have to deal with your philosophical theories because I don't understand them. But I am certain that they are harmful to the party.'

"But popular reaction was tremendously positive toward my position. Letters flooded the office of *Borba*,* and people throughout the country agreed with me. I must say that my stand toward the party in the last month that preceded my fall from power was not entirely correct. I wanted to place my views before the country, to leave a trace. At the same time, however, I did not try to form a faction, although a majority of the Central Committee sympathized with me. I just wanted to express my views, come what may. I remember that in those crucial days I kept repeating a simple phrase, a naïve phrase, but I kept saying it to myself and my wife and friends: 'It is better to be an honest man than a cabinet minister.'

"I had always wanted to be a writer and I thought at that time that I had already lost twenty years, that I had vacillated long enough between politics and literature. I believe that throughout my life I have been a moral personality. I was forced during the war to do things and use tricks. That is a part of revolution and politics. But I was never disloyal toward my comrades. Later they accused me of all sorts of sins; they said I was trying to restore the old bourgeois system. Villages such as Gostivar, Glamoc and my own Kolasin passed resolutions calling me a traitor, a Trotskyite, a revisionist and other names. I have never regarded myself up to this day as a traitor to socialism. What I argued for in 1953 and 1954 was the need for free discussion within the party and the establishment of another socialist party. I felt a need for pluralism in the socialist world.

"But I didn't anticipate that my ouster would be a personally painful affair. The face of my world was transfigured. At first I plunged into an erotic crisis, something that was completely out of character with my normal self. Every other woman in the street seemed attractive to me. I managed gradually to bring this crisis under control. Then I realized that I was in an absolute vacuum.

* The Communist party newspaper in which many of Djilas' articles were published. Its circulation at the time was in excess of 700,000 daily.

People whom I had known for a long time, for whom I had done many favors, did not know me anymore. A policeman was placed in front of my home. Those who entered the house had to show their identification cards. Communism is a closed world. In a sense I didn't exist anymore."*

He wanted to think, to get away from the capital and map his future. What better way was there than taking a trip on a raft down the Tara and Drina rivers, testing his courage on treacherous waters in their vertiginous loops through the mountainous wilderness. He was forty-three years old at the time, and he realized that he had misread the importance of the organization he had helped create. But he also felt that he was not cut out to practice clique politics and that it was the ruling oligarchy's thirst for power that had brought about his downfall. They were afraid of democratization and of free debate even within the party that he had advocated. *They* had lain in waiting for a moment—and that moment came when he took his ideas before the country—to drive him out. He was not acting against the party; he had understood that "most mistakes we had made could have been avoided had we had a minimal degree of intellectual freedom within the party." He was willing to bow out of politics without much fuss, feeling he could make a fresh start as a writer, that the writer in him had been in abeyance during the years of his political career when he had had to play the Marxist ideologue and philosopher, but that in the solitude of his new life he could make up for the lost time.

He plunged into writing, doing a number of short stories and an autobiographical account of his childhood, *Land Without Justice*. He was, however, completely unprepared for the orchestrated campaign of scorn and vilification that awaited him. His literary works were automatically rejected as unsuitable. His public image at home had to be destroyed. At the same time Tito seemed to have offered Djilas as a sacrifice to Moscow. The Soviet-Yugoslav rapprochement in fact came immediately afted Djilas's ouster.

"They simply wanted to kill me intellectually," Djilas told

* Eric Bourne, the veteran Balkan correspondent for the *Christian Science Monitor*, once told me that in 1954 he and his wife went to the Yugoslav Drama Theater in Belgrade. "The Djilases were there, but we were the only ones who talked with them. A number of Djilas' former colleagues were in the audience, but they walked past him as though he didn't exist."

me,* "I was not to exist anymore. What else could I have done except to seek contact with Western publishers and journalists or to die spiritually? But I would have died spiritually had I recanted. I could have accepted all sorts of sins against the party and they would have perhaps permitted me, in time, to publish my literary works. But my makeup is such that I could not have written a thing. You can say something to the effect that you had done harm to the party, but you can't deny the kernel of your personality and your thoughts. If you break this kernel you are through. I think that an intellectual who allows himself to be morally quashed is finished. Why don't you have good writers in Russia, except for the dissenters?

"I have always felt that it was not correct on my part to go to Western publishers, to use Western newspapers to speak out; yet what else could I have done?"

Autocratic regimes have a multitude of means to silence a free-spirited man. Most of them were used on Djilas, but to no avail. One sentence uttered by Tito to a group of foreign journalists in the winter of 1954 revived in Djilas his old Montenegrin streak of rebelliousness with a peculiar intensity. Djilas, Tito told the journalists, is dead, he is "a political corpse."

"That was enough," Djilas told me, "to bring my mind and instincts into a state of rebellion." He was not dead, the announcement was premature. He began giving interviews to Western reporters in Belgrade. In January 1955 he was tried on charges of spreading hostile propaganda and sentenced to up to three years in jail. The term was made conditional. In November 1956 he published an article in *The New Leader* supporting the Hungarian revolution and was promptly arrested and tried. Sentenced to three years of strict confinement, he was dispatched to Sremska Mitrovica to the same prison where he had served a term in prewar Yugoslavia. But before his arrest, he had completed *The New Class*, which came out in New York in 1957. Another trial was held and he was given an additional six-year term for trying to "compromise" socialism. In

---

* A former top secret police official most intimately involved in calibrating repression against Djilas told me during a private conversation in the winter of 1975 that Tito "wanted to destroy Milovan in every respect, except physically. Tito saw him as a personal threat. While encouraging Djilas to write his article in 1953, Tito talked privately with top people in the party. He would take you aside and say, 'By God, don't you think Djido (the nickname for Djilas) had gone too far.' " Tito used the same technique against Rankovic in 1966.

prison he wrote several books, two of them on toilet paper; he was granted conditional pardon in 1961. Once out of jail, he wrote his *Conversations With Stalin*, which was published in May 1962 in New York. He was again arrested and sentenced to five years in jail on charges of revealing state secrets. He was released from jail on December 31, 1966. Meanwhile, his books continued to be published abroad.

When I met Djilas in 1973, he seemed like a man who had come to terms with himself. Suffering had made him wiser, more introspective, combining the alternate boldness of purpose and prudence of action. The long imprisonment had left a mark on his health. His back was weak and he had to wear a specially designed hard medical collar to support his neck. He was also receiving regular medical treatment for certain painful muscular conditions. He never told me about this, but his wife Stefica once whispered to me that I should seat Milovan in a chair with a hard back, then explained the reason for her request.

It seemed to me at times that he almost must have wanted to go to prison. I asked him how he felt now about his political role in the postwar period, especially about his virtually dictatorial powers in the field of culture and ideology. He touched on a number of aspects of revolution with the blend of sympathetic understanding and a criticism that was slightly surprising. "I felt that I was involved in intellectual oppression, that I was doing a job which was rather dark and which was not honorable. But that was how it had to be in such a system."

He had turned toward literature because he was determined not to permit life to dwindle into a kind of idleness and frustration. Then, Tito's scorn and harshness mobilized all of Djilas' resources into his struggle for intellectual survival. He finished *The New Class* in less than six months. Why did he feel that "strange and demonic" delight in debasing himself against his own background? He had been full of bitterness. "When I sat down to write *The New Class*, suddenly everything became clear to me."

But it was somewhat uncanny to hear him talk about the prison world and about isolation which helped him analyze his views and contemplate his own limitations. "When I was arrested in 1956 and taken to prison, I heard other inmates saying, 'Who's the new guy?' and there was a half-crazy inmate who recognized me and he kept saying, 'Why, he was the second man in the land, right after Tito, but that was not enough for *him*.' And others looked at me in bewilderment."

The fall has been precipitous, from the closed circle of old comrades at the pinnacle of power to a prison ward where most inmates were either hardened criminals or thieves. His first term from 1956 to 1961 was especially difficult since he was imprisoned by his old comrades. His heresy was part of a shift in his thinking; he had come to the conclusion that the system he had helped found was unjust. His heresy did not involve an active rebellion against the ruling party. More than anything else it was a personal confrontation with the moral dilemma of the political life. "I was not a completely moral person," he told me.

In prison he had time to reflect on cosmic themes about mankind and destiny. I had the impression that he had thought at the time that prison was the only way in which he could purify himself, test his courage and atone for his sins. His second term in prison brought him spiritual peace and quiet. "It was as though I had become a medieval monk, a more integral person," he said. "I felt I could go on living this monastic life forever. I became more sincere and open, with myself and others. If I sin now, I recognize it for what it is; twenty years ago when I sinned I would not admit it to myself."

He felt that he had not lost the struggle with Tito, whose political talents he esteemed greatly. "Of course, the purely ethical position is weaker than power," he said once. "Any policeman here can arrest me, haul me up for an investigation. But you cannot defeat a man with an unshakeable moral position; you could destroy him, annihilate him physically, but you can't defeat him."

He was, he said, more completely in control of his own world than at any time before. Ironically, he was only theoretically free; special limitations on his movements have been in effect for years; he was, by some miraculous action, denied the right to buy an apartment in Dubrovnik even after the sellers agreed on a deal and accepted Djilas' money; he was not allowed to rent a house in Hercegnovi, a city about an hour's drive away from Dubrovnik; he is refused a passport to travel; and none of his books can be published in Yugoslavia.* His wife and their son Aleksa are allowed to travel.

---

* However, the Institute for Study of International Labor Movement in Belgrade bought the Yugoslav copyright for Djilas's *Memoir of a Revolutionary*. The institute director is the wife of Milos Minic, the deputy premier and foreign minister.

Aleksa, indeed, has done his university studies in Austria and England.

Although he has been an atheist all his life, Djilas's intelligence seemed to me to be fundamentally religious. He felt ideology had to be totalitarian in character "to be able to carry conviction." Religion, on the other hand, he saw as a living thing trying to locate man's place in the cosmos. He believed that philosophy was a form of religion. He didn't believe in God. "I'm not a religious man," he said, "but that itself is a form of religion."

Talking about this subject, I felt, as I had already felt in reading his books, that he was a man in search of humanistic values. More than any other of Djilas's work, *Njegos*—a long biography of the nineteenth-century Montenegrin prince-bishop who was also the greatest poet in the Serbo-Croatian language—reveals his own world. Like Njegos, Djilas was always a writer and a politician. He saw Njegos's fundamental dilemma in the circumstances imposed upon him—"to kill and to be humane, to do evil while fighting evil."

In Montenegro in the first part of the nineteenth century, Djilas said, "This was both logical and commonplace, reasonable and just— the struggle for survival but based on ethical principles."

Djilas felt that this had been his dilemma. He had finally opted for the ethical alternative. "I am happier than I ever was before, even when I was in power. Now I live in my own world. I don't seek power. I would accept it, if by some strange combination of circumstances I was called back. But I can live happily without power."

12

Culture: A Drive for Enlightenment

HOWEVER IMPERFECT TITO'S SOCIALISM HAS BEEN, ONE OF ITS GREAT accomplishments has been the introduction of what for want of a better term can be described as the modern spirit. Deeply conscious about their country's backwardness, the Communists impressed upon themselves and others the absolute necessity of raising the cultural level of the population. The key word was *kultura*, or culture, which was invested with a specific meaning. The leaders have spoken about communism being the penultimate stage in the evolution of man's society, yet until relatively recently their people were in a preindustrial stage. So the leaders have stimulated a romantic reverence for *kultura*, which in their minds embraces fields ranging from literacy and education to life styles, literature and the arts. Which was, in effect, a drive for enlightenment, a yearning to cast off the inheritance of underdevelopment and move up to the cultural and economic level of Western Europe. What else has been the purpose of the revolution? In trying to quickly bridge the vast gap between rhetoric and reality, the leaders tried to make a kind of merger between the ideals of modern socialism and the concepts of enlightenment.

The drive for enlightenment in the immediate postwar years had a liberating effect on the hitherto unprivileged people, who suddenly were given a chance to engage in activities formerly reserved for a privileged few. If there was a clear problem at the time, it was that *kultura* was identified with new institutions, new buildings, new libraries, new journals. There was too little time to plan, to think. Local leaders confronted the party's tasks by resolving problems piecemeal, by establishing institutions without thinking about future financing or overall needs.

In quantitative terms, the three decades of Communist rule

produced impressive results. In 1945 Yugoslavia had three universities, one liberal arts college and one separate law school; in 1975 there were 158 universities and colleges in Yugoslavia. In terms of the number of college students per 10,000 population, Yugoslavia outranked all West European countries except Sweden and Holland and all East European countries except the Soviet Union. In the period between 1957 and 1974 Yugoslav medical schools graduated 29,871 physicians and dentists.* In 1974 Yugoslav publishing houses published 13,063 new titles, 11,776 of them by Yugoslav authors; the number of daily and weekly newspapers stood at 1,989; the number of periodicals at 1,150; a total of 3,252 public libraries—and this excludes about 10,000 school and college libraries—were maintained; there were sixty year-round professional repertory theaters with the combined attendance of 4.3 million persons in the 1973–74 season; more than 8 million persons visited the 371 government-supported museums in 1974; the country had nine separate television stations and 190 radio stations.†

Younger sophisticated Yugoslavs are frequently given to pooh-poohing the emphasis placed on mass culture and education, dismissing Tito's cultural policies as superficial and imitative. I have come to believe that this view fails to take into account one crucial factor—that imitation can ultimately change substance. The drive for enlightenment coupled with the country's openness toward the West (in which perhaps the massive influx of tourists played a key role) created competitive pressures to acquire kultura. Suddenly old churches and ikons—which lay neglected and ignored for many years—were rediscovered not only as objects of tourist attraction but as a source of cultural continuity. I remember spending a day with Gerhard Ledic, a Zagreb art critic, who has amassed a priceless collection of medieval books and artifacts, along with one of the most complete collections of primitive paintings and sculptures I had seen. He had collected most of it, he said, in the fifties when he worked as a roving reporter. Old, elaborately carved wooden chests

* All figures quoted in the annual publication of the Yugoslav Statistical Bureau.

† According to the League of Nations' statistics for 1938, Yugoslavia was at the bottom in Europe in terms of the number of radio sets per capita—one set per 65 Yugoslavs. Albania, which was next to the last, had one set per 37 persons. It was estimated that in 1974 there was one radio set per two Yugoslavs, and one TV set per seven persons.

were junked at the time, he said. "Now you've got to pay a fortune for an old chest. Even the peasants are collecting them."

Kultura had caught fire throughout the countryside. A few yours ago officials of the Library of Congress in Washington were amazed when they received a request from the public library in Vranje, a small town in South Serbia, for the expensive 108-volume National Union Catalogue. "Only the top-notch libraries in the world have this catalogue," one Library official told me. "The British Museum Library has one copy. Why in the world did Vranje ask for it?" And my *New York Times* colleague in Belgrade, Ray Anderson, once returned from a visit to the dusty Serbian town of Leskovac telling about its professional repertory theater, whose main door frequently got broken by eager playgoers. Leskovac, he said, "is a theatrical producer's dream—not only every seat at every performance is occupied, but the people crowd the wall aisles as well."

Frequently one comes across vulgarized or even tragi-comic attempts by rural communities to gain status through culture. One such story, which could well fit into Balzac's France, was related to me by Milic Stankovic, a well-known painter of the surrealistic school.

Stankovic, an energetic man in his forties who sports a Lenin beard and who is deeply religious, is first and foremost an exceptional craftsman. His paintings display an element of fairy-tale enchantment and deep religiosity that prevents their being "modern" in the way De Chirico or Max Ernst are. Milic's talent was first recognized abroad, later at home. He had established his own "school" in his native Machva village, about one hundred miles west of Belgrade.

Stankovic, who on the basis of his reputation commands high prices, was commissioned by the leaders of Bjelo Polje, a backwoods community on the border of Serbia and Montenegro, to do a large mural for their newly built hotel in 1975. The men of Bjelo Polje wanted to add a touch of class to the new establishment, and they felt that money spent on a reputable artist would buy just that.

Since the mural was to tell something about the Bjelo Polje area and its history, Stankovic's theme focused on an eleventh-century monastery in Bjelo Polje where in 1192 the first written document of the Serbian nation, the *Gospel of Miroslav*, was written.

The original monastery had disappeared long ago, but the gospel survived, the only thing of note to be associated with Bjelo

Polje. In fact, Bjelo Polje has been more backward than most other Yugoslav communities because it had remained under Turkish rule until 1914. "What else could compare to the first written document in a nation's history," Stankovic reasoned as he painted his mural.

Stankovic had almost finished the mural when ominous warnings reached local party chiefs that the work was "religious—through and through." Heated arguments ensued, the chiefs demanding that portraits of several local Communists who died during World War II be painted in the foreground of the mural to give it a measure of "socialist" content. The painter had to compromise. The formal unveiling was scheduled with all the town notables to attend. The hotel, after all, was the main establishment of Bjelo Polje and a prominent local citizen was selected as its director.

The day before the scheduled unveiling Stankovic, instead of signing the work, painted a self-portrait in its lower right corner inside a decorative medallion. But then he felt the need to balance it off with a medallion in the left corner in which he sketched a portrait of the hotel director. When the mural was unveiled, the small portrait of the hotel director touched off a storm. The festive crowd —including some of the director's rivals—among them the mayor and the local party secretary—stared at the small portrait in the left corner as though the rest of the vast mural did not exist. "Why should he be immortalized?" "What about Jovo?" "And Milan!" "Isn't Marko more deserving?" In the uproar the mural was covered again with bed sheets and Stankovic was told to "correct" his work.

I ran into Milic a few days after his return from Bjelo Polje. "Imagine, all the dignitaries wanted to be in the mural," he snapped. "They felt it should be a group picture of sorts." He refused and painted the two medallions over.

The problem with Yugoslav culture is that it is governmental. One can take it for granted that only a determined authoritarian government could have stimulated a cultural revival on a mass scale. But all authoritarian governments fear freedom because they cannot tolerate a diversity of opinions. That freedom is intimately bound up with the whole question of culture can be seen in Yugoslavia. The government has tolerated freedom of expression in the visual and performing arts, which has led to an explosion of talent in these two fields throughout the country. A number of Yugoslav painters, such as Ljuba Popovic and Vladimir Velickovic, have established solid international reputations. I was impressed by talented Macedonian painters, such as Petlevski and Naumovski, the entire primitive Hlebine school of Croatian painters led by Ivan and Josip Generalic, Rabuzin and Ivan Lackovic, by the Bosnian graphic artist Mersad Berber, and by the work of the Slovenian school of graphic artists.

Younger men in the party have outgrown the paranoid period when they tended to read political significance into every form of art, including painting and music. But the absence of freedom is still evident in literature and film. Here the line of confrontation between authority and talent is clear; but what tips the balance in favor of authority—or the other way around—is not always clear. I followed with interest the career of one young writer, Mirko Kovac, who during my stay was practically read out of the official world of culture and then readmitted to it. Both actions—each as abstract and incomprehensible as the other—illustrate the unpredictability and arbitrariness of officially sponsored culture.

Kovac was among the more successful young writers, with four literary prizes to his credit. He had published four novels, several dramas and television screenplays and numerous short stories.

In 1972, when his novel, *The Wounds of Luka Mestrovic*, won critical acclaim, Kovac was thirty-four years old. Critics were enthusiastic about the irreverence he showed in fictionalizing his childhood memories of how the Communist Revolution was imposed on the small village in Hercegovina where he grew up. He revealed that the men who carried out this task were often clumsy and frequently corrupt, including secret police officials who were arresting men in order to seduce their wives. In Kovac's books one also senses obscure misgivings about popular myths, especially about the inevitability of progress. Isn't this one of our delusions? he seems to ask.

In the same year the Communist party and civic leaders of Valjevo, a small town about sixty miles southwest of Belgrade, voted to establish an annual literary prize in honor of their most distinguished citizen, novelist Milovan Glisic. The idea had been percolating in Valjevo for some time, fueled in part by a desire to upgrade the town's distressing reputation as one of the less enlightened communities in the country. The final push involved a timing element—in the fall of 1972 the town was preparing to celebrate the 125th anniversary of Glisic's birth. Glisic, who spent his lifetime in Belgrade, where he was chief of the National Drama Theater, wrote extensively and with considerable intellectual force about rural life' in the nineteenth century. He had also translated into Serbo-Croatian nearly all the major works of Tolstoy, Gogol, Goncharov and Chekov.

Acting on the advice of established literary critics, the leaders of Valjevo decided to award the first Milovan Glisic Literary Prize to Mirko Kovac for his *The Wounds of Luka Mestrovic.* An elaborate certificate was designed and printed. The prize also carried an equivalent of seven hundred dollars in cash, which was handed to Kovac by the mayor of Valjevo in the presence of the local political and cultural elite led by Gvozden Jovanic, deputy culture minister of the Serbian Republic. The ceremony was followed by a formal dinner in the house where Glisic was born in 1847.

Mirko Kovac, whose muscular physique and large nose belie his instinctive shyness, became embarrassed and confused when he realized that none of the dignitaries around the dinner table had read his book, except perhaps for the blurb on its jacket. He left Valjevo after dinner, as soon as coffee was gulped down with the help of generous quantities of *vinjak,* a potent local drink.

Less than six months after this festive event, in the spring of 1973, Kovac and his latest prize became a source of controversy. Just who started the fuss is unclear. But some vigilant members of the National Veterans Union, which is run by the dogmatic old partisans of World War II, began writing letters to major Belgrade newspapers attacking Kovac as a leader of the "dark wave" in Yugoslav literature. The Valjevo chapter of the Veterans Union, in a resolution filled with sinister warnings, demanded that Kovac be jailed and all his books burned.

The controversy created a crisis in Valjevo's town hall. The mayor, whose culpability seemed evident from the press photographs of the award ceremony, was quickly ousted. His Communist colleagues in the town leadership now claimed they had been misled into sponsoring the affair without having read Kovac's book. They voted to correct the mistake by formally stripping the first Milovan Glisic Literary Prize-winner of his prize. On the reasonable assumption that he had already spent the money, they asked Kovac to return only the colorful prize certificate. And just to preclude a future recurrence of such embarrassing ventures into "high culture," they quietly abolished the prize altogether.

For Kovac, newspaper articles filled with dark intimations inaugurated a period of official disgrace. Publishers, editors and producers steered away from his texts. In 1975 he became respectable again and his new drama was shown on Belgrade television. During his disgrace he had kept silent. He had done it to survive, and it was typical of the price the noncomformist intellectuals in general were paying to ensure their participation in cultural life.

Yugoslavia's cultural scene is such a muddle that one hardly knows how to begin to describe it. It is unique in the sense that it is an Eastern, Western and Mediterranean culture at the same time.

Geography, not history, has come to dominate the thinking of Yugoslavs. The Orthodox Serbs and Macedonians, who had come under the religious and cultural influence of Byzantium, had developed an artistic and spiritual style of their own before they were plunged into the darkness that the Ottoman Turks brought upon the lands they conquered in the fourteenth century. When Serbia again emerged as a geographic entity in the early nineteenth century, its people were less altered psychologically than the Croats were from the Austro-Hungarian domination. The Serbs had accepted much from the Turks in the way of mannerisms, cooking and life style, including the Oriental proclivity for contemplative indolence. But the Serbian myth and the glories of the medieval Serbian kingdom were preserved in the collective memory of the people.

Things were different in Croatia and Slovenia. The Croats were partitioned under Hungarian, Austrian and Venetian rule. The Turks ruled Croatia for about one hundred years, but that was in the seventeenth century. The Croatian elite was either Germanized or Magyarized. And yet the people, despite their humble social position in the Hapsburg Empire, had lived in the world of Europe and under the civilizing influence of the Roman Catholic Church. In the nineteenth century, when nationalism infected the Austro-Hungarian empire, the Croats and Slovenes developed an intellectual life far more advanced than that in Seria. But what they had exploited also held them back. They were torn between their desire to belong to the world of Central European culture and the necessity to develop their own national culture. For the latter, they lacked a forceful national myth. For the former, they were spurned by the Austrians and Hungarians. As late as 1867 the Hungarian leader Count Andrassy articulated his nation's contempt for the Croats by telling the Austrian Chancellor Beust, "You look after your barbarians and we will look after ours."

What all Yugoslavs shared, however, was a humiliating heritage of subjugation. Their languages and traditions were preserved through the centuries by peasants in the mountainous areas, which remained outside the constant ebb and flow of conquering armies that vied for the control of the overland road to Asia.

In the midst of the struggle for national liberation, both the Roman Catholic Croats and the Orthodox Serbs had a visionary and ecumenical concept of Christianity, and both nourished a sense of Yugoslav nationalism—against foreign rule. The Croatians were in the forefront of the Yugoslav national movement. Perhaps the most important figure in the movement, Josip Strossmayer, the Roman Catholic bishop of Djakovo, regarded all Yugoslavs as one nation and saw in the religious differences no obstacle to common national existence.*

Cultural and religious differences became important only after the creation of Yugoslavia in 1918. Once the cause that originally brought them together no longer existed, the ethnic issue became the paramount problem in the country. The nationalist feud between the Serbs and Croats stirred deep passions. Matters that once brought the two peoples together, such as the common language, became a source of division. The Serbs and Croats, somebody once told me, are "two peoples separated by the common language."

Culture became a field of political struggle. Just as patriotic intellectuals in the nineteenth century—in their singleness of vision —wrote historical accounts that resorted to fiction and exaggeration to exalt Slavdom, their twentieth-century colleagues continued the tradition by writing similarly to exalt one Yugoslav nation above the other.†

What most of these accounts tended to obscure was the fact that except for folk arts and crafts Yugoslav peoples had lived for several centuries without any recognizable national culture of their own.

---

* Ljudevic Gaj, a Croat linguist and editor, was the organizer of the Yugoslav movement, which at first went under the name of the Illyrian movement. The Croat poet Petar Preradovic was the first to use the term Yugoslav, as the common name for all South (or Yugo) Slavs when he dedicated his first book of poems, published in 1846, to the "fair sex of the Yugoslav people."

Many Croats, however, saw their political future within the Austro-Hungarian empire. But their attempts to gain internal autonomy and equal status within the empire were repeatedly frustrated by the imperial elite, especially by the Hungarian nobles, and this eventually forced the Croats to turn toward a Yugoslav state.

† The best panoramic account of modern Yugoslav history is contained in Viktor Meier's *Neuer Nationalismus in Sudosteuropa*. C. W. Leske Verlag, Opladen, 1968. Meier is a Swiss national who is the Balkan correspondent for *Frankfurter Allgemeine Zeitung*. He has spent more than twenty years in the Balkans.

There were individual flashes of outstanding cultural importance. The Slovene cleric Prímoz Trubar, for instance, translated and published the New Testament into Slovene in 1582. Or Juraj Krizanic, a Croatian Roman Catholic priest and a scholar of considerable accomplishment, who was the forerunner of two important currents that would reappear in Yugoslav lands in the nineteenth century—Yugoslav unity and militant pan-Slavism. Krizanic went to Russia in the mid-seventeenth century to seek Russian help for the liberation of South Slavs. Ironically, he wrote his main work, *Politics: A Discourse on Power*, in Siberia, where he had been exiled for fifteen years by the Tsarist government.*

But these are lonely figures on the intellectual landscape of the subjugated South Slavs prior to the nineteenth century. There were, of course, other Yugoslavs, especially Croats, who achieved distinction as artists and scholars, but only after migrating to Austria, Italy and Germany. Among them were such exceptionally gifted men as the fifteenth-century architect Juraj Dalmatinac, who worked in Italy, and the eighteenth-century mathematician and astronomer Ruger Boscovic. But all men of exceptional talent made significant contributions after they were assimilated by other cultures—another tradition that has continued into the twentieth century.†

* Krizanic served for a time as a Kremlin librarian and tutor to Alexis Pavlovich, the future tsar. Princeton historian James Billington, in his *The Icon and the Axe*, says Krizanic was less badly treated under Alexis than other exiles. He was given a pension and freedom to write. In his prolific writings, Krizanic addressed himself to the economic, legal and political aspects of statecraft. Writing in a mixture of Russian, Latin and Croatian, he foresaw a great destiny for Russia and her domination of Eastern Europe. Among other things he advocated women's liberation and urged the abolition of the institution of dowry. "In matters of marriage, the law should be the same for men and women." His ideal was enlightened monarchy: "Among all the sins that make a king hated by God and men, the major one is tyranny." And he saw Russia helping the Yugoslavs achieve their national independence and sovereignty. "All nations curse foreign rule and consider it the worst shame, misfortune and humiliation. The disgrace is lesser if a nation had been conquered by arms than if it has allowed itself to be deceived by alluring words." The reason for his long exile is not known.

† Of the four Yugoslavs who won Nobel prizes, only one, the writer Ivo Andric, worked in his native land. The other three, all chemists, spent their adult life abroad, Lavoslav Ruzicka and Vladimir Prelog in Switzerland and Frederik Pergl in Austria. The two great Yugoslav physicists, Nikola Tesla and Michael Pupin, lived and worked in the United States. Tesla discovered the rotating magnetic field, the basis of practically all alternating-current machinery. Pupin devised means of greatly extending the range of long-distance telephone communications.

In a sense it is almost impossible to understand the cultural scene without keeping in mind this complex inheritance and the amplitude of differing civic and cultural resources. For Yugoslavs, the need for cultural continuity was a political and existential imperative in the nineteenth century. In the twentieth century this need led to the emergence of strident ethnicity.

The Slovenes in the north seem to be the only ethnic group to have overcome the psychological traumas suffered because of a humble past. An essay included in an official book about Slovenia and written by novelist Primoz Kozak describes the Slovenes as a peasant people whose national consciousness dates to the 1848 "nationalist renaissance" within the Austro-Hungarian Empire. Kozak wrote:

> It is in the nature of a peasant to want to be the master of his own land, and to be if not better than his neighbors, then at least as good. This gave rise to two basic and characteristic aims: on one hand, a desire for independence and social emancipation (which must be emphasized, since the Slovenes were for centuries the lower, working and subjugated class in society); and on the other, the desire to obtain whatever they had been deprived of through the centuries. Therefore, we can safely say that the Slovene national consciousness is expressed in the demands they make for themselves and their people: to acquire and appropriate everything that the modern world has produced which is of any value.

It is this sober and rational attitude that perhaps accounts for the remarkable cultural and economic development of this small nation over the past century. Struggling to assert their national existence, the Slovenes have developed a sense of common purpose and a covert yet very strong feeling of nationalism. Even the Slovene Communists are not an exception. A prominent Yugoslav leader told me how at the end of World War II, when partisan forces entered Slovenia in pursuit of retreating German forces, Serb Communists were baffled by the attitude of their Slovene comrades. "Our Serb soldiers started destroying Roman Catholic roadside chapels. They had been told that the movement was against religion and they acted accordingly; I remember Kardelj and Boris Kidric and other Slovene leaders kicking up a fuss. They were furious, and I must admit that I didn't understand them at the time. Aren't we against religion, I asked them. 'Yes,' they said, 'but all those roadside chapels are a part of our national heritage.' "

There are two other elements which, no doubt, have contributed to Slovenia's unique development. One is the Slovene language, perhaps the most archaic of all Slavic tongues and not easily understood by other Yugoslavs, which makes it hard on Communist cultural watchdogs in Belgrade to detect liberal or other "deviations" in Slovene literature and culture. Novelist Beno Zupancic told me that his first books, in which he questioned Communist romanticism and illusions in the 1950s, baffled his like-minded colleagues in Croatia and Serbia. "They told me they couldn't get away with such material, they couldn't get it published to begin with." The other element, equally if not more important, is the fact that Slovenia borders on Italy and Austria. This geographic factor has to be taken into account constantly by the local leaders. "You can't expect the Slovenes to compare themselves to the Bulgarians and Albanians," Slovenia's prime minister, Andrei Marinc, told me in the spring of 1976. "They compare themselves to their neighbors, the Italians and Austrians." The remark provides a clue about the Slovenes' view of themselves, as well as the pressures they feel to catch up with their neighbors.

Other Yugoslavs—especially intellectuals—are prone to dwell upon the real or fictitious glories in their history, conveniently ignoring the painful fact that their ancestors had lived for centuries in what could only be described as a cultural and political void. I recall a Macedonian guide explaining with absolute conviction that the tenth-century fortress, which overlooks the town of Ohrid in Macedonia, was built by the "Macedonian Emperor" Samuilo—despite the fact that Samuilo was a Bulgarian king whose domain extended into Macedonia.* Young Croatian exiles in the United States who hijacked a TWA jetliner in September 1976 forced the Washington *Post* to print their manifesto in which they state that "after a full thirteen centuries of continuity as a legitimate state, Croatian state sovereignty was abolished" by Yugoslavia. And I recall young Serbs, speaking with equal conviction, maintain that Dubrovnik, the tiny Dalmatian oasis of freedom with a history of mature statecraft and independence, was populated by the Serbs—although the city's ethnic composition has been overwhelmingly Croatian. Finally there's Bosnia, the central province whose population is a mixture of Serbs and Croats. About 1.5 million of them, or more than 30 percent of

* The same claim is made in the April 1976 issue of the Yugoslav monthly magazine *Review*.

the province's population, are of Islamic faith, Yugoslavs whose ancestors accepted the faith of the conquering Turks five or six centuries ago. Are they Croats? Or Serbs? Tito's regime resolved the problem that had bedeviled relations between the two largest ethnic groups by declaring the Moslems a separate Bosnian Moslem nation. But can one create a nation by decree?

Originally, the Yugoslav Communists had planned to create a new Yugoslav "socialist" culture. They had viewed ethnic tensions in the period between the two great wars as "class" conflicts between small ruling groups against the background of intolerable poverty and despair in a wretchedly underdeveloped country. Education, literacy, urbanization and social services would quickly overcome Yugoslavia's institutional softness, its lack of common political and cultural experience and its religious and ethnic differences.

But after 1965 Tito stopped talking about a "unitary socialist Yugoslav culture." By then most Yugoslavs, and most of the Yugoslav Communists, had long abandoned the rhetorical vision of a New World. "New generations," an elderly Yugoslav university professor told me, "began to look for human links with the past, trying to understand their cultural heritage. The Marxist leaders were, after all, dogmatic fellows who believed the world was plastic. They were brimming with the naïve self-assurance of autodidacts—for that is what they were before the war. Suddenly they were faced by unforeseen results: increasing pressures for creative freedom among the young and talented people on one hand and a remarkable renascence of nationalism at the regional level, on the other. The regime saw political challenge implicit in both, and devised a fairly ingenious response."

Among his numerous political talents, Tito possessed the gift of adopting the ideas of his potential enemies and critics as his own and then using them in achieving his objectives. He resisted the revival of nationalism for a long time before changing his views and policies to become a champion of national cultural rights in the late sixties. All nations and national minorities in Yugoslavia now enjoy rights of cultural self-expression—but within the framework of "Yugoslav socialist commonwealth." The "ethnic key," a mechanism introduced to ensure a fair share of jobs and influence to each national group, also carried over into the field of culture. Each Yugoslav has certain rights as a member of his ethnic group.

Pressures for creative freedom posed a different and more serious problem. At stake was the individual's right of expression, or freedom of speech, which ultimately would legitimize the right to challenge the political system. In the absence of a free political life, these pressures were expressed in Aesopean language in the discussion of cultural and national issues. But here the regime had to draw a line. "In a system like ours," one Yugoslav politician told me, "you've got to control the security establishment and information in its broadest sense." Responding to the pressures, however, the regime opted for the collective over the individual. National cultural expression became a collective right of each ethnic group. This was in line with economic decentralization. But "collective" rights can be controlled by the Communist party while at the same time providing a degree of pluralism—sometimes real, sometimes fictitious—that fuels hopes for real, long-term cultural freedom. Such policy also provided grounds for cooperation with intellectuals. Tito has always sought conciliation—not confrontation—in his dealings with intellectuals, using threats and honors, bribes and concessions, to co-opt them into the system. It has been a brilliant form of gamesmanship: keeping them off balance, dangling privileges in front of them, whispering into their ears ominous words about the Russian threat and about the position of intellectuals within the bloc, so that they became overwhelmed with the concessions granted and with their own good position.

Concessions were many. Unlike the rest of the Communist world, the Yugoslavs had joined in on most of the cultural movements of the twentieth century—abstract art, op and pop art, jazz and rock, folk rock musicals, modern dance, stream of consciousness novels, surrealism and electronic music.*

Nor did the regime erect barriers against the flow of information from the West. Yugoslavs can easily purchase a variety of Western newspapers and magazines in street kiosks, foreign books in bookstores. I have frequently seen books on sale that would be regarded as poisonous in other East European countries. All this gave the country a unique flavor—communism unlike the one practiced in Eastern Europe.

But there are contradictions. A Yugoslav can buy the complete works of Leon Trotsky and read them to his heart's content, but he

---

* A Zagreb writer-composer team of Alfi Kabiljo and Milan Grgic came up with a musical on Watergate less than three months after the fall of Nixon in 1974.

cannot publicly espouse Trotsky's views without risking imprisonment. He can enjoy Herbert Marcuse's books, but should he write
something along the same lines he could not hope to get it published
in Yugoslavia.

This is the style of Tito's censorship. It is less complete than
that of Brezhnev and other Communist leaders, but it is still a serious obstacle. Dissenting opinions are not entirely suppressed, but they
are presented through esthetic and symbolic subterfuges so obscure
that the general public cannot grasp them. The authorities, more
out of a sense of prudence than a commitment to democracy, are
willing to reason with nonconformists and bring them around to a
compromise. The young Croatian nationalist poet Goran Babic,
whose poem "Croatia Is Burning" came out at the height of the
Croatian crisis and inflamed nationalist sentiments, was not punished. He was made an editor of the Zagreb journal *Oko* instead. But
three journalists of the now defunct *Hrvatski Tjednik*, which published Babic's poem on its front page, have been given prison terms
of up to three years.

Those who refuse to be seduced are treated differently. Matija
Beckovic, perhaps the most important young Serbian poet who is
also a very independent-minded person, is periodically denounced in
the press, his "crime" being that his father was a member of the
Chetnik royalist guerrilla force. Beckovic's father was killed during
the war, when Matija was five years old.

What is intriguing about such public attacks is that they do not
entail financial hardships nor are they ever directed against the
members of the offender's family. In Beckovic's case the public attack meant that for several months he could not get anything
published, but eventually he was allowed to publish a new book of
poems. The pernicious aspect of the attack, however, involved psychological and social pressures on the poet. Written by a prominent
Communist and poet, Oskar Davico, the attack amounted, in the
view of Yugoslav intellectuals, to a call for psychological lynching.*

A dialogue in such situations is hardly possible. The weekly
Komunist, which published Davico's attack, refused to print
Beckovic's letter to the editor. It also refused to print letters of two

---

* Davico was an accomplished poet before World War II. Since the war,
however, he has turned into an ideological watchdog; he had close links with
the secret police, UDBA. In 1966 he published a poem celebrating the UDBA.

prominent Communist writers who came to Beckovic's defense. I discussed the matter with Beckovic in the summer of 1976, a few months after the publication of Davico's article. Beckovic was philosophical about it, even found a humorous aspect to such periodical attacks. "In 1962, when I published my first collection of poems, those who wanted to attack me in the press were saying my father was a Chetnik," he said, laughing. "In 1963, when my second book came out, they promoted him. Now he was a Chetnik *vojvoda* [a high rank in the guerrilla organization]. By 1968 he was already one of the major Chetnik leaders. The truth is that my father had been a lieutenant in the old Royal army and joined the Chetniks in 1941. He was an insignificant man."

But nonconformists are a distinct minority. From my office I gained another, perhaps reassuring, insight from the regime's point of view. Tito's policy toward the intelligentsia has been successful. Most intellectuals seemed satisfied with concessions and adjustments that have diluted the authoritarian strain of the system. Even in private conversations, when they grumbled and complained, their main concern seemed to focus on the need to preserve all their cultural and economic rights. And nothing reinforces their position as much as an allusion to the conditions within the Soviet bloc.

Television and the movie industry, because they command the largest audiences, are under the strictest controls. I was rather surprised to find such technical proficiency among Yugoslav film makers, who were obviously under the influence of American cinematographers. I met several prominent directors and came away with the impression that they were all highly paid but frustrated people. One of them, I recall, was unusually open in revealing his frustrations. He started out being extremely loquacious. He was hoping to get an Oscar nomination for his latest movie. A story about the movie published in the Washington *Post* would help him, he said. But soon his talk became filled with dark intimations. "It's difficult to make a really good film here, because *they* get in on the act, tell you to cut this, change that," he said. But, he added, fixing his large blue eyes on me, he had managed to "sneak in" some ideas which are "totally unacceptable" to the regime. I had seen his movie and was unable to discover any heretical tinge in it. He triumphantly mentioned a sentence in a brief scene and invested it with oppositionist sentiments. If he were to win a measure of international recognition, *they* wouldn't dare massacre his stuff in the future. I tried to find out who *they* were and how *they* exercised control over him, but he wouldn't be precise about it. He was a typical example of the director who had achieved local fame and became affluent by playing along with the censors.

Those who refuse to compromise are either silenced or driven out of the country. One of the most talented, Dusan Makavejev, was indicted in 1973 on a criminal charge of derision "of the state, its agencies and representatives," following a belated party outrage over his film *Wilhelm Reich: Mysteries of the Organism*. Although the film won acclaim from critics at the Cannes festival and elsewhere in the West, it had been shown only to a few selected audiences in Yugoslavia. Another Makavejev movie, *Man Is Not a Bird*, was selected by Vincent Canby of the *New York Times* as one of the Eleven Best Films of 1974. The plot of this film, made in the late sixties, centers on a moody, introspective engineer who, against his better judgment, has an affair with an attractive but much younger woman in an industrial town. The actual—but implicit—subject is Tito's Great Social Experiment. *Mysteries of the Organism*, which is done in an avant-garde manner, is far more explicit. It shows Makavejev as a disciple of Dr. Reich, the Austrian-born psychoanalyst who considered sexual repression the basic cause of political repression and fascism. The movie is structured as a collage, mixing different threads of a fictional plot with documentary footage in a way that makes the distinction between the real and dramatized very thin indeed. The plot itself is a love story about a Yugoslav girl and a Russian man. The political message is presented through the use of old newsreels and films. But although these juxtapositions are complex and although Makavejev satirizes both the socialist and capitalist worlds, his films were deemed subversive. Some of his scenes were perhaps not obvious to the average viewer in the West, but they were immediately recognizable to the East European viewers, such as, for instance, the linking of the documentary footage about Stalin and excerpts from Nazi movies supporting the nations of racial superiority. Makavejev's message is that political repression—rather than sex—is pornographic. Once the party censured Makavejev, he was roundly denounced in the official press.

The controversy over the film did not center on its sexual explicitness—a Danish pornographic movie was being shown in Yugoslavia at the time—but on its political message, which implicitly criticized Tito's authoritarian style. Makavejev, who was born in 1932, went into West European exile, and in 1975 directed the film *Sweet Movie,* a French-Canadian production.

The Makavejev affair generated political and intellectual tensions in the Yugoslav film industry as well as in the Academy of Theater, Film, Radio and Television in Belgrade. Several professors were ousted from the Communist party and nonparty staff were sharply censured. One of the censured professors was Alexander Petrovic, whose film *I Even Saw Happy Gypsies* won the Jury Prize at the Cannes Film Festival in 1967. He was denounced for having given a high grade to a student whose graduation project, an avant-garde film titled *The Plastic Jesus,* offended Marshal Tito "in an especially rude manner" and equated "the values of fascism with those of socialism." The student's film, which was made in the style of Makavejev, contained newsreel scenes of Hitler, Stalin and Tito combined in a manner offensive to the Yugoslav censors. It was never publicly shown. The extraordinary thing about this incident was that Communists in the Academy saw nothing wrong with *The Plastic Jesus,* and the film came to the attention of the authorities only after the student who made it had been inducted into the army and drew attention to himself with some unorthodox statements. The army intelligence started inquiring into the young man's background and learned of the film.

The two incidents proved to be a serious setback for Yugoslav cinematography in the seventies, as the regime sought to impose cultural orthodoxy to a great degree. To get around it, film makers revived interest in the late nineteenth- and early twentieth-century satires on rising middle-class consciousness and the beginnings of the dissolution of moral values in the countryside. This became especially attractive for television producers, who are censored far more severely than anyone else. Old texts were dramatized and staged in a setting suggesting contemporary scenes and problems.

TV programming also has to conform with Yugoslavia's international position. Third World movies, regardless of their quality, are aired at prime times. To counter the popularity of *Kojak* and *McCloud,* the Yugoslavs have sharply increased imports of Soviet and East European TV films. I made it a point to watch a thirteen-part series, *Benjovski,* made by a Czech television company in collaboration with the Hungarians. The series was so banal, and its propaganda message so crude and transparent, that it stood out among a crop of similar programs. Its plot revolved around Moritz Benjovski, a Polish count serving in the French Imperial Army of the nineteenth century, who is sent to Madagascar to quell a native rebellion. From the outset Moritz sees that the natives were fighting for a just cause, and he tries to take their case before the emperor. The very sight of French officials in Paris, who are to decide on Count Moritz's presentation, makes it clear that neither he nor the natives have a chance. Meantime, Moritz contracts yellow fever and is nursed back to health by the natives who, having realized that he is a just European with a pristine pure heart, elect him their king. A few other French Imperial Army soldiers join Moritz's royal administration. They are good guys, and all good guys have Slavic names. Moritz's program is all détente: national independence, peaceful coexistence, noninterference in internal affairs, bilateral trade. As far as weapons go, Moritz tells his native counselors, "there are other places where they could be bought." The most dramatic moment comes at the end when the French treacherously lure Moritz away from his camp and kill him. The Pole's death symbolizes the defeat of a Madagascar independence movement in the nineteenth century.

In the decades before World War II, there appeared in Yugoslavia several first-rate novelists and poets. Most of them were leftists, viewing the contemporary world either in Marxist terms of class conflict or probing to comprehend the country's social development through the nineteenth and twentieth centuries. Perhaps the most important figure among them was Miroslav Krleza, the great, highly cultured Croatian writer of Marxist persuasion. Although the kingdom of Yugoslavia was by no means a great democracy, leftist intellectuals were allowed to publish their works and run their journals without any great difficulty.* The outstanding figure among non-Marxist writers was Ivo Andric, a career diplomat who served as the Yugoslav ambassador in Berlin up to the moment of Yugoslavia's destruction by Hitler in 1941.

Both Krleza and Andric belong to the same generation of Yugoslav intellectuals, having been born in the last decade of the nineteenth century: Krleza in Zagreb in 1893, Andric in Travnik,

* Marx's *Das Kapital* was published in Serbo-Croatian by a Belgrade publishing house in 1932. It had been translated by three Communists, Mose Pijade, Rodoljub Colakovic and August Cesarec, the first two doing most of the work while serving prison terms.

Bosnia, in 1892. Krleza, who was of bourgeois background, was graduated from the Hungarian Royal Military Academy in Budapest and served briefly with the Austro-Hungarian Imperial Army. After the Great War, he took up the Marxist cause, edited several leftist newspapers and magazines, and published more than twenty books, including novels, short stories, dramas and essays. Even his ideological enemies before World War II had regarded Krleza as one of the most important and talented Yugoslav writers. After Tito came to power, Krleza became a leading cultural figure, served as a member of the Central Committee, president of the Yugoslav Writers Union and became an intimate of Tito's.

Andric, on the other hand, came from a mixed Croatian-Serbian family of artisans and as a youth joined the revolutionary student organization that carried out the 1914 assassination of Archduke Ferdinand. Andric was not a part of the assassination plot, but he did wind up in an Austrian prison. He studied philosophy and took his doctorate at the Graz University in Austria in 1920 before joining the Yugoslav foreign service. He wrote quietly during the next two decades while serving in a number of European capitals. In 1941, a day before Hitler's attack on Yugoslavia, he returned home from Berlin. He then went into retirement, in Belgrade, under German occupation, and completed his three major works, among them *The Bridge on the Drina*, for which he won the Nobel Prize for Literature in 1961. After the Communist takeover in 1945, Andric was quickly co-opted into the Communist party, elected president of the Yugoslav Writers Union and a deputy of the Federal Assembly. He remained a widely respected but elusive figure until his death in 1975.

In some respect, the two men present a very sharp contrast. Krleza, a lifelong Marxist, has been preoccupied by the terror of the destruction of Central Europe in World War I. His *The Croatian God Mars* shows how the horror of war results in the debasement of human values. His dramas, such as *The Glebmay Family*, are based on the concept of the moral fall of a particular social class that finds itself incapable of adjusting to modern conditions. For all his leftist activism and polemics, Krleza has managed to retain an independent voice, a quality that eventually brought him at odds with the Yugoslav Communists in the seventies. Unlike Krleza, who addresses himself to the upper tier of sophisticated Yugoslavs who had been exposed to Western education and who can cope with West Euro-

pean ironies, Andric as a writer is steeped in the tradition and folk-
lore of his country and its backward and multinational society. He
views ancient national myths and legends as having a greater hold on
the habits of mind than the vagaries of political and ideological
change could ever have. Without doubt, Andric is the greatest master of Serbo-Croatian. In his chronicles of the past of Yugoslav
peoples—the Serbs, Croats, and Moslem Slavs, all living in the
claustrophobic world of Visegrad, the town where Andric spent his
youth in Austrian-occupied Bosnia—the novelist combines the severity of a clinical psychologist with the compassion of a peasant
grandmother.

What Krleza and Andric have in common, however, is the fact
that during the three decades of socialism they have not produced
anything of exceptional value. In Andric's case, *all* his novels were
completed before 1945. Krleza has written one massive novel since
1945, but it comes nowhere near the artistic quality of his previous
works. Why? I asked several thoughtful Yugoslavs the question. They
responded by saying that the fate of Andric and Krleza symbolizes
what has happened to writers of exceptional talent—and there were a
few dozen or so of them before World War II, men who sought to
grasp the fundamental social changes that lie behind national conflicts. The left-wing intellectuals among them became a part of Tito's
Great Experiment, at first enthusiastically trying to perform
through their writing what Djilas in the immediate postwar years
described as the function of socialist art—"to give artistic works to
the masses [and] to arm those masses with the lethal weapons of
knowledge and fervor." Those who were non-Marxists, or who like
Andric had been closely identified with the old royalist system, either had to lay low or to subject themselves to a self-discipline which
would keep them in the good graces of the regime.

From this followed another fact—which the regime found extremely unpalatable. It was among the dedicated Marxists, which
included a crop of talented Communist writers who grew up under
Tito's socialism, that restrictions and censorship gave rise to pressures for intellectual freedom. "We realized that something is very
wrong with the system," one leading Marxist novelist told me. "We
discovered lies within the system and within ourselves."

Krleza, Petar Segedin, Branko Copic, Miodrag Bulatovic, Mesa
Selimovic, Dobrica Cosic and other Communist intellectuals have
been the ones who criticize the regime. Writers like Andric or Milos

Crnjanski—another royalist who went into exile to England but then returned to Yugoslavia—have been silent.*

While the tradition of wartime struggle was still alive and the ideology still enjoyed its prestige as a revolutionary and moral force, Marxist intellectuals accepted the regime's assumptions as a guide to the practical political life and worked for Communist objectives. In time, however, it became evident to most of them that the realization of the socialist hope was more and more remote and questionable. Long after "class enemies" were destroyed and the "remnants" of the old system abolished, the Communist leaders were not prepared to grant to its supporters the gamut of freedoms that the former royalist regime had granted to its Marxist enemies. "Our leaders are, fortunately, not as dogmatic as the Soviets," one writer told me. "Ours know that they can't abolish freedom to think and feel. But they can and do prevent freedom to communicate."

The regime has tried to test what it regards as acceptable limits to free speech. But, as Prvoslav Ralic, a doctor of philosophy and a ranking man in the party's ideological commission, put it to me, "We'll not tolerate the misuse of creative freedom, the use of culture for political ends. Here you enter into the area of political struggle."

The problem, of course, is that the ruling oligarchy determines what is the "misuse" of creative freedom and the standards keep

---

* Andric, whose literary accomplishments are outstanding, was privately criticized by other writers for being a miser and a man interested in his own thought as a sort of self-contained system. His conversion to communism was perceived as insincere by the leaders. Djilas told me that when a group of Communists in a formal meeting proposed that Andric be admitted to the Communist party, the writer actually never said that he wanted to join. "If the comrades say so," Djilas quoted Andric's evasively affirmative reply. The Yugoslav leaders, however, sought since 1943 to attract as many prominent literary figures as possible, bringing into the partisan army such well-known figures as the poet and children's story writer Vladimir Nazor, who was then in his seventies. Andric, however, was the most important convert. His about-face, however, reinforced Andric's penchant for privacy. About a year prior to his death, I tried to persuade Andric to grant an interview for a journalistic profile. On one occasion he agreed in principle but suggested I meet a friend of his, a literary critic, to discuss details. "Are you going to ask him any questions about his career before the war?" the critic asked me after a long discussion. Yes, I said, I wanted to sketch a portrait of Andric the man and writer. "Then I can assure you that Mr. Andric will never agree to an interview," the critic said. "Since you're going to ask such personal questions, the answer is going to be no." The critic was right.

shifting according to national climate. Changes such as the break with Stalin to rapprochement with Khrushchev, to the Czechoslovak invasion, as well as numerous other zig-zags in internal policies, have produced shocks that have taken away much of the romantic fervor and have given way to cynicism. The successful introduction of democratic education and the *kultura* drive in general have proven complicated in the absence of free competition for advancement. There are pockets of creative vitality, but they are few and far between. The intelligentsia by and large has been seduced by privileges and by their own appetite for material well-being, which the regime nurses cautiously as a hedge against their rebellious proclivities. Yugoslav leftists who are in contact with leftist groups in Western Europe are often baffled by their idealism. I recall meeting Danilo Kis, one of the leading young poets, a few days upon his return from France, where he had spent two years as a lecturer at a French university. "It's so nice to be back," he said laughingly. "You know, there are so many Communists and leftists in France, it is positively annoying."

13

Innocence Lost

ONE DAY IN VOJVODINA, IN THE HOT SUMMER AFTERNOON WHEN EVERY-one seemed to be taking a siesta, I drove over a deserted country road with an American diplomat, Irving Pernick. He was new to Yugo-slavia, but he had undergone language training in Washington and spoke good Serbo-Croatian.

As we swung around a long curve, we suddenly came upon a funeral procession. Tall poplars along one side of the road had ob-scured it—a horse-drawn cart carrying the coffin, followed by a priest and a handful of relatives and friends—so that we didn't get a chance to determine whether it was a Roman Catholic or Eastern Orthodox funeral. For Vojvodina is the quintessence of the Balkans: races and religions coexist within an almost claustrophobic range—the Serbs, Hungarians, Croats, Ukrainians, Czechs, Slovaks, Romanians, Ruthenians and Gypsies. Tens of thousands of ethnic Germans who had once owned farms on this fertile plain had been forcibly de-ported to Germany and Austria immediately after World War II when anti-German passions were running high. But the landscape still bore the imprint of Germanic neatness: farm houses shaded by tall poplars set in precise geometric forms seemed hauntingly peace-ful. Even the silhouettes of Roman Catholic and Orthodox churches from a distance looked so indistinguishable as to suggest a fusion of architectural conceptions. The Orthodox ones had been built with-out the traditional onion domes. The spires of Catholic churches are not high and sharp but rather bulging. Both types seem a curious blend of baroque and Byzantine.

As we spoke about the complexities of a multiethnic country we suddenly noticed two motorcycles approaching us from behind at great speed. When they caught up with us we saw policemen signaling us to halt. This seemed highly irregular, especially since we had distinct diplomatic tags on the car and had committed no traffic offense. "Haven't you seen the funeral?" one of the policemen thundered, looking distressed but obviously assuming that we could not possibly understand what he was saying. "They must have seen it," he said to his colleagues. Then he turned to us, angrily gesticulating as if to emphasize the point. "There was the priest, and the hearse and people in black. You should be ashamed. You didn't have the decency to stop and let the funeral pass in peace. In this country we have a law that requires you to stop. But you don't need a law to tell you that. It is basic decency . . ." We listened without saying a word as he repeated himself one more time. Then he waved us on to continue our trip and turned toward his colleagues, saying contemptuously, "Diplomats, eh? Barbarians!"

I recall this otherwise insignificant encounter because it illuminates one of the central Yugoslav traditions—respect for the elemental aspects of life, such as birth, death, baptisms, weddings, and key religious holidays. We had obviously offended the policeman's sense of propriety. He may have been infuriated by what he took to be foreign insouciance. Just possibly he may have been a friend of the deceased. I don't know. But in a country where people have been in psychological or physical combat with each other, as well as with hostile foreign neighbors, the moments of great adversity or of exceptional joy show the Yugoslavs at their best. In everyday life there is a certain roughness they show toward each other, an indifference toward the other's views, the feeling that the best way to settle accounts is by a display or a threat of force. With the possible exception of the Slovenes, Yugoslavs have great difficulties in accepting the concept of corporate morality. But when their reactions depend on their own spontaneity, they are capable of extreme acts of individual bravery, consideration, self-sacrifice and kindness. And then their impulse toward compassion, the simplicity and directness with which it is displayed and the authenticity of feelings involved, suggest reactions of an earlier Christian era.

Indeed, bubbling under the deceptively modern surface of Yugoslav life are strong currents of primitive Christianity, a syndrome of traditions and feelings inherited from an innocent past which still permeates all ethnic communities and provides moral underpinning for individual actions. Despite more than three decades of antireligious propaganda, the values inherent in the traditional way of life still frame the outlook on the world of most Yugoslavs.*

But unlike the Eastern Slavs, the Yugoslavs are a Mediterranean people distrustful of mysticism and religious abstractions and devoted to the pleasures of good living. Largely as a result of their underdevelopment they have traditionally assimilated the structure of the faith without learning much about the dogma, or even caring about it. Their religion is humane rather than doctrinal, a way of life they had derived from nature and experience. I have found mostly ignorance when questioning Yugoslavs about the Christian dogmatic tradition. Over the years religion has become a symbol of ethnic identification, a vessel of tribal existence. Hence the religious dimension to the tribal feuds.

A Croat is a Roman Catholic because he was born into the faith just like a Serb is Eastern Orthodox for the same reason. They may look alike, speak alike, play alike and behave alike but they *know* that they are different because of their religion. It is impossible to switch religious affiliation. A Serb who turns Roman Catholic forfeits his tribal identity, and vice versa. I knew a lady who bore one of the most famous Hungarian noble family names and who probably had little Croat blood in her. Yet her Croat nationalist sentiments were diamond-hard. When she told me she was a Croat she did so with a beatific smile and an air of self-contentment as if she were describing an extraordinary personal accomplishment. And I have met several Serbs whose names and features suggested a mixture of races and religions but who were as assertive about their Serb identity as if they were heirs and lineal descendants of the medieval Nemanja princes.

The paradox, of course, is that organized religion suffered an enormous moral setback during World War II when some members of both Orthodox and Roman Catholic lower clergy joined extreme nationalists in a fratricidal Serb-Croat war. Once the Communists

* In 1975 a poll conducted by the Institute for Social Research at the University of Zagreb looking into religious persuasion of students in fifty high schools in the Zagreb area revealed that 32 percent of the students believed in God but 70 percent celebrated religious holidays. Only 17.5 percent declared themselves atheists and 26 percent accepted Marxism as the basis of their world outlook. Although the inquiry guaranteed anonymity, it can be assumed that at least some of the students were reluctant to state their true feelings in view of the official hostility toward religion.

took power, the Churches were immobilized. Tito's propaganda immediately sought to project the criminal behavior of a relatively small number of clerics onto the Church hierarchies in general, charging that they had sponsored or encouraged wartime massacres. Alojz Cardinal Stepinac, the archbishop of Zagreb and leader of the Croatian Roman Catholic Church, was tried and convicted on these charges.*

The violent intrusion of Tito's regime had been so unexpected, and Marxism as the state creed so completely alien to the Yugoslavs, that they instinctively turned toward their churches. To a certain degree the regime was committed to atheism and "scientific socialism" as the moral foundations of a new order. But their violent attack on religion was mostly political. They smashed political parties and proclaimed their determination to eradicate any organized opposition. The Churches were organized and they, like most of the people, resented the false god of atheist Russia that was destroying Life's pattern. So the regime surrounded religion with walls of restrictions, and its secret police infiltrated Church ranks. Outspoken priests were arrested and some churches shut down. The basic objective of the regime was to destroy the image of the Croat and Serb Churches as spokesmen for their respective ethnic communities.

The Croatian Church, although young, was viewed as a far more serious opponent than the Serbian Church.† Throughout Serbian history, the Orthodox hierarchy has preached submission to the State, even during several centuries when secular power was in Turkish hands and when the Church had to accept an awkward accommodation with the Turks in order to survive. Moreover, the supreme leaders of the Church are located in Belgrade, which made the hierarchy more pliable. This is not the case with the Croatian Church, whose supreme leader is the Pope sitting in Rome. The leaders of the Church are outside Yugoslavia, the Croatian Church is better organized and intellectually stronger, and above all its pecu-

---

* A former senior Communist official intimately involved in the Stepinac trial told me privately that the authorities had evidence at the time that Stepinac had complained about atrocities committed by the Croat fascist government. In retrospect, the informant said, the only problem of Stepinac was that "he didn't take a public stand on the issue."

† Although Croats accepted Christianity a thousand years ago, they managed to persuade the Vatican only in 1852 to grant them their own Church by the establishment of the archbishopric of Zagreb.

liar identification is with Croat nationalism—all this has made the Croatian Church more formidable. Even today, the Croatian Church is probably subjected to more police scrutiny than any single institution in Yugoslavia. As a result, many Croat nationalists feel they are being held in subjugation by *Belgrade*, the word used pejoratively, since in Croatia it carries the dual connotation of Serbs and primitivism. Perhaps this official pressure accounts for the militancy of Croatian nationalists. An American diplomat who served in the Consulate General in Zagreb told me that he was dismayed by the intolerance of the Croats toward non-Croats that he detected while pursuing consular business through the countryside. Typical, he said, was the reaction of his Croat maid when he decided to take his family on a tour of medieval Serbian monasteries.

The maid, he said, professed to be baffled by their travel plans, suggesting he was a reckless adventurer preparing to take his family into what she regarded as the equivalent of the unexplored parts of Africa. When, after their trip, the diplomat was sorting out his color photographs of Serbian monastries, the maid spotted the picture of a medieval icon of the Virgin Mary. "Ah," he said, imitating the maid, whose voice implied that she didn't have the slightest idea, "do they have Virgin Mary, too?"

Foreigners are too easily disposed to ignore awkwardly complex Church-State relations in Yugoslavia. The government, for instance, has found it advantageous for foreign policy reasons to ensure a normal development for the Moslem religious community. All visiting Arab and Moslem politicians are invariably taken to Sarajevo—a city with nearly one hundred mosques and the center of Moslem culture in Yugoslavia—where the skyline is dominated by slim minarets and where they can hear the muezzin calling the faithful to prayer. Since the collapse of the Ottoman Empire, the Yugoslav Moslems, almost two million strong, have tended to accept uneasy accommodation with any government in power. Men with Moslem names are often sent as ambassadors to Moslem countries. Since the 1973 world oil crisis, Arab oil producers have become increasingly important for Yugoslav industries. The Yugoslav government has established close economic and political ties with many of them, especially Libya and Iraq, and has been putting out repeated feelers to Saudi Arabia, which does not maintain relations with Communist countries. An Egyptian diplomat told me that during President

Sadat's visit to Yugoslavia in 1974, the then Yugoslav finance minister, Janko Smole, told a senior Egyptian official: "Please tell the
Saudis that we're not against religion. Tell them that our Islamic
community is flourishing, as you have seen yourself."

Nor does the government have special problems with the
Roman Catholic Church of Slovenia, or with the Macedonian
Orthodox Church. (The establishment of the latter in 1966 was
sponsored by the Macedonian Communists.) It is the tribal feud
between the Serbs and the Croats—burdened by the umbilical link
between ethnicity and faith—that has cast religion into the political
arena. This is a crucial point psychologically—for religious intolerance reflects ethnic animosities rather than anything created by
organized religion. The Churches have to take into consideration
the undertow of Serb and Croat nationalism which, in the absence of
free speech, is difficult to gauge.

Are ethnic animosities due to a lack of education? Or underdevelopment? I asked such questions in separate talks with Orthodox
and Roman Catholic officials. Orthodox spokesmen were oblique
and uninformative in their responses, as if they had grudgingly come
to terms with the limits the State has set for the Church's activities.

In Zagreb, however, Roman Catholic spokesmen were more
forthcoming. They were testing the limits in a dialogue with the
authorities, a somewhat uneven contest, since the authorities could—
and frequently did—ban issues of *Glas Koncila*, the weekly publication of the Zagreb archdiocese, while using the entire range of
information means at their disposal to promote *their* side of the
dialogue.*

That the old values still hold and that the people resort to the
old defensive processes can be explained perhaps by the absence of
any other distinct set of values. Tradition and history have helped
them create sets of reactions against recurrent confusion and law-

---

* In 1973 an issue of *Glas Koncila* was banned for having carried a poem by
Ivan Filipovic, titled "Fatherland's Consolation." Filipovic, who wrote the poem
in 1852, at the time the Zagreb archbishopric was established, was imprisoned by
Austro-Hungarian authorities for harboring seditious ideas. In his poem he urged
the Croats to keep their faith, cautioning them that "had we been wiser, had we
dreamt less and instead acted reasonably, we would have been closer to our
goals." An official statement about the court decision to ban *Glas Koncila* said
Filipovic's poem could be interpreted as "an allusion to our current political
situation."

lessness. But their age of innocence, which had lasted so long, ended almost overnight. Enormous changes have been taking place before their very eyes. I was reminded of this when, a few weeks after my arrival in Yugoslavia, I ran into a childhood friend. It was an accidental encounter in a café, a quick drink, a short outburst of reminiscences. As a child he had lived in a lovely modern apartment building near a park where well-to-do people lived before World War II. During the war a German officer or someone associated with the Germans moved into the building in an apartment a Jewish family had been forced to vacate. The new occupants fled the premises at the war's end, leaving intact the antique furniture, paintings and just about everything else. The part I remember clearly is that a Communist officer took over the apartment a few days later, and then brought his entire family from his village. This included a grandmother, who arrived with a goat. The proximity of the park, of course, provided ideal conditions for keeping the goat in the apartment. I had never seen the grandmother taking the goat to the pastures in the park, but I had heard my friend speak about it. "The family must have liked goat milk," my friend said with a smirk when I recalled the story. "What happened to the family with the goat?" I inquired. "Well," he said, "the old man retired as major general, both his daughter and son finished college and the son spent a year as a Fulbright scholar in the United States. No more goat milk for the general," he added, laughing.

How many rustics have traveled this distance? They had surged into war-ravaged towns and cities depleted of life—Tito's partisans, trusted cadres and village Communist enthusiasts—to take over the administration and reshape the world. They were given good jobs, apartments and privileges, and they were told that a "new dawn" was just rising on the horizon. Their almost naïve belief in the power of education led them to believe that people could be molded. But that was thirty years ago. Now they're older, fatter, more sophisticated, better dressed and without illusions.

That first wave of migration was followed by others—peasants trying to escape rural poverty, having to compete for jobs and living in squalid quarters that mushroomed around every big city. Then came the migrations to Western Europe, all of which amounted to the type of social and physical mobility the Balkans had never experienced before. And the automobile in a country so complex and so diverse became—to use George Ball's phrase—"an ideology on four wheels."

Today Yugoslavs are grasping for the symbols of middle-class status. I have seen numerous manifestations of this, such as the production by Yugoslav firms of fake Louis XVI furniture, the faddish hunger for paintings, icons and antiques in general, the irresistible urge to spend vacations in Spain, southern France, Greece or Italy. (In July and August of 1976 nearly 800,000 Yugoslavs were holidaying in Greece alone.)

I have known people who have acquired priceless collections of Russian miniatures, icons, antique furniture and Oriental carpets. But then there were other symbols: Yugoslavs furiously polishing their small Fiats and Volkswagens on a Saturday afternoon; an old peasant woman dressed in the traditional black garb who came to our street on Thursdays in a black Mercedes selling fresh lamb; young men in jeans and plaid shirts looking like young men anywhere in Western Europe. (An American woman, who with a group of college girls had visited Yugoslavia every summer for the past ten years to attend folk dance festivals, told me, "In the sixties, we were an instant attraction in Yugoslavia, since we wore different clothes. Now we all look alike. By looking at you they don't know whether you are a Yugoslav or a foreigner.")

It is this lurch into the modern age—guided by "crass materialism not socialist materialism," as one writer put it to me—that had weakened organized religion more than any atheistic propaganda of the regime. But the resulting, often uncomfortable contrast between inherited traditions and habits and institutions created by modern technology was leading Yugoslavs back toward the old values. The feeling of vulnerability generated by the loss of the relative security of pastoral existence becomes greater when people realize that there is no going back. Nerves are tense, pressures come from all directions. (In 1940 the number-one killer in Yugoslavia was tuberculosis, while in 1976 it was heart disease.) The changes have been too rapid and the government has been too inept in controlling and shaping society's transformation. Without doubt no government could have done it easily. The problems are natural for a country that only recently has come into contact with the rest of Europe and, in fact, with the rest of the world. The Yugoslavs have been so engrossed in catching up and so assiduous in their bourgeois acquisitiveness that they never realized that what they wanted most they also feared. They gained a higher living standard, but they lost the sense of security.

Tito's experimentation contributed to a beleaguered form of

life. He has positioned the country between East and West, with the government clinging to the rhetoric of the East and the people looking toward the West. The jargon of the party is incongruous with the reality; it is the jargon of someone who doesn't really know what he is supposed to be doing. The Communists have lost their faith as well. Party spokesmen are no longer sure why they are addressing the people, except to remain in power. "We talk a great deal," one Communist official told me. "But you've got to if you want to get ahead. Why worry, we're living well." And if there is an underlying psychological malaise in the land, it comes both from the restrictions the government fixes on the individuals and from a sense of confusion and vulnerability caused by freedoms inherent in an urban, mobile society.

The loss of idealism among the young has led to widespread cynicism. I recall a conversation between two high school graduates that I overheard riding a streetcar in Zagreb. "I think I'll join the party," one of them said, "then things become easier. At least I know I'll get a job when I finish college." The other youth acknowledged the utility of the proposal. He cited examples but wondered what his parents' reaction would be. It seemed as though they were involved in mapping a train route that would take them to a desired destination, rather than joining an organization that is supposed to demand total ideological commitment.

The trouble is that after more than three decades in power the Communists have been unable to develop civic and cultural resources whose range would include political tolerance and respect for institutions. But, as a Yugoslav sociologist otherwise critical of the regime pointed out to me, "We all long for harmony but somehow the notion that a clash of opinions involves physical struggle is imbedded in our consciousness." Where the real failure lies, he said, is in the official state creed. Communist rank and file and even the leaders may not believe in the Marxist rhetoric but they use it to justify their monopoly of power. "They cannot afford an open forum to serve as a clearing house for different ideas because that would threaten their power. What else could you say?"

But that is an old story. What is new in the stream of Yugoslav life is an emerging middle-class culture and a mixing of races and religions regardless of the humdrum of government. Ricky Silberman, the wife of the American ambassador and an astute observer in her own right, pointed this out to me in a dramatic way. She had befriended a Yugoslav couple whose children have a unique set of grandparents: a Roman Catholic, a Moslem, an Eastern Orthodox and a Jew. Mika Spiljak, the former prime minister, told me that one out of each three marriages in the 1970s involves partners of different religious affiliation.

While the young enter into mixed marriages with sophomoric recklessness and abandon, their relatives go through traumatic experiences and family dramas. Friendships among people of different ethnic groups are not only possible but often exceptionally deep and warm, but mixed marriages challenge the blood attachment to the tribe. Even atheist intellectuals and party members privately seek to discourage mixed marriages. Among many such incidents I recall one because of its stereotyped routine and accompanying drama. A young Moslem girl from Sarajevo had fallen in love with a Croatian boy. The girl's father, who served as the director of a major Bosnian firm, was violently opposed to his daughter's liaison. The boy's father held a less exalted job but equally strong sentiments against a Moslem bride for his son. Both families suffered agonies of apprehension at the thought of the prospective calamity. Both mustered relatives and friends to help exert pressure on the young people in love. By the time these maneuvers reached their raging pitch, with each side arguing that their good name would be dragged to dust, the young people eloped and got married. The girl's father, upon hearing the news, suffered a mild heart attack. The boy's father, while withstanding the shock, announced to his relatives that he was casting a "curse" on his son. For nearly a year the two families had no direct contact with the newlyweds, until the first grandchild was born. The baby acted as a catalyst for reconciliation. Both the girl's and the boy's fathers were party members and it was only in public that their disagreement continued. In their family circle they could let their hair down. Ethnic animosities have their own lingo which is employed routinely and which is understood by everyone.

Although mixed marriages are not about to resolve Yugoslavia's ethnic problem, they are an expression of profound social turmoil and of the advent of an urban, cosmospolitan world. Various nationalist and religious spokesmen I talked to denounced this trend, worrying that the ethnic dedication felt by previous generations could not be forcefully transmitted to the young. Ironically, those Yugoslavs who have voluntarily opted out of their tribal mold nowadays find themselves at a disadvantage. "I'll never make ambassador," a senior bureaucrat in the Foreign Ministry told me privately. "I left my republic twenty years ago, and I have lost all contact with people there. Today, you have to be nominated by your republic for ambassadorships." His complaint epitomized the complexities of ethnic policies in Yugoslavia. Ambassadorships, and everything else, is distributed on the basis of the "ethnic key."

British historian A. J. P. Taylor has described Tito as "the last Hapsburg," an apt reference to the problems involved in holding together a multinational country by giving each ethnic group the fullest possible stake in the survival of the commonwealth. Yugoslavia's problems are similar to those of the old Hapsburg Empire and Tito's solution is similar to the one Archduke Ferdinand is said to have contemplated prior to his assassination in 1914. Except that Tito has set his policies into motion and that his aim is the creation of a Communist confederation.

Will it work? Despite ethnic issues, I saw a country becoming, despite itself, increasingly united. The greatest cohesive force is the economy, which has brought about the emergence of a self-conscious middle class. In a world of consumerism, man's attention is inevitably diverted away from spiritual and political issues; daily preoccupations with material things have thinned out the intoxicating air of Balkan anarchy. It was as if Yugoslavs were feeling, perhaps dimly, an alienation from themselves, an emergence of a way of life that somehow is not theirs. For the first time they have lived through three decades of peace. For the first time they have—at least in a social and spiritual sense—become a part of Western, industrialized society. But at the same time this entry into Europe has demonstrated Yugoslav backwardness and accentuated the compulsion to overcome it. Paradoxically, Tito and his colleagues set out after the war to force modernization on a reluctant country. Three decades later the people had a clear preference for things modern, but the rulers were holding back on cultural and political changes to accompany the consequences of economic development and were unable to offer spiritual guidance or enlightened political reforms.

A leap across the Atlantic and we were home, the first time in more than three years, and suffering from shock. We had been thinking, all the time we were in Europe, how much better off we were in the States. So terribly patriotic. My son's picture of America was one of candy bars lying in the street. "We have no police in Washington," he used to tell our Yugoslav maid, pointing to a policeman who was stationed twenty-four hours a day in a small booth near the entrance to our house. But Karin and I had also tended to remember the most pleasant things from the past, especially material comforts.

We had been away during most of the anti-Vietnam turbulence in the late sixties, when we lived in Moscow, and we had missed most of the Watergate trauma as well. Living in a world of authoritarian regimes, it frequently occurred to me how relatively insignificant President Nixon's misdeeds must have appeared to the people who have always lived under tutelage, under laws composed by distant lawgivers on whom they had no influence. The spectacle of a sitting President being forced out by the pressure of public opinion was completely alien to their experience and thoughts.

For a while after our return I felt as though we had come to another foreign country. The scars of Vietnam and Watergate seemed to me to have left the country less sure of itself and more worried about its future. But then I began to work, trying to sort out my impressions of Yugoslavia, seeking a thread of logic to link them together. The more I thought about it, the less easy it was to formulate them. It was, after all, unfair and misleading to compare Yugoslavia with the United States or with Western Europe. One had to compare her with her East European neighbors.

And the Yugoslavs have done quite well indeed. They have maintained political independence and sovereignty and have introduced a degree of freedom not known in the Soviet bloc.

I recall the opening, in May 1976, of a new railway linking Belgrade with the Adriatic port city of Bar, the largest and most complex single enterprise of its kind ever undertaken in Yugoslavia. It took a quarter of a century to build the 476-kilometer link between Serbia and the Adriatic Sea, and it will probably take even longer to amortize its cost. The railroad literally cuts through some of the most inaccessible mountain territory—nearly one third of it, or 115 kilometers, consists of tunnels—and clings to the rocky formations of south Serbia and Montenegro like a tendril. Foreign journalists were invited to ride the first train through the high pastures and the pine forests of the Sandjak mountains and then through a jumble of crags and heavy boulders hanging along the fringes of bald and arid Montenegrin ranges. What I had failed to realize at the time was the psychological need for this railway. More

than a century ago the two independent but weak Yugoslav states—
Serbia and Montenegro—had planned to build a communication
link between Serbia and the Adriatic but were explicitly forbidden
to do so under the terms of the 1878 Congress of Berlin, where the
great powers gave the Hapsburg Empire the right of blocking such
construction at will. After the Berlin Congress, Serbia was put in a
position tantamount to being an Austrian protectorate. For Tito,
who grew up in the Hapsburg Empire and was forced to live both in
and off a foreign culture, the building of the Belgrade-Bar railway
was an act of the independent Yugoslav spirit as much as anything
else.

But foreign policy has claimed a disproportionate degree of the
top leaders' attention, clearly at the expense of domestic issues.
True, all the changes of the past three decades have improved the
quality of Yugoslav life and have brought the political system to
the edge of pluralism. And perhaps, just perhaps, that after Tito and
the old-guard Communists leave the scene, the Yugoslavs will be
ready for a political reform and further liberalization. As long as
Tito and his top aides are in charge, however, the system will adhere
to the current Marxist mold regardless of how much it has con-
strained the natural development. Nor does the mold provide room
for further liberalization, for it is built by layers and layers of clear
rationality based upon a few utopian assumptions and shored up by
internal security forces and governmental controls over the information media.*

Setting aside rhetorical pretensions of the regime, the Marxist-

---

* The security-information tandem is unusually important. I recall visiting
with Uco Krstic, a prominent former operative of the internal security police,
UDBA, who distinguished himself on numerous occasions. Among other things,
Krstic had captured General Mihajlovic, the royalist war minister, who was
hiding in the Serbian mountains long after the Communists took power. Krstic
had held a number of sensitive positions, the last being that of Yugoslav consul
general in Munich (a post reserved for top-ranking UDBA operatives), before
he was ousted after the fall of Rankovic. A sophisticated man with a severe,
alert face, he looks like Hemingway; a burly, strong man with a white beard
living in the village of Jermenovci and writing his memoirs. He told me over
drinks in the village café that he was assigned in 1954 to organize the press department for foreign journalists in the Yugoslav Information Ministry and that
he had headed that department for several years. What struck me as illuminating
is the fact that an agent who had pulled off the most important security coup in
that period by capturing General Mihajlovic would be assigned to organize the
press department for foreign journalists.

Leninist notion that a Communist party has the right to hold power indefinitely in the name of the socialist revolution is the basic assumption of legitimacy held by the men who rule Yugoslavia. Given their outlook and their conception of the country and of their own political future, they are always driven to certain highly predictable decisions that will protect their monopoly of power. And yet they have the illusion that their tireless dissimulation and insincerity will eventually create a genuine Yugoslav commonwealth and that by a miracle called historical determinism a society will emerge in which ethnic differences can be transcended without free and open discussion.

14

Whither Yugoslavia

IN THE WINTER OF 1976 BELGRADE'S DIPLOMATIC COMMUNITY WAS buzzing with one of those periodic rumors about Tito's failing health. A tabloid newspaper in neighboring Austria had originated the speculative reports that the old marshal was near death. From then on everything was predictable: the wire services picked up the speculation and diplomats made the usual cautious inquiries; as in previous years the Yugoslav press said nothing; and, also as in previous years, a week or so after the circulation of the rumor had picked up enough steam, a photograph of Tito hunting in the Bosnian mountains popped up one morning on the front pages of the papers without any specific reference to foreign speculations. Tito holding a rifle over the body of a dead brown bear at his feet—the annual bear-hunting picture. Except that as he had grown older, his hunting exploits seemed less believable and the temptation to crack jokes on this account greater and greater. "What's happened to the two guys who were holding the bear?" intellectuals would say privately, grinning at those annual bear-hunting photos.

It takes imagination for a Westerner to comprehend Yugoslav hypersensitivities. Partly, and only partly, this is due to the nature of the system. An autocrat, whose rule is never fully legitimized, is always insecure about his power and always concerned about foreign perception of his country's political stability. The deeper reason is in the Yugoslav past. It telescopes easily: Yugoslav lands were often invaded and plundered, and most of the people lived in serfdom for centuries, without a state in the dangerous and rapacious world of the Balkans in which the strong devoured the weak. Whatever there was of the old Slav civilization had dissolved, except the old myths and a knowledge of the world's basic order and a long roll call of battles most of which they had lost to stronger races. The people who had to absorb the shock had invested with bogus glory those medieval battles in which the enormity of defeat spelled the end of their political independence—the destruction of the Croats led by Petar Svacic at Gvozd and the annihilation of the Serbs at Kosovo. When they finally emerged into the modern world in the nineteenth century, real power eluded them. Power surrendered long ago to Vienna, Budapest, and Istanbul was now shared by London, St. Petersburg, Berlin and Paris. Great powers telling them whether they could build a road or a railway on Yugoslav lands and controlling local leaders through financial subsidies, loans and promises of diplomatic support.* So the people know that foreign relations is a very serious business for Yugoslavia. Officials seem prepared to go to any length to maintain an illusion of strength and stability, including random brutality against domestic dissidents and supervision of information that filters abroad.†

* Prince-Bishop Peter II (1813–51) of Montenegro, whose impoverished tiny principality could not exist without foreign assistance, told a Serb diplomat, "I like Russia, but I do not like having to bear the price of its aid on every occasion. I am tired of it and wish to throw off that yoke." He also said something that illustrates the image the United States had even in the remotest corners of Europe in the first half of the nineteenth century. He had long wished to visit the United States, adding, "It is proper for free Montenegro to receive aid only from a free country such as America, seeing that it cannot get along without aid."

† At the time of the 1976 rumor about Tito's health, my editors ordered me to the Middle East because of the Lebanese civil war. But prior to my departure they insisted that I update an obituary written by Anatole Shub, who was the *Post*'s Belgrade correspondent in the mid-sixties. The updating involved three lengthy paragraphs which I found impossible to transmit by Telex. Each time I attempted a transmission, my link with the *Post* communication center would be interrupted. I tried to phone in the material but was told that all phone lines to Western Europe were down. Then I realized that the material, written in the style proper for obituaries, was suggesting that Tito had died. So I established Telex contact with the Belgrade exchange, which is also monitored by security officials who can and do disconnect lines when matters of great importance are suddenly being transmitted, and advised everybody that Tito is very much alive and that I was engaged in transmitting a routine update of his obituary. Several times I typed out that Tito is not dead and then proceeded to transmit to the *Post* without interruption. This was not an isolated incident. Yugoslav authorities, of course, would never admit the existence of communication and mail censorship. I have met, by accident, two persons working as language specialists for the security agency's foreign language surveillance who told me in private conversations that they occasionally had to translate my phone conversations and private letters from English into Serbo-Croatian. They cited details from my private correspondence to establish credibility. On one occasion the censors apparently misplaced five photographs portraying a Yugoslav family on vacation and put them in one of my monthly expense-account packages. *Post* accountants in Washington were baffled by these pictures, which were not men-

It became clear to me during my long sojourn in Yugoslavia how foreign relations have come to dominate the minds of the men there. The country, after all, had been created at the Versailles peace conference following the turmoil of World War I. And the men who ran the country in the period between the wars were all small-town politicians whose power was based on parochial loyalties and religion. In their efforts to go beyond the old nationalist abstractions and to come to terms with the modern world they were at the mercy of imported ideas and institutions. But the Yugoslav kingdom never really had a chance to succeed. From the very beginning the knives were out for King Alexander, who was an able administrator but who could not offer an acceptable vision to all ethnic groups. His assassination was carried out by terrorists who were supported and trained by Italy and Hungary, both of them with territorial claims against Yugoslavia and both seeking to destabilize her. From that point on, the leaders were involved in stopgap policies and plans, always aware of the chilling prospect of a collapse. It came when Hitler dismembered the country in 1941.

In contrast, Tito had no ethnic or parochial loyalties and was an "internationalist" in the true sense of the word. At first he sought to play a larger role within the Soviet bloc but then, after the fateful quarrel with Stalin in 1948, he was forced to maneuver in rough international waters, something he relished doing and something he had mastered as no one had in his people's history. So Tito, the son of a Croat peasant, became by trial and error the first Yugoslav statesman of international stature, and with a concept of an all-Yugoslav commonwealth, gave the world a new idea of the country.

Thus foreign relations provided a sense of direction for his mulish and pugnacious people. There it was—his activism, the can-do, the instinct for timing and maneuvering that forced him and the country onto the world scene, utilizing the Cold War struggle between East and West and getting credit from both sides while at the same time becoming the guru of the Third World, the only

---

tioned in the cover letter, and inquired by Telex what to do with them. They mailed them back to me, and I phoned a senior official in the Ministry of Information and explained the problem. The pictures, I said, should be returned to their rightful owners. The official agreed to that. But when my secretary attempted later in the day to deliver these photographs to the official she failed. By then it was clear that if they accepted the pictures, they would in effect acknowledge the existence of mail censorship.

European among Africans and Asians. His age alone commanded respect. He learned how to hide his warts and how to dim the hidden fears which had propelled him to power in the first place. His most important lesson in Marxist theory came a few months after he took power. The Russians wanted to reopen operations at the large Bor copper mines in southern Serbia. They would put in new mining equipment, and Tito would pay for it in kind by letting them have half of the mined ore. He wanted them to pay at least something for the copper, since the country was hard pressed and since he knew that the French, who had operated the Bor mines before the war under a similar arrangement, had payed substantial amounts of hard currency into the royal treasury each year. But the Russians said no, that's not the socialist way of cooperation. I asked Djilas how the Russians justified their stand. "They used Marx's theory of value," he said, "arguing that the ore had no value while lying in the ground. And we knew that that was only a new form of exploitation."

Yet Tito remained a Marxist after the 1948 feud with the Russians, except that he branched off on his own. And there was something inherently contradictiory in Tito as the first Marxist king. The country was vulnerable and weak, and yet his ambition to harness its potential was enormous. So he started to build relations with all countries, promoting trade and cooperation and trying to build a web of weak links which could serve as a cushion to possible blows by the world's mighty nations. Foreign policy became his focus, his personal domain. He told Senator Edward Kennedy in 1974 that the two men he admired most were President Nasser of Egypt and President Kennedy. Both died young and both became legends. What he really admired was their ability to inspire millions with their vision and their rhetoric, and project their image on the world. Tito never dreamt small dreams but he could not transmit them in an inspiring way. He had to struggle, maneuver, bluff, cajole and dissimulate. He was at his best in diplomatic struggle and close-range maneuvering, having that brilliant sense of how far to push. "They really believe in international law," Tito told a close associate at the time of the 1954 crisis over Trieste, referring patronizingly to Kardelj and other senior leaders who felt Yugoslavia should go to war with Italy because Yugoslav claims on the city were just. Tito had ordered general mobilization not to wage war—he thought at the time he wouldn't get Trieste anyway—but to strengthen his hand in diplomatic bargaining for a greater chunk of the Istrian Peninsula, which he got.

A natural diplomat, his strengths are Russia and the pressurized atmosphere of Communist diplomacy. Since the death of Stalin he has sought to recover a place in the Communist world, but on his terms only. It was easy with Khrushchev, in whom Tito immediately recognized an element of the bully. So Tito snubbed him publicly during their first meeting in 1955, before one of the largest crowds of foreign journalists ever to descend on Yugoslavia. When he instructed the translator not to translate Khrushchev's arrival speech at the Belgrade airport, he must have assessed the situation with instant clarity. One had to deal with a bully right away, especially if the bully had overextended himself and had virtually no fallback positions. And Khrushchev, by coming to Belgrade, had overextended himself. It has been more difficult to deal with Brezhnev, Kosygin and company because theirs has been a government by committee. They're slow, deliberate and cautious. Tito is privately scornful of these weak men who seized power but did not exploit it thoroughly. Tito has always searched for a weakness in his opponents and he knows Soviet weaknesses inside out. His experiences with Russia date back to 1915. At that time the current Soviet leaders were small boys. He drew on his experiences in the Comintern when he was an insignificant official with the pseudonym of "Walter." (Stalin met him for the first time at the end of World War II and always referred to him as Walter. Tito had felt that Stalin did so on purpose, trying to place him on the defensive by reminding him of his past as a Comintern agent.) His knowledge of Russian weaknesses and hidden fears was the source of his strength. Later he seized upon American ignorance of Russia as a leverage in diplomacy and played upon the anti-Communist paranoia of Washington until Washington began to view him as an acceptable Communist, a good Communist. He was still trying in the fifties, to impress the Americans sometimes in small and not too subtle ways. Like dragging Mrs. James Riddleberger, the wife of the American ambassador, to show her his bear. The Riddlebergers were making their farewell call in January of 1958, and Tito had just had a cave built inside his compound in Belgrade. The bear was in hybernation, but he insisted on waking it up and pushing the dozed animal to the front of the cave so that Mrs. Riddleberger could see it. Like an Oriental potentate, he slipped on a special protective glove and teased his leopard for the benefit of his guests. Always showing his prowess and seeking to impress. Only in the sixties and especially in the seventies, when his world-wide connections cemented his reputation, would he have no time for ambassadors. His eyes on History, he was like an old miser constantly trying to protect and enlarge his investment, which he did in a spectacular way during his 1977 triumphal tour of China. Not only did the Chinese Communists take back their earlier denunciation of Tito's "revisionist" policies, but Mao Tse-tung's successors began to study Yugoslavia's self-management as a possible way to motivate China's disaffected workers and stimulate economic growth.

Tito's activism in foreign affairs has introduced a new way of looking and feeling in the once static world of Yugoslavia. For a long time his policy departures were a matter of words alone, the people serving as a background for his fantastic, innovative schemes. But then—gradually at first—the government granted the people the long-coveted freedom of movement, and Yugoslavs began to discover for themselves Africa, Asia, Latin America and, above all, Western Europe. The great migrant rush was, next to the Communist revolution, the single most important social development.

I recall a story told by David Binder, the *New York Times* correspondent in Belgrade in the early sixties, of Yugoslav peasants who, having acquired new tractors, tried to test them just as they used to test their oxen—they tied two tractors with chains and had them pull in opposite directions to determine which machine was stronger. And ruining the tractors in the process.

But that was before the country had opened its borders, before the Yugoslavs had entered Europe. I found Yugoslavia in the seventies a country that had absorbed an enormous amount of Western know-how and wisdom, but at the same time it was a country unsettled by the turbulence and the cruelties of the modern world. The quick penetration of industrial civilization seriously bedeviled the judgment of the people, who remembered the time when the Yugoslav world stood still and the issues were simple. A new hyperactive, mobile society saw Western Europe as its frame of reference. Only a few decades before, clan and religion had defined the individual. Today Yugoslavs are submerged in a world of air conditioners, Xerox machines, outboard motors, country cottages and various other features of middle-class, Western existence. All of it came too soon. "We are like a people who moved to Xerox machines without ever knowing of the existence of carbon paper," one Yugoslav sociologist said, which, I thought, explained the difficult relationship between the modern and the primitive in Yugoslavia.

Strobe Talbott, who was *Time* correspondent in Belgrade, told me a story which I found more touching than funny. He and his wife had to run an important errand and hired a cab. The cab, moving in the heavy rush-hour traffic, started gasping, then suddenly stopped. Its engine had broken down and the prospects of finding another cab at that hour were remote at best. Mrs. Talbott was moaning in despair, since she sensed that they wouldn't be able to make their appointment. The driver must have gotten the gist of her complaint, although he didn't understand English. For him the breakdown meant a loss of face. "You know," he said, turning to the Talbotts and throwing his hands up in the air, "we've been under the Turks for five hundred years." A perfect explanation!

I have heard the same argument used in one form or another by senior government officials. It was the last line of defense when they had to acknowledge that in their own debilitating way they too could foul up things. The legacy of foreign rule!

The problem is that Yugoslavs have had to respond to too many new ideas at once. They are attracted by industrial civilization yet it seems alien to them, an imported thing that has yet to blend with the native cultures. I began to understand the Aristotelian idea of culture as a factor in distinguishing between a good and a perverted form of political system. That system, Aristotle had argued, is the best that most closely matches the views, customs and traditions of a community. What struck me was the growing discrepancy between the complex and conflicting objectives of the government on the one hand and the changing realities of Yugoslavia on the other. In the very success of Yugoslavia's entry into the modern world lay the seeds of her ideological ruin.

It may turn out to be an illusion that technology and modernity can create a sense of cohesiveness and help the country gain an idea of itself. Yugoslavia is a country without a past. A real understanding of the past means free inquiry, which the regime thinks it cannot afford, and so history books are rewritten. What is promoted is industrial civilization, which in turn creates economic growth, the loss of faith, the end of the clan, the end of respect toward venerated traditions—in short, a spiritual chaos.

I gained an impression from talking with Alexander Grlickov, a man of exceptional intellectual lucidity and one of the most impressive leaders, that the surge into modernity was a deliberate ploy to create a new socialist civilization by destroying the old. But the experiment had to be controlled to prevent a new middle-class consciousness from forcing any realignment of political priorities or shifts of power. The result is a moral void, a feeling of emptiness in which people revert to the old ways that may be irrelevant to modern conditions but are all they have.

The other part of Tito's foreign policy, his balancing act between East and West, has made it possible to maintain stability. I recall meeting a Yugoslav film director in Prague. She was Croatian but she sounded like a genuine Yugoslav patriot after two weeks in Czechoslovakia. "You know," she told me during dinner, "we Croats and Serbs argue all the time and hate one another but we'll stick it out together. Whenever I go to one of the other socialist countries I realize that ours is a pretty decent country after all." I met her in Belgrade a few months later. By this time the memories of her disgust with Soviet-style socialism were dim, and so was her Yugoslav patriotism.

To maintain a sense of unity through foreign policy, the leaders have to have chronic crises. Even if the Russians were to completely write off Yugoslavia, the Yugoslav regime would have to maintain an illusion of some kind of an Eastern threat. The people may aspire to being like the Swiss, who have their neutrality honored by others. But for Tito and his associates, this would spell a political collapse. Hence the constant motion and activism. Hence the importance of China, the Third World and Eurocommunism. Hence also continued dark hints about enemies of Yugoslavia in the West, where Yugoslavia in fact has very few enemies, with the exception of Yugoslav émigrés, who by and large belong to weak political movements (and some of whom periodically have to resort to terrorism to keep their ideologies afloat).

But the Russians have not written off Yugoslavia, though following the 1948 feud, Stalin had wanted to do just that. Yugoslavia was declared a capitalist country run by fascist agents and American stooges. Tito was trapped and he knew it. But he survived by creating his own brand of socialism, his own true interpretation of Marx and Lenin. He charged the Kremlin with revisionism and accused Stalin of having perverted the dogma. From then on the Russians could not write him off, for Titoism was a poisonous ideological challenge, an alternative religion which had to be contained or destroyed.

What was subsequently shown to be a brilliant balancing act was also a trap Tito had built for himself and his country. He was locked into it, and both his power at home and prestige abroad depended on Yugoslavia's unique standing in the Communist world. A part of it, yet independent—definitely not a satellite. An alternate center of Marxist learning which could successfully mobilize other independent-minded Communists, such as the Italians, the French, the Spaniards and the Romanians in a common front against Russian ideological hegemony. In reality this independence of Tito's was possible only in the context of East-West competition. Of course only a diplomat of exceptional talents could maneuver successfully in such a situation, yet the situation was created by competing ideological currents.

Yugoslavia today is a country without an ideology. A hardening antipathy to communism of the Soviet type coexists with a rather widespread acceptance of socialism, but socialism of the type practiced in Sweden. Apart from a general commitment to socialism, Titoism was long ago reduced to a set of practical policies—independence, nonalignment, self-management, market socialism and an open-borders policy. This in fact is Tito's legacy.

Tito has lived too long. The people have gotten accustomed to his paternalistic rule and to the illusion of stability he has created. He has traveled a long road, from a merciless tyrant to a benevolent autocrat. Along the way he loosened up the leash considerably, and nobody expects him to loosen it anymore. He talked about democracy and freedom for the people and granted them a measure of freedom which, by comparison to what they had been used to, seemed considerable.

Actuarial tables say the end of the Tito era is near, and the country is waiting. It has been waiting for some time. And the longer it waits the greater the gulf between the existing power structure and changing attitudes and values. For many people in top positions the temptation is strong to speak openly about such changes, but since that would be tantamount to political oblivion, they keep silent. This results in a curious type of split personality among the higher echelon, who speak with passion but who don't believe what they say. They are committed to carrying on Titoism even after Tito, which may turn out to be difficult, for Titoism—not merely a set of policies—involves charisma, political magic and illusions.

After the passing of charismatic leaders, countries invariably turn inward. Big foreign policy dreams normally fold like an accordion. Lesser men get bogged down in big domestic problems. And Tito is leaving his heirs with the most difficult question before the country: How much individual freedom can be permitted?

He has grappled with it for years, side-stepping it in many ingenious ways, claiming that what he wanted to achieve was a real kind of freedom that does not exist either in the West or in the East—"direct democracy" at the local levels of self-managed socialism. He has taken a series of half measures: consumerism, the open-borders policy, ethnic rights, the freedom of movement, economic integration in Western Europe—all of which were to divert attention from the central question. Whenever there were stirrings in the country, he was shrewd and sensitive enough to perceive them and to incorporate them into his policies. This has helped to diffuse some of the restlessness. But most significantly, he was the man who knew how to handle the Russians and Americans. He turned his country of twenty-two million into an independent force in international affairs and as a result was regarded seriously by other world leaders.

Tito's heirs will not have the charisma or reputations to sustain the Titoist illusion—the illusion that something unique and new has emerged at the juncture of East and West Europe, that new Marxist truths have been discovered. In Yugoslavia one is aware—perhaps more than in most other Communist countries—that communism is a mosaic of half-truths, that it was based upon a misunderstanding of nineteenth-century Western European ideas transplanted into the backward world of Slav Europe in the twentieth century. Here and there imaginative minds trying to grasp the message seized upon kernels of truth. The genius of Tito lies in his obliviousness to ideological scholasticism and his obsessive insistence on practical policies of development. He has sought to bring about a cultural renaissance and an industrial revolution in a mere three decades. His has been an era of innovative mimicry. His heirs will have to deal with a country that has assimilated, however imperfectly, the ideas and technology of Europe. And Tito's old magic, with its power to move the people, will no longer be there.

This is Yugoslavia's problem. It would be impossible today, short of a cataclysmic civil war or direct Soviet intervention, to turn Yugoslavia into a people's democracy of the East European type. And it is equally impossible for Tito's successors to quickly turn the country into a Western democracy. So cornered, they would probably have to perpetuate Titoism without Tito, to protect their own power.

But the status quo cannot be maintained for long. Tito's heirs will have to either move toward reforms or find new props to hold up the autocracy.

Any meaningful reforms born of insecurity could provoke an active Soviet policy of subversion in Yugoslavia. The Russians, who lack a reliable outlet to the Mediterranean, view Yugoslavia as a strategic piece of real estate. If changes are to take place, the Russians would expect them to be in the direction of greater orthodoxy, rather than liberalization.

I believe a return to greater orthodoxy is an unlikely option. If anything, Tito's successors are likely to face internal pressures against the restrictions on freedom and against the arbitrary rule of the party oligarchy. The country has become more complex and more sophisticated. New generations are bursting with talent, brains and entrepreneurial industry, for which there are only limited outlets. They have grown up in an age of foreign travel and national enlightenment, ignorant of real Communist dictatorship and the awful anxieties it breeds. Old policies of pacification through prosperity and ethnic rights simply do not work with generations that do not remember the deprivations and degradations of the past and are instead comparing themselves with West Europeans and demanding similar economic and political liberties.

Even West European Communists have posed an uncomfortable challenge to the Yugoslavs by publicly endorsing the concept of political pluralism. The rhetoric of Eurocommunism makes Yugoslavia's position enormously complicated. Either, as the French Socialist Jean-François Revel suggested, all Communist regimes are Stalinist to a greater or lesser degree, with Yugoslavia representing the lesser; or the public commitment to parliamentary democracy by the Communists of Italy, Spain and France does in fact represent a genuine new departure that could provide Tito's heirs with a model by which they could introduce political pluralism.

Hence, the question which intrigues Yugoslavia's neighbors and other Europeans is "After Tito, what?" Confident forecast is impossible. The Yugoslavs have proven to be unpredictable. Even among the men slated to take power there are different attitudes toward domestic and international issues. Above all, there is the implicit assumption that the Russians will put heavy pressure on Yugoslavia in an effort to acquire Adriatic sea bases and other strategic advantages, and to reduce the heterodoxy of the Socialist world. This has been true all along, except that such speculations also envision a Soviet military intervention. This view, however, ignores the realities of Soviet global strategy and the fact that the Russians have not taken military action in Europe outside their sphere of influence agreed upon between Stalin and Churchill in October 1944 at Moscow. (Yugoslavia was the only East European country where the Soviets were not given dominant political influence; it was split fifty-fifty between East and West.*) What the Russians have tried to do, and undoubtedly will continue to do in the future, is to encourage more orthodox elements in Yugoslavia and at the same time to exploit nationalist tensions. These are parallel efforts. Their appeal is directed at those people in the establishment, mostly pseudo-intellectuals in the party and army, who entertain doubts about the emerging industrial civilization of Yugoslavia and who yearn for restoration of a world of security and simplicity. For these are the men near the levers of power who may be prompted into action by a revival of nationalist quarrels and the prospect of another collapse.

Most of the younger politicians, men such as Dolanc, Grlickov, Kiro Gligorov and others, are bright, intelligent, pragmatic and committed to a modern Yugoslavia. But regardless of their personal views, they are all boxed into the Titoist trap. With the exception of the ailing Kardelj, all ranking Yugoslav politicians suffer one enormous disadvantage: they do not have a national constituency, and so their policies most likely will be tactical, motivated essentially by insecurity. They will continue the same policies in the intermediate period, invoke the same justifications, play the same game. They will most likely respond to pressures for political liberalization and freer expression but within parameters that preclude fundamental reforms. I do not share apocalyptic views held by many Western ex-

* Ironically, Stalin's backing of Tito and the strength of Tito's wartime movement prevented a dismemberment of Yugoslavia at the end of World War II, an idea advanced by Roosevelt, who proposed as late as 1944 that Serbia be detached from the rest of Yugoslavia and restored as a separate country.

perts about Yugoslavia's future; she will most likely survive Tito's departure without major turbulence.

A task of great magnitude will be the establishment of a consensus among regional barons on the shape of the successor regime and its policy course. In the mid-seventies Tito's experiment already seemed to have run its course. Life had been getting better and there was hope that if would get even better in the future. But the country seemed to have reached the point where it was ready for the ultimate test, the test of personal and economic freedom without which all previous social experiments seemed like an illusion pepetuated by an oligarchy to retain its power. Although the old marshal's magic still worked and his prestige was still high, there was a strange flavor of stagnation. For the new, younger men, this will be a dialectic situation. They have helped set in motion an improbable process of changes and reforms. In their lifetime they have seen how the country has been transformed by education, electricity, technology and induced upward mobility. But despite these achievements, the people are still denied the right to pursue their destiny in a free political environment.

It was difficult for me to pierce more than half the layers of hints, contradictions, meanings and intentions in a stream of information I had gathered. The ethnic feuds seemed real enough to me, yet I heard Yugoslavs say with conviction that the ethnic issue is being used by the ruling group to divide the country and to postpone indefinitely the granting of individual liberties. I heard both Serb and Croat intellectuals argue that the 1971 crisis in Croatia was a popular movement against the authoritarian strains in Tito's regime and that the regime eventually fought back by casting the Croats into the role of separatists and spoilers and telling others, "See what happens when you loosen up? The Croats want to destroy the State." I could not judge the truth of this for myself. Yet there is a strange contradiction between the regime's insistence on independence and sovereignty on one hand and the one-party rule at home on the other. Also contradictory is the regime's attitude toward the Soviet bloc. The Yugoslavs want to be a part of the Communist world but not subject to Soviet bloc discipline.

Professionally, I have viewed Yugoslavia in a geopolitical context. It is, after all, Europe's potential "explosion point," the precarious country which is easily provoked and unpredictable. I have spent many evenings with my diplomatist friends dissecting Yugoslavia's political scene, guided not so much by convictions or morality as by rationality. What an extraordinary experiment! How much more humane and tolerant the Yugoslav system is compared to that of the Soviet or Chinese. The continued existence of nonaligned Yugoslavia is clearly in the interest of the West. Isn't it still an attractive alternative for other East Europeans who live under the Soviet yoke? An important piece of territory denied the Soviet Union? A Trojan horse in the Communist world?

But privately my views and feelings were more complex. I considered myself at home in Yugoslavia, and yet I knew that it could never be my home. The people and ideas which had framed my view of the world were not there. Beyond that, living as I did for three years in two worlds—the world of the Western community with its noisy receptions, its elaborate dinner parties and its myopic self-satisfaction, and at the same time in the urban world of Yugoslavia wallowing in indecisions and incomprehensible new problems—I realized the exorbitant human price paid for the existence today of a Yugoslav State. For generations they had engaged in violence as a form of social action, seeking to gain freedom; and the Yugoslav Communists have given them an independent country without, as yet, granting them personal liberties.

I recall visiting Arsen Popovic, a friend of my family, who emigrated to the United States during World War I, but who returned home just before the outbreak of World War II. Archie, as they called him in St. Louis, Missouri, was seventy-nine. Still vigorous and alert, he was delighted to see me and proud to display his English. I knew his personal history: he had always wanted to go to America to make his fortune and was saving money as a young man. When World War I broke out, the banks collapsed and his savings vanished. So he made his way to France, walking most of the way across Europe and somehow gathering enough money for passage in steerage. He settled down in St. Louis, first working in a Swift meatpacking plant, later in a warehouse that was owned by one of my aunts. Finally in 1937, having saved $28,000, he decided to return to the Old Country, where he bought a house and placed the remainder of his savings in a local bank. When World War II broke out, the bank collapsed and his life savings vanished. After the war the Communists confiscated his house and he could not return to America because the government would not permit emigration. Besides, he had a family. Both of his sons eventually became engineers, and supplemented Archie's meager pension.

He has cursed the day he left St. Louis a million times at least, he said. And when he talked about America, his eyes grew misty and his images became swollen with ebullient praise. I thought for a moment that he had recaptured some of the illusions of youth. Or his vision of America was completely distorted. For I knew that his life in St. Louis was not exciting—long hours in the packing house, working in streams of blood reaching up to his knees, then six days a week sweating in the warehouse, resting on Sundays, living his life in a rooming house and denying himself creature comforts to save money. So I gently reminded him of his life in St. Louis. And he said yes, life was hard in those years, and before he mastered English, kids used to throw stones at him and call him "Polack"—what kids called immigrants who didn't speak English. But, he explained quietly, "I was free, free. You know what it means. Free." Later he shuffled down with me to the gate and clung to my hand to put off the moment of parting so that he could warn me adequately not to be taken in by all the talk about freedom in socialism.

Bibliography

Adamic, Louis. *The Eagle and the Roots.* New York, 1952.

Armstrong, Hamilton Fish. *Tito and Goliath.* New York, 1951.

Auty, Phyllis. *Tito.* London, 1970.

Brzezinski, Z. K. *The Soviet Bloc: Unity and Conflict.* New York, 1963.

Campbell, John C. *Tito's Separate Road.* New York, 1967.

Deakin, F. W. *The Embattled Mountain.* London, 1971.

Dedijer, Vladimir. *Tito.* New York, 1953.

Djilas, Milovan. *The New Class: An Analysis of the Communist System.* New York, 1957.

———. *Land Without Justice.* New York, 1958.

———. *Conversations With Stalin.* New York, 1962.

———. *Memoir of a Revolutionary.* New York, 1973.

———. *Wartime.* New York, 1977.

Halperin, Ernst. *The Triumphant Heretic.* London, 1958.

Hoffman, George W. and Neal, F. W. *Yugoslavia and the New Communism.* New York, 1962.

Jelavich, Charles and Barbara. *The Balkans in Transition.* Berkeley, 1963.

Johnson, A. Ross. *Yugoslavia in the Twilight of Tito.* The Washington Papers, 1974.

Kennan, George F. *Memoirs, 1950–1963.* Boston, 1970.

Lendvai, Paul. *Eagles in Cobwebs.* London, 1969.

Lowenthal, Richard. *World Communism.* New York, 1964.

Maclean, Sir Fitzroy. *Eastern Approaches.* London, 1949.

Rubinstein, Alvin Z. *Yugoslavia and the Nonaligned World.* Princeton, 1970.

Rusinow, Dennison. *The Yugoslav Experiment, 1948–1974.* Berkley, 1977.

Seton-Watson, H. *Eastern Europe Between the Wars, 1918–1941.* Cambridge, 1945.

———. *The East European Revolution.* London, 1950.

Seton-Watson, R. W. *The Rise of Nationality in the Balkans.* London, 1917.

Shoup, P. S. *Communism and the Yugoslav National Question.* New York, 1968.

Silberman, Laurence H. "Yugoslavia's 'Old' Communism: Europe's Fiddler on the Roof." *Foreign Policy,* Spring 1977.

Sulzberger, C. L. *A Long Row of Candles.* New York, 1969.

Ulam, A. B. *Titoism and the Cominform.* Cambridge, 1952.

Vucinich, Wayne S., ed. *Contemporary Yugoslavia.* Berkley, 1969.

West, Rebecca. *Black Lamb and Grey Falcon.* New York, 1941.

Zaninovich, George M. *The Development of Socialist Yugoslavia.* Baltimore, 1968.

Index

Riddleberger, James, 188–189, 236
Roberts, Walter, 125
Romania, 94, 104, 164
Roosevelt, Franklin D., 188, 243
Rössel, Agda, 100
Rusinov, Dennison, 36
Russia, Imperial, 122, 123, 127, 204, 233
Russia Revolution, 122
Ruzicka, Lavoslav, 204

Sadat, Anwar, 135
St. Louis, Missouri, 245–246
St. Louis Post-Dispatch, 16
Saljic, Tihomir, 33–34
Samuilo, King of Bulgaria, 206
Savin, Jogan, 105
Saudi Arabia, 22, 223
Segedin, Petar, 38, 39, 215
self-management, 94–107 *passim.*
    See also 108–112, 131–134;
    basic organizations of
    associated labor, 105–106;
    criticism of, 160–161, 170–171,
    172, 241, 242
Selimovic, Mesa, 215
Serbia, 18, 21, 22, 26, 64, 65, 92,
    102–103, 129, 202–207, 229–
    23; influence of the military,
    147; kingdom of, 24; Orthodox
    Church of, 24, 25, 160, 219–
    223. *See also* ethnic key and
    ethnic tensions
Serbian Academy of Arts and
    Sciences (Belgrade), 36
Shub, Anatole, 233
Simic, Andrija, 83
Silberman, Laurence, 150, 154
Silberman, Ricky, 226–227
Slovenia, 18–20, 26, 64, 65, 89,
    92, 104, 110–111, 202–207

Smole, Janko, 223
Solzhenitsyn, Alexander, 153, 178
Sonnenfeldt, Helmut, 154
Spain, 225; Civil War in, 70, 123
Spiljak, Miko, 28, 114, 227
Stalin, Josef, 59, 97, 98, 113, 117,
    122, 124, 125, 132, 134, 138,
    166, 167, 186, 188; pact with
    Hitler, 143, 212, 217, 234, 236,
    239
Stankovic, Milic, 198–199
Stefanovic, Milivoj, 164
Stepinac, Cardinal Alojz, 221
Stojanovic, Svetozar, 172
Strossmayer, Bishap Juraj, 35,
    203
Sulzberger, C. L., 126
Supek, Rudi, 171, 175
Svacic, Petar, 233
Sweden, 112, 118, 141, 158, 240
Switzerland, 79, 81, 111, 141

Tadic, Ljubomir, 162, 169–175
Talbott, Strobe, 238
Taylor, A. J. P., 228
Tennyson, Alfred Lord, 182
Tesla, Nikola, 204
Tetovo (Macedonia), 163–164
Thorez, Maurice, 124
Time, 238
Tito, Josip Broz, 4, 15, 18, 26, 27,
    28, 29, 59, 60, 61, 88, 99, 105,
    114, 115, 116–117 *passim.*, 138,
    139, 140, 141, 153–155, 160,
    162, 176, 177, 184, 185, 187,
    207, 212, 214, 225, 228, 233,
    240, 241–245; Comintern and,
    123–124; Croats and, 38, 109–
    110, 113, 133, 147; cult of
    personality and, 118–119, 129–
    130; Djilas and, 166–168, 188–
    194; Eastern Europe and, 126,

About the Author

DUSKO DODER was born in Yugoslavia in 1937 and came to the United States after World War II. After graduating from Washington University, St. Louis, he studied philosophy at Stanford, and earned master's degrees in both journalism and history at Columbia. He worked in several domestic bureaus of the Associated Press and was a Moscow correspondent for United Press International before joining the Washington *Post*, where he has been an assistant foreign editor, a State Department correspondent, and a foreign correspondent. From 1973 to 1976 he was chief of the *Post*'s East European bureau. Mr. Doder has also reported for the *Post* from Canada, Cuba, Somalia and the Middle East. He has been awarded several fellowships, the last from the Woodrow Wilson International Center for Scholars, Smithsonian Institution, where he wrote this book. Mr. Doder is now on the *Post* staff in Washington, where he lives with his wife Karin and their son.